To Prof. [ ]

with my best regards

[signature]

15/5/2023

INSIDE AN ARAB MIND

Selected Works of Mohammed Jaber Al-Ansari

Translated by Riyad Y. Hamzah

Copyright © 2022 Riyad Y. Hamzah

All rights reserved.

ISBN: 9798835183876

Cover Design by Sahar R. Hamzah

Testaments on the Intellectual Projects of Mohammed Jaber Al-Ansari by Arab Scholars

"If there were anyone to be considered the best representative of Ibn Khaldun's way of thinking in the 20th century, Mohammed Jaber Al-Ansari would definitely be one of them. The importance of what Al-Ansari did and is still doing in terms of historical analysis and political thinking is his presentation of a view and theory that could be called "believing realism" as opposed to "materialistic realism" that controls Arabic political thinking."

- *Khaled Al Haroub -Khulood Amro*
Cambridge Book Review

"With the work entitled *The Arab and Politics: Where Is the Flaw?* Al-Ansari presents to us a new way of looking at things. I see it as an answer at the end of this century to questions posed at the beginning of the 20th century. This is an invitation for writers and researchers to analyze this study, and a call for the Arabic reader to read the book and thereby find himself more aware and knowledgeable…and that, in itself, is the beginning of the ultimate change."

- *Prof. Abdul Al Hamid Ismail Al-Ansari*

"As an Arab reader, I kept looking for a chance to say that, in my opinion, the publication of Dr. Mohammed Jaber Al-Ansari's book about the territorial state opened a new path in analyzing the development of Arabic society."

- *Ismail Bandy*

"In theorizing about a compromise in the Arab way of thinking and Arab society, three attempts, as far as I know, were made. These are: *The Equivalency* by Tawfiq Al Hakim in 1955, *The East, the Artist* by Zaki Najib Mahmoud in 1961, and *The Arabic Middle: An Ideology and Application* by Abdul Hamid Hassan. The point of view of Al Hakim is from the eye of the artist, as is that of Zaki Najib Mahmoud, although with more philosophical depth, while Abdul Hamid Hassan fluctuates between the artist and the researcher. Finally, comes the book of Dr. Mohammed Jaber Al-Ansari, *Arabic Thinking and the Conflict of the Antagonists,* as if he follows the same line of thinking, but this time with more depth, more comprehensive and fundamental, and even more documented than his predecessors."

- Syrian writer Mohammed Kamel Al Khatib

"Whether we like it or not, there are writers in our Arab countries from the "center" and writers from the "edges." The center is represented by the capitals of Arab culture, Cairo and Beirut. Writers who do not reside in these two will not gain significance, even if they are important. I remembered that while I was reading two very important intellectual works by Dr. Mohammed Jaber Al-Ansari. The first was *The Political Dilemma for the Arabs and the Position of Islam* and the second was *Renewing the Renaissance by Discovering and Criticizing the Self.* The two books actually represent some of the Arabic enlightenment thinking during this period."

- Lebanese critic Jihad Fathal

"The book…the writer…and the project. The book was written in modern language, the language of intelligent dialogue based on accurate details and information. I hope that this book will be reprinted so that it reaches all concerned individuals in the different parts of the Arab World."

- Dr. Shukri Ayyad
In his critique of Al-Ansari's book The Changes in Thinking and Politics

"Dr. Mohammed Al-Ansari has a writing style that combines the accuracy of science and beauty of art. There is no complexity in his style. He presents to us a wonderful

image of purity of expression."
- *Raja'a Al Nakkash*

"One of the most distinguished writers who presented a detailed study on the *tawfiqiah* was Mohammed Jaber Al-Ansari. While the study of the *tawfiqiah* by Zaki Najib Mahmoud and Abdul El Hamid Ibrahim is dominated by a descriptive nature and personal analysis, the study of Al-Ansari is closer to the argumentative nature aiming to overcome this *tawfiqiah* (reconciliation)."
- *Mahmoud Amin Al Alim*

"As much as the Al-Ansari critical project uses the previous way of thinking, it uses it with more depth and surpasses it. The most important thing in it is the daring in the presentation of his ideas."
- *Strategic Egyptian intellectual Al Sayed Yassin*

"The true critique of understanding reality was not achieved by political movements but by the efforts of an elite group of Arab intellectuals. One of them is the distinguished Bahraini intellectual, Dr. Al-Ansari, in his book, full of rich thoughts provoking deep contemplation."
- *Iraqi politician and intellectual, Aziz Al Hajj*

"Al-Ansari presents a very ambitious project containing a lot of adventure, a lot of effort, and a lot of excitement, too."
- *Jordanian thinker Mo'nis Al Razaz*

"To me, the works of Al-Ansari are entertaining and argumentative and have their own enigmatic nature."
- *Jordanian writer Fakhri Saleh*

"Electric shocks for the Arab mind…Al-Ansari threw out a burning ball of ideas…will Arab intellectuals consider it or will they be afraid of burning their hands?"
- *Arabic poet and writer Dr. Ghazi Al Gosaibi*

"A book that keeps away many of the nightmares that haunt me. It requires more than one reading. What transparency in the book! Jaber Al-Ansari, where have you been hiding?"
> - *Syrian writer in Paris, Dr. Ghassan Al Rifai*

"Al-Ansari, the pioneer of the institutional methodology for statehood in contemporary Arab sociology."
> - *Dr. Abdullah Al Zihani*
> *Sana'a University (University of Sana'a)*

To Dawn

CONTENTS

Preface by the Translator...i
Introduction by the Translator...ix
Selected Translations of the Works of Mohammed Jaber Al-Ansari...xiii
I. The Philosophic Project xv
- A Philosophical Project for the Arabic Intellect…or an Ideology Bypassed by Conflict.................................1
- The Contemporary Political Significance of the Historic Viewpoint in Question...87
- Towards a Sociological Approach that Views the Crisis at its Roots..104
- Western Civilization in Its Confusing Mirrors 112
- The Only Issue We Do Not Research 128

II. Social Dimensions of Arab-Islamic Civilization 131
- An Insight into the Roots: The Responsibility of the Past towards the Crisis of the Present 133
- The Arabs and Progress: Where Is the Flaw? 144
- The Problem of the Arab Social Makeup: Minorities…or Multiple Majorities? 162
- Arab Boundaries: To Get over It… Draw It First!........202

III. Cultural Perspectives from Bahrain 225
- The Harbor for Memory: The Harbor of Our Lost Reality..227

- Television: A New Stone Age? The Culture of Image …And a Caution about Mankind's Mental Backwardness...…...244
- Labor: A Short Story …...…………...…………………...254
- Desert Journey of a Sea Bird: A Poem ……...…………..262

IV. Intellectual Interview ……………….…..……………..265
- Mohammed Jaber Al-Ansari's Intellectual Project: An Inquiry………………………………………………..267
- About the Author……………………………………...…..317
- About the Translator……………………………………….319

PREFACE

In this incalculable information age, a time when human knowledge can be possessed by all those who seek it, the boundaries that divide humanity have begun to erode, little by little, until our cultures have become like water pools with walls that constantly collapse, eventually forming one river that is ever searching for a single path. This is an age in which the world has become one sea, with shores that interlink and intertwine. Yet because this sea is so vast, there are many pockets along the shores that have very different climates. Each culture retains a history and flavor that is uniquely its own.

One of the phenomena of this age is increasingly easy access to, and interest in, histories and cultures that are not our own. It is for this reason that translation has come to have an immeasurable influence on the acquisition of world knowledge of various cultures and societies.

The process of intellectual exchange is slowly undergoing a change as more and more areas of the world gain access to greater means of communication and self-expression.

Innovation first develops in the mind. As human beings, we have tools of expression for that innovation. Our hands have a limitless variety of abilities to create. Art with the stroke of a brush or the molding of clay. Music with the strum of a string, the pounding of a drum, the stroke of a keyboard, or the flutter of fingers upon a flute. Our feet, too, are capable of amazing skills. Gaze upon the artistry of a calculated leap into the air at a ballet or be dazzled by the agility and speed with a ball at a football match. Such things are without boundaries and can be appreciated and admired without regards to one's culture, history, or language.

But the world of ideas, philosophy and literature, are not so easily grasped and shared. These things can only be expressed through language and communication. Languages, like human beings, live and grow, weaken and grow stronger. There are numerous languages around the world, each spoken primarily by the people of the culture in which it is based. However, the dominant language in the world, the language of the most powerful, most productive, or most innovative, becomes an essential tool for making the literary artists, philosophers, and leading thinkers of other cultures known to the rest of the world.

This is not a modern concept. Earlier forms have occurred whenever a civilization grew strong enough to enforce its domination, as well as its language. Greeks, Romans, Arabs, Turks, Dutch, Spanish, French, British, American. All have extended their language as a means of achieving understanding throughout the world.

The dilemma comes when the voices of intellectuals, and creative and innovative people are not heard because their languages are not the ones easily assessable to the rest of the world, are not the languages proven to be the most effective in a particular era or age. How many great actors, writers, scientists, etc. has history bypassed because of the limitations placed upon them by lack of exposure due to their native languages? In order to benefit from this process, one must grasp the intricacies of the dominant language and learn to use it as a means of self-expression.

Translation is the invaluable tool to bridge the gap between the various cultures of the world and the West. It is language, whether original or translated, that shortens the distances in the gap of understanding. And there is no greater means of honoring intellectuals than to translate their works into the dominant languages so that greater numbers of readers may have access to their works. The West knows Edward Said and Khalil Gibran because they wrote in English, and it is easier for those of the West, understandably, to stop there than to take the trouble to search beyond. If *Midaq Alley* and his other works had not been translated into the languages of Europe, the Noble Prize would never have made its way to Nagib Mahfouz, although he is famous among the readers of his own language, and he has made the world interact with his works. It is in this bridging of the gap between the East and West that I choose to participate with this effort.

The significance of people and countries does not come from their size or the languages they speak. The Kingdom of Bahrain is at the eastern border of the Arab World. If a stone were thrown from the Far East, the first place it would land in the Arab World would be Bahrain. This small archipelago nation has produced numerous precious beautiful pearls, and I take this opportunity to introduce to the readers of the English language, one of Bahrain's pearls, Mohammed Jaber Al-Ansari, one of the prominent intellectuals of the Arab World.

Mohammed Jaber Al-Ansari was born in Bahrain and began his education there before traveling to Lebanon to attend university. For decades, he has been a prolific writer in all aspects of the media with columns in newspapers, articles in magazines and refereed journals, books, poetry, short stories, and literary critique. With degrees in Arabic literature and Islamic culture, he has mixed literature with political sociology, giving his works an interesting blend of flavors unique to his work.

Mohammed Jaber Al-Ansari served as the Advisor for Cultural and Scientific Affairs to the King of Bahrain, His Majesty King Hamad bin Isa Al-Khalifa, and is well-known and respected throughout the Arab World for his intellectual treatises on the role and position of the Arab World in modern times. He has published more than twenty books, many of which have become bestsellers, and some are used as textbooks in university classes throughout the

Arab World. He is a man who, through his own efforts, ambition, and hard work, has pursued knowledge in all its aspects, and continually contemplated the world and the progress of life, society, and civilization.

Mohammed Jaber Al-Ansari has been recognized for his contribution to intellectual thought in various parts of the world on different levels, honored by numerous countries in the Arab World from Morocco to Oman, and been given numerous medals of honor and awards of appreciation by highly prestigious cultural institutes, governments, and heads of state. He has spoken in countless intellectual forums and engaged most of the most distinguished and renowned intellectuals of the Arab World in intellectual debate.

His writings are published in Arabic. Having worked with him as a colleague and followed his work for more than thirty-five years, I have undertaken the task of presenting a selection of his works translated into English.

I will not be modest and say that this was an easy task. His works are erudite and profuse, touching upon history, politics, literature, philosophy, sociology, and social psychology, and I have devoted years of my time and effort to reading them all and translating a select few.

This collection includes works that are his most well-known and indicative of his general ideas, intellectual projects, and opinions on many issues at the international, regional, and local levels. I have translated selections from his published works that constitute his reflections on various issues that have dominated intellectual thought in the Arab World during the past several decades. I have also included a lengthy intellectual interview conducted with him by the late Syrian intellectual and writer Turki Ali Al-Rabeao, the most significant interview among Al-Ansari's numerous interviews, revealing his insights and opinions on matters of interest in the Arab World.

As a scientist who has always been greatly interested in the scientific renaissance in the Arab World, I came to realize that coming to terms with this issue was not just a matter of having well-stocked laboratories and imported chemicals and reagents and having access to international journals. The scientific renaissance of the Arab region is much more complex and far-reaching. The solution to this issue, like other issues of society, lies at the door of politics, sociology, economics, philosophy, and religion. The status of science in the Arab World is a reflection of all these fields.

In my quest to understand the causes and possible solutions to the dilemma of minimal advancement in scientific research in the Arab World, I studied countless tomes concerning the history and development of science and education, which quickly led me to broaden my search into the associated fields of politics, economics, sociology and religion. This search made clear to me the absolute intertwining of these fields, that knowledge is an ever-widening circle that encompasses all fields of intellectual research before bringing you back to where you began. The advancement of one cannot be sustained without accompanying advancements in the other aspects of life. To enjoy a scientific environment has much to do with achieving a healthy political environment.

This search also led me to realize that one of the leading intellectuals and authorities on these same issues was residing just down the hall and one floor up from me at the university. Mohammed Jaber Al-Ansari has been publicly concerned with these issues for five decades, delving into the ideologies and actions that have dominated the Arab World for centuries, fearlessly asking the most sensitive and daring questions, and refusing to fall for the easy answers.

As he has said, "The most important means to prevent

callousness and extinction in the life of cultures and nations is the ability to look back and reevaluate the basis, the beginnings, and the tracks...Let us start by asking the questions. To live in a forest full of sincere, bleeding questions is better than to live in a fort of answers that are stubborn and resolute ignorance."

Though others have attempted to answer the questions that have plagued the Arab World, the problem is that very few are asking the right questions to begin with.

As Al-Ansari states, "We have heard a lot of answers from people before us and others, and the answers sounded great and elegant, well-articulated and confident, but unfortunately, they did not save our nation from the pain and loss it is living now. We, the sons of this Arabic generation, have to ask our questions...to reach our answers and to discover our truth. They say that there is no clear correct intellect, and we say, because we have not started asking the clear basic questions."

Al-Ansari has spent his life dedicated to two intellectual projects dealing with the status of the Arabs in the modern world. His first project focuses upon the study of the makeup of the Arab intellect, and he has written a comprehensive history of Arab intellect in the twentieth century. In his conglomeration of research, he has tried to unveil the intellectual configuration of Arab intellectual doctrine in its indecisive reconciliatory approach and works for compromise and reconciliation regardless of what appears in its doctrine as radical revolutionary. He explains this as going back to the severe contradictions in the Arab reality that would enable this.

The Arab defeat of June 1967, whose repercussions swept the Arab World, was one of the decisive influences upon the development of Al-Ansari's intellectual pursuit and made him recognize the necessity of putting knowledge before ideology, of studying the reality of Arab society as opposed to the ideological dream of what the society should be.

Al-Ansari's second intellectual project focuses on diagnosing the political sociology of Arab societies and the historical makeup that continues to influence the nature of Arab political regimes, including how this has contributed to blocking democratic national reforms in the Arab World. He focuses on analyzing social reality rather than celebrating the political idealism that fuels Arab society with false hopes and expectations while ignoring the realities of the modern world.

In addition to these two intellectual projects, studying the intellectual component and makeup and the social makeup of the Arab reality, Al-Ansari has been greatly influential in the development of the cultural and literary renaissance of the Arab World. He has published numerous works in the fields of culture and literary critique and has published numerous examples of his literary prose, short stories, and poetry. He has contributed to the beginning of a new literary movement in Bahrain and in the Arabian Gulf since the early 1960's, pointing out that Arabian Gulf culture is not a culture "made by oil."

Al-Ansari has also conducted extensive research on eastern civilizations in Asia at the time of Arab retreat and predicted the rise to power of the Far Eastern nations, like China, in his publications five years before the publication of *The Clash of Civilizations and the Remaking of World Order*.

The vast amount of Al-Ansari's significant and influential published work made it extremely difficult to simply choose what to include in these translations. There were three perspectives in the choice. A large section of his writing has had a great impact on Arab intellectualism, but much of this is directed towards Arabs. I wondered if this would be the best choice to translate into English.

Or should I choose that which, when translated, will serve towards elucidation for the West in order to better understand the Arab intellect? Or should I choose samples of his works that show the development of Al-Ansari as an intellectual over the decades, with his many contributions to literature, sociology, history, religion, strategic studies, philosophy, and politics?

Working together with Al-Ansari to make our selections, we decided that some part of all three of these aspects should be translated. Perhaps I have not been fair to all three, as there is far more still to be read and translated.

There is a famous Arabic proverb that, roughly translated, means that just because you cannot achieve the whole, it does not mean that you should simply leave it all behind and not achieve at least a part of it. I cannot include translations of all his many works in this collection, although I believe that his work should eventually be translated into at least English and French in its entirety. But I include a number of the major works of Mohammed Jaber Al-Ansari in order that this Arab voice may be heard beyond the boundaries of the Arab World, and in this way, we will have done service to our culture and to our civilization.

This then is an invitation for you to be introduced to Mohammed Jaber Al-Ansari.

Riyad Y. Hamzah

June 1, 2022

INTRODUCTION

The first time I ever met Mohammed Jaber Al-Ansari was in Beirut in 1975. I had just turned sixteen years of age and I was a freshman at the American University of Beirut (AUB) in Lebanon.

At that time, having recently returned to Beirut from a trip to my native country of Bahrain, I had gone to visit a friend, a fellow Bahraini residing in a neighboring dormitory, to deliver gifts sent with me from my friend's family. As I entered the lobby of the dormitory, I encountered other friends, and we stood for a moment chatting in the lobby. One of my friends pointed to a distinguished-looking man standing nearby and said to me, "That's Mohammed Jaber Al-Ansari."

I recognized him immediately from his many photographs in the newspapers. I had been reading his articles in newspapers and magazines for many years back home in Bahrain, where he was a well-known, yet rather controversial, figure in the national political arena.

From 1969 to 1970, Al-Ansari had served as the Bahraini Director of Information, the equivalent of a Minister of Information in the era before Bahrain attained its independence from Great Britain in late 1971, and he had left his administrative position to pursue a scholastic career not long before Bahrain officially declared its independence.

Al-Ansari had also been writing articles for several Lebanese newspapers in Beirut, which was no mean feat at that time for a writer from the Arabian Gulf. Beirut in the 1970's, before the civil war began in 1975, ruled supreme in the world of Arab intellectualism and culture, rivaled only by Cairo in Egypt.

The Lebanese and Egyptian newspapers were the most distinguished, respected, and widely read newspapers in the entire Arab World. For a writer from the Arabian Gulf to be able to publish his articles in one of these newspapers was a great achievement. Al-Ansari was the first writer from the Arabian Gulf to attain such honors.

While I was in Beirut, a radio announcer once referred to him as "the *Lebanese* writer, Mohammed Jaber Al-Ansari." The people at the radio station just assumed he was Lebanese and had not bothered to check on the veracity of their statement. I had a good laugh over this mistake, but I admit, I felt a sense of national pride for his accomplishments, knowing that people were paying attention to what a Bahraini writer had to say, trying to argue and debate his ideas and to counter and contradict his statements. This incident spoke volumes about the perception of the status then of Arabian Gulf intellectuals on the international level in the Arab World, but also about the success of Al-Ansari himself as an intellectual. It may seem funny to say that simply being mistaken for a Lebanese was a form of praise, but in a way, that is precisely what it was.

At the time of our first meeting, I think I just wanted to get a good look at the Bahraini who had achieved this level of fame on the regional level. I had heard that Al-Ansari was working on his Ph.D. at AUB, gaining the distinction of being the very first Bahraini to work on a Ph.D. from AUB.

My friend led me over to him, and I was introduced for the first time to Mohammed Jaber Al-Ansari. We shook hands and exchanged the usual pleasantries. He asked how I was enjoying Beirut, I said I liked it very much. We said good evening, shook hands once more, and I departed in order to meet with my other friend and deliver the gifts from home.

Our meeting was very brief, lasting no more than a few

moments. He was courteous and friendly, and I remember thinking of him as a very pleasant and polite person.

With the outbreak of civil war in Lebanon, I left Beirut in 1975 to complete my university studies in the United States. I spent the next nine years studying in the United States, achieving my Ph.D. in Biochemistry in 1984, after which I returned home to Bahrain.

In that year of 1984, I had my second encounter with Dr. Al-Ansari, now at a different university, the newly established Arabian Gulf University in Bahrain. It began again as a very brief meeting, the exchange of pleasantries, the shaking of hands. But this encounter did not last only a moment, as the previous one had. We were to begin working in the same place, the Arabian Gulf University, and this encounter lasted for more than thirty-five years.

And in these thirty-five plus years, the world has changed many times.

SELECTED TRANSLATIONS

OF THE WORKS OF

MOHAMMED JABER AL-ANSARI

I. THE PHILOSOPHIC PROJECT

A Philosophical Project for the Arabic Intellect... or an Ideology Bypassed by Conflict?

In: *Arab Thought and the Conflict of Antagonists*. Beirut: Arabic Institute for Studies and Publishing, 1996, pp. 587--649.

(1)

The dialectics of Arab Islamic culture aspire towards *tawhid* (unification) as an ideal objective. The unity of God, of belief and law, of religion and state, of religions in one continuous religious message, the unity of civilizations into a comprehensive one of peoples in one belief and of nations into one nation, and in brief, the unification of all facts into one word; one final, eternal, constant word.[1]

(2)

Our world however, in its essence, is based upon contradictions and disagreements in abundance. Unification in the abstract sense is a far-fetched achievement and an ambitious undertaking – with its purified perfection – in our world ridden with duality. It is an ideal we aspire and work towards, but as achievement, a remote possibility.

(3)

How then can we cross the great chasm between God and Man, between the sphere above and the world beneath, between the transcendent ideal and the profane reality in its multiplicity and contradictions? Will we give in to a reality of strife, accepting duality? We who are unitarians?

(4)

Although our worldly reality prevails with no achievement on our part of the unification ideal in its completeness, we do attempt what approaches it. We attempt reconciliation, which is the drive of the mind and the soul approaching godly oneness.

Reconciliation is our ascent to oneness and our tether.

By reconciliation, we face contradictions, narrow the gap between them, and eliminate as far as possible what there is of opposition in order to emerge with that which expresses our passion and urge for the achievement of unification, with that which resembles but falls short of it, since our worldly reality is other than godly reality.

Thus, by reconciliation we rise above duality, approaching the level of oneness and by this, we overcome multiplicity and reach the threshold of unification.

Reconciliation remains our worldly expression that achieves, if falling short, our ideal unitarian belief.

(5)

As much as reconciliation and harmony between elements approaches unification, symbolizing redemption and sanctuary, the struggle between conflict and multiplicity becomes a return to polytheism, representing destruction.

Because of this, there has been confirmation systematically of the oneness of God, the wholeness of belief, the comprehensiveness of order, the total agreement on the *Sunna* (orthodoxy, based upon the prophet's way of life), the unity of the group, to follow one religious leader, and the one direction to which all Muslims pray.

Multiplicity in terms of godliness is polytheism and atheism, which is unforgivable.

Multiplicity in terms of religious belief is refusal and deviation from adherence to the *Sunna*.

Multiplicity in terms of the state is the return to polytheism or being tempted astray, which threatened the unity of the group.

(6)

In the course of the interaction of civilizations, the principle of unification and reconciliation was a fundamental measure among other standard measures of acceptance and refusal.

Islam had direct interaction with the dualism of Manichean Persia within its own territories and accepted absorbing Greek influences. However, it absolutely refused – in accordance with its unification and reconciliation principle – the adaptation of this striving dualism, or any positive interaction with it, or ignoring the effect of its reflection in its literature and thought.

Dualism became *zandaqa* (free-thinking). *Zandaqa* in its most evident sense is the worst kind of atheism.[2]

This Persian *zandaqa* was fought, just as Arab pre-Islamic idolatry was battled against.

(7)

The efforts of the caliph Al-Mahdi in the war of atheism and the uprooting of Manichean dualism[3] is paralleled only by those efforts of the caliph Al-Ma'mun regarding the comprehension of Greek rationality and the encouraging of translation from Greek philosophy.[4] Furthermore, this philosophy – with its two branches, the peripatetic Aristotelian and the neo-Platonic – has its beginnings, like Islam, in the principle of unification.

This is the foundation, in our opinion, of the historic and fertile meeting between Islam and Hellenism, for Peripatetism pertains to Aristotelian (formal) logic which places in the forefront the principle of "non-contradiction," and sees Being as a logical whole in harmony with itself, initiated in its wholeness by one Prime Mover. Neo-platonic thought develops from the idea of "the one" primal being from which all the cosmos emanated beyond the material world.

The solid common ground and basis upon which religious faith meets with Greek rationality in classical Islamic reconciliation is not only due to the general metaphysical assumption of a unique divine source for both revelation (which is God's gift) and mind (which is God's creation),[5] but it must be realized that there is a true and specific correlation between the principle of unification and the refutation of polytheism and multiplicity in Islam on the one hand, and between the concept of self-harmony and the refutation of self-contradiction in Aristotelian logic, on the other.

Islamic unification traces all things back to the One and Only One, the essential single sublime, in harmony with itself, beyond contradiction or multiplicity: "If there were, in the heavens and earth, other gods besides God, there would have been confusion in both." (Surah Al-Anbiya 21:22.)

Aristotelian (formal) logic on the basis of its essential saying on "non-contradiction" – that is to say, "A" is indeed "A" and it is impossible that it is a "non-A" (which is what modern dialectical logic will refute) – sees in Being a logical oneness that does not allow self-contradiction.

In addition to this is the idea of 'the unity of truth" that coincides with this logic and "which has its roots in neo-platonic Greek tradition."[6] This idea was "the only logical path available to Muslim philosophers for justification by means of their methods of philosophy and for convincing the *mutakallimin,* Muslim theologians, and to satisfy the mind's lusting for self-harmony."[7] Thus did the Islamic and Greek viewpoints basically meet – the first in terms of the unknown and the second in terms of logic – upon the necessity of establishing a unifying vision of the world.[8]

This is what gave depth of perspective between Islam and its principle of unification and Greek philosophy with its Aristotelian logic, in as much as it separated Islam from Persian dualism. In our opinion, had the Greek mind been dual or doubting on the question of God's divinity and the unknown, the harmonious encounter would not have occurred. (This is to be elaborated upon presently regarding the crisis of neo-reconciliation in its encounter with the modern European mind and its dialectical nature).

The meeting of Islam and Hellenism was not limited to philosophy and to *Kalām* (systematic theology), but included stylistics, interpretation, criticism and grammar. It is right to say, therefore, that the two most important elements that the Arabs rendered in Islamic culture as a whole were subjected to the rules of Aristotelian logic, and these are religion, in both its *Kalām* aspects and jurisprudence and its language and grammar.[9]

It is for a reason that Islam ignored the vital Dionysian element, tragic and spontaneous in Greek heritage, and rather focused attention upon the later factor, the Apollonian, of order and intellect, and of unification which began with Socrates and that Nietzsche considered as antithetical to the first factor, and the cause of deterioration of the art of tragedy and the fall of the age of tragedy, and of innate heroism in Greek civilization.[10]

(8)

It is most probably because of this unifying perspective concerning Being, and the selectivity of measuring up against the principle of unification, that Arab Islamic civilization did not develop a clear interest in investigating the true nature of tragedy in human life, nor in depicting it or creating its modes of thought and aesthetic forms.

Islamic thought chose to relate to the unifying and intellectual factor in Greek civilization, while ignoring the aspect of tragedy therein. Thus, the live historical proof that it did not correspond with the spirit of tragedy (the phenomenon of the struggle between two forces in Being). This failure to respond to Greek tragedy, as we see, is a continuation of the Islamic viewpoint *vis à vis* the struggle of Persian dualism, and an adherence to the spirit of reconciliation which refuses the dialectics of the struggle.

With the absence of that dramatic aspect of Greek tragedy from the cultural perspective of Islamic civilization, both Arabic and Islamic literatures became void of the drama of theatrical art (in the sense of tragedy).

Within the spirit of reconciliation, where it is always necessary that the sharp edge of conflict be alleviated, and where points of agreement are brought to relief, tragedy dies, or never actually does take root, and what prevails is the literature of the one voice, the literature of the unified self in its lyrical capacity and in its singular key. (Maybe this reconciliatory explanation partially clarifies the absence of the art of tragedy in both ancient and medieval Arabic literature.)

Naturally, this prevailing aspect was not limited to literature alone. Within the domain of faith, *Kalām* did not focus on elements of stress and tension within the religious experience as much as it focused on the formation of unifying principles of faith that were absolute and mental.

Thus, Islamic tradition never witnessed anything similar to "The Confessions of Saint Augustine." When Al-Ghazali produced "*al-Munqith min al-Dalal*," (*The Deliverance from Error*), he was not concerned with revealing personal psychological ailments and his experience of doubt, but he presented a mental record as guide and as witness to the designed faith and to serve as a blocker to personal agony within the religious experience.[11]

If Al-Ghazali allowed for Sufi *dhawq* (mystical experience), he also rendered it esoteric, not to take the form of confessions or expression that grant disclosure and depiction.[12]

It is quite probable, moreover, that the spirit of reconciliation played a role in the near disappearance of a literature of candid confessions or autobiography. This is because the viewpoint of reconciliation does by nature overcome fragments of difference and ignores contradictory details that are worrisome in life, seeing these as superficial appearances that need to be overcome in order to reach into what is beyond of unity, of essence, and wisdom that derives value from the experience and does away with whatever suffering or worrying had come before.

Literature of confession and autobiography only thrive with the focus on detail fragments and points of difference in the life, self and mind, other than the factors of doubt and of tension it brings to relief. Such are matters that have mostly not been given special attention or carefully recorded in the art of Arabic writing (with the exception of certain Sufi literature.)

(9)

As regards the higher level of the self's entity, beyond the agony of tragedy and a shattered self, towards its redemptive merging and unifying, the spirit of reconciliation becomes a motivating and positive factor. This is because reconciliation – when it is authentic, honest, and in harmony with the nature of its era* - it does in fact succeed over the agony of tragedy, thanks to its fusion of opposites into an organic mix. Consequently, it causes a state of togetherness and sense of inner peace, of harmony with the self, to prevail, while the edge of tension in thought and mind is alleviated, both on the individual level and within society. In its inner construct, civilization then becomes one of harmony where conflict and mental or psychological collapses are rare, and therefore the phenomenon of suicide disappears in the history of the nation.

The truth is that the absence of the suicide phenomenon in the history of Arab Islamic civilization has drawn scholarly attention and become ground for various interpretations and explanations.[13]

Perhaps our awareness of the characteristics of reconciliation within the spirit of this civilization will shed light on the bases of its immunity against that psychological sickness, for once reconciliation is absorbed deep within all powers of self and mind (with no fabrication to cover-up hidden agony) then the germ of falling towards conflict and suicide disappears and the self is filled with the happiness of unification.

(10)

The advent of intellectual revolution in modern times brought a double challenge to the two factors of classical reconciliation, the Aristotelian mind and Semitic faith, especially what they share in regard to a vision of unification. On the one hand, a transformation occurred in the definition of logic from the consistency of formal (Aristotelian) logic, which is based on the principle of self-harmony, towards the dialectic of Hegelian logic, which in one aspect is based on the principle of an inner contradiction, which became an absolute requirement for the achievement of the oneness of things and the oneness of the cosmos itself.

On the other hand, the transformation of the definition of the mind, especially regarding metaphysics, from a mind that is objective, firm in its belief and astutely confident (Aristotelian) to a mind that is idealistic, cautious, of frail self-confidence and idiosyncratic faith (Cartesian – Kantian), or a mind that is sensual, experimental and questioning. Thus altered the relationship of the mind to religion from an absolute reality, stable as established by Averroism and Thomism, to a problematic issue, open to question, unstable and lacking that old, sustained balance between the two factors. This problematic issue reached its peak with the insistence of the scientific materialist mind on relating the source of heavenly faith to its earthly and tangible equivalents and its confinement within its limitations.

With the revival of reconciliation at the hands of Mohammed 'Abduh and his school, and the return of the efforts toward reconciliation between faith and mind, neo-reconciliationists ignored the significance of the radical change that occurred regarding the concept of the mind, from Aristotelian objectivity to the idealism of Descartes and Kant, and this qualitative leap in the concept of logic of which the most acknowledged category became the principle of self contradiction, inherent in the nature of things and their inter-relation, in the nature of evolution, as in the nature of all Creation.[14] This principle, if not difficult for Christianity to reach from the perspective of a rationalized comparison between the triplet (thesis, antithesis, synthesis) and the mystical divine Trinity (the Father, the Son, and the Holy Ghost), it is certainly not easy for Islam to accept, unless Islamic thought were able to create some kind of depiction of a positive relation between pure unification and the dialectic, that is based upon the interaction of opposites; the purpose therein being the realization of the sought-after unification. (It is significant to note that Hegel, who originated the idea of the dialectical trinity, came to the world of philosophy from the world of theology. It is not improbable, therefore, that this trinity extends, whether consciously or by faith and instinct, from the Christian trinity creed, especially that Hegel had rationalized the revelation, creed, and the absolute.)

Not having reached the point of depicting this relation, up to the present time, constitutes, in our opinion, the missing link within the series of meeting points between neo-reconciliation and the "logic" of our age. It is also the cause of the abortive efforts of reconciliation that never did achieve a true starting point for a solid ground to coordination between the philosophy of unification and the phenomenon of dialectics.

The achievement of historic reconciliation between Islamic faith and the Greek mind because of their common unifying characteristics does not necessarily signify the absolute compatibility of faith and mind in all times. It became necessary to comprehend the significance of the series of intellectual revolutions occurring in modern times.

Modern Islamic thought, however, did interpret modern European civilization as a revolution against traditional Christianity.[15] But do not find in this thought sufficient alertness to the fact that, in one important aspect, it represented a revolt against Aristotle and Aristotelian logic, as the philosopher Bernard Russell noted in his *History of Western Philosophy*.[16]

It was up to the revival of reconciliation to determine that particular mind with which Islam had, in the past, reconciled, and the nature of the mind which it confronts in the modern age, and to distinguish between them:

1. That mind with which Islam reconciled is characterized by self-harmony, which is contrary to the dialectical axiom by which the modern mind is characterized.
2. The mind is confident in its constituents, undoubting of its objective awareness of metaphysical truths, contrary to the modern mind which began with criticizing itself and doubting it methodologically, modifying its visions and metaphysical reaches, diminishing consequently its capacity for sure comprehension of Being without the tools of experimentation and the senses or the idealist self-perception, all of which methods need decisive and confident conviction.
3. The mind believes in God upon the objective bases it has established for itself and in which it has trust[17], contrary to the modern mind which doubts the capacity for objective comprehension of divine truth, and which traces the question of faith back to a subjective intuitive logic, as with Descartes, or to a moral necessity as with Kant, or inserts Nothingness within the core of existence making of faith the outcome of dialectical contradiction, as with Hegel. For Descartes has transferred the focal point of the mind's thinking process from the interaction with the external world to interaction with the self; that is to say, from Aristotelian induction to Cartesian intuitive deduction, while its key to certainty was in his incapacity to doubt that he is doubting.[18] Thus the acquiring of knowledge altered from being an objective process evaluated by rules of logic – as laid down by Aristotle – and became a subjective conceptualization where the mind starts from the direct intuition of its subjective being before all else. Kantian philosophy developed this direction further by distinguishing between pure reason – incapable of proving the existence of God – and practical, moral reason which was focused upon certainty, thus stripping proofs of God's existence from their

pure intellectual foundations, and thus making of the question of divinity a noncommittal moral issue (contrary to Aristotelian proof).[19] Then came Hegelian logic with its pertinence to the principle of inherent self-contradiction in Being, making the conflict the twin of unity and its necessary requirement, its other face, thus completing this mental revolution.[20]

Here then resides the most difficult of modern reconciliation dilemmas, for whereas classical reconciliation used to find staunch support in a Greek philosophic mind which believes in its nature, new reconciliation attempts relate to a mind that is developing, revolutionary and doubting. There lies the difficulty of establishing reconciliation based upon sound and fixed foundations.

(11)

Of the effects of this dilemma, we find that when Ibrahim Al-Labban called for the interaction of Islamic thought with religious European idealism, he was satisfied to accept its religious outcomes, and he did not give attention to the nature of its understanding the mind by which it reached its subjective conceptual faith, nor did he address the central problem in terms of the method by which to reconcile the principle of Islamic unification and dialectical discourse…is it possible for Islamic unification to absorb part of the concept of strife and contradiction in order to reach total unity, as in the case in the philosophy of dialectics?

On the other hand, the two Arab Thomists, Youssef Karam and Charles Malik, were in harmony with the spirit of classical reconciliation by ultimately returning to Aristotle, and then criticizing modern idealism.[21] In its Thomist interpretation, Aristotle's definition of the mind is that the mind is in harmony with true traditional faith as prescribed by the modern Catholic Church.[22]

Nevertheless, from this standpoint, they confirmed their

classical tendencies, contributing nothing new to the field of contemporary reconciliatory thought. It is our assumption that they did not open ways of reconciliation or positive interaction between religious thought and the modern mind. After all, the return to Aristotle does not resolve the problem that is suffered by contemporary reconciliation.

As an alternative to returning to Aristotle to revive the believing classical mind, other reconciliators, such as Al-Aqqad for instance, followed up more recent schools of faith in contemporary philosophy, as represented for example by Bergson, Nikolai Berdyaev, and Karl Jasper, to prove the return of the European mind to faith after the long journey of questioning and of doubt, and they deduce from this the possibility of reviving reconciliation and its inevitability.[23]

This selective attempt, however, ignores an important aspect in the history of the mind's evolution, also ignoring that these recent schools of faith are a dialectic extension to modern skeptic rationalism, and an organic growth in that tree, which can neither be understood nor appreciated without return to the roots of original mental formation against which those schools appear to have revolted. Add to that, the tension and tension contained in this same new faith, inherited from the intellectual revolution at the source. This is an aspect that Islamic reconciliation ignores when it refers to that faith.

(12)

Another dilemma reconciliation suffers, shared with those that came before, concerns those periods of change in civilization, of work towards creating new directions in the life of nations, which demands admitting to the truth of the strife, being participant therein, its acceptance in fact as in thought, with obedience to its rules, and giving it precedence over reconciliation and proximity for a period of time.

The reconciliation viewpoint, which by nature avoids strife, ignoring its demands and requirements, may not be the appropriate concept or the most suitable idea for such changing times.

Its moderate stance in the conflict between new and old puts the two parties – according to its own rules of equivalence and balance – equals, and does not lead to a definitive result where the new overcomes the old, which is an ultimate necessity in the creation of a new direction in history and civilization.

Thus, although reconciliation is valid for ages of stability and cultural prosperity that are settled and well-balanced, it is unsure whether it stands good for periods of historical decisiveness where circumstances necessitate the rejection of one direction for the benefit of another different direction.

Islam itself did not at the outset take a stance of reconciliation between its new conviction and the old ones. It digested several factors from the latter. But it vigorously integrated them – after sifting – into its own faith and order, while it violently battled against the pre-Islamic creed until the matter was decided in its favor and it prevailed. Then it established its reconciliatory equations in the wake of its victory and stability and according to its own conditions and values.

Perhaps the prevalence of reconciliation over contemporary Arab "revolutionary" thought can interpret the failure of this thought to establish a complete revolution, decisive and having pronounced characteristics, for reconciliation, by nature, needs a fair amount of time to ferment and mature, being a developmental outcome of circumstances and not a sudden outburst of revolt. Furthermore, reconciliation is a complex construction of existing elements, while revolution criticizes the existing complex structure and prevalence of one element over the other in a decisive manner. Hence the radicals' criticism of the moderate Pan-Arab stance that it were in fact, non-revolutionary.[24]

(13)

Does this mean then that the idea of contemporary reconciliation is unsuccessful and is doomed to be sterile?

The real spirit of genuine reconciliation requires that the thinker be aware of the essential core of those two orders between which he reconciles, so that he focuses on creating a harmony between the axes of each. Once the proximity is established between the essences of the two systems, then it is possible to remove the contradiction and establish reconciliation between its branches and parts.

Reconciliation between Islam and socialism, for example – if ever there could be scope for reconciliation between them – needs to begin with the understanding of the spirit of Islam and the essence of socialism so as to discern the possibility of a core reconciliation between them (if there is any). As for the selection of as aspect of Islamic law to prove its being analogous to a aspect of law in socialism, this would not represent a true reconciliation between both sides. This limited style of selection is what led to the existence of a redundant accumulation of works closer to syncretism than they are to reconciliation in contemporary thought. (See the definition of "syncretism" in the section "The Reconciliation Phenomenon," *Terminology*. See also Saliba, *The Dictionary of Philosophy*, 1/336-7.)

In addition, the situation requires that reconciliatory thought decide which of those currents of modernity are nearer to its spirit in order to be reconciled with it; just as when Islam selected from the Greek civilization its peripatetic and neo-platonic philosophies at the exclusion of others. We believe it is wrong to adopt the saying of Mohammed Farid Wajdi that Islam accepts all that civilization brings.[25]

If modern reconciliation is to be a useful idea, then it must sift through modern currents to discover what is most compatible with it in all honesty and scrupulousness. It should also sift through the various interpretations of Islam itself to discover which is capable of reconciliation with the selected contemporary current.

Embarking upon a series of partial reconciliations between aspects of Islam and others of modern civilization is a vicious circle with no end. Islam, after all, has a rich heritage with multiple facets, and modern civilization is an unlimited and varied entity. It is easy to select similar partitions and gather these to reveal tens of reconciliatory equations between them.

We should understand clearly that if reconciliation does not reach the level of "synthesis" by the fusion of both paths into a new vital and active unity, it will remain an incomplete compound and a useless syncretism.

Reconciliation will not attain the level of organic synthesis unless it accepts the nature of the conflict and comprehends the dialectic. Because synthesis does not become truly molded except when amidst the fervor of struggle and mature interaction. For such an interaction – which includes both truths of the struggle and of reconciliation together with the nature of things – is what merges antithetical elements, fuses them to emerge unified and strong, invulnerable to the shattering which artificial and deliberate reconciliation is prone to, upon the confrontation of challenges.

This means that Arab thought should go beyond the "equivalency" of Tawfiq Al-Hakim. This equivalency, which represents a transitional stance between old reconciliation and new dialectical discourse, allows for the conflict only in order to redeem a lost balance, while it does not allow for its continuum in order to achieve a new unity, both elements having been fused. It retains old or existing dualities in an eternal equilibrium, as in Manichaeism, with no sublimation or progress towards the level of synthesis, of a new organic outcome surpassing it to a higher qualitative degree.

The failure to recognize the importance of the conflict of opposites – before its synthesis and unification – will lead to the failure to recognize one of the most important truths of this age, its thought and its civilization, in addition to the consequences of hybrid forms that lack efficiency, authenticity and stability.

True and authentic reconciliation to which the Arab unification tendency aspires cannot mature and become complete, in our opinion, unless a certain amount of conflict and interaction is undergone between its two opposite elements, Salafism and rationalism, in an open, free, civilized confrontation.[26]

(14)

The inevitability of this encounter requires that reconciliation take into consideration – in the sense of a comprehensive and total awareness – the positions of Salafism and the rational both, before it attempts a forced synthesis of its own equations. Synthesis or proximity perforce is what will befall reconciliation in the long run, causing its internal instability, vulnerability and eventual speedy deterioration, since it would lose control at times of crises – no longer able to check the two bolting and mutually repellant stallions that draw its medium vehicle.

This pursued objective towards an understanding requires before all else, shedding light upon the positions of each viewpoint in order to comprehend them within the context of their own disciplines and their root points of origin, before embarking upon any attempt to achieve proximity. This is a necessary step that we do not find taken by modern reconciliationists with the preliminary objective and theoretical thought required to pave the way towards establishing their aspired balance of forms.

The outset of the contemporary "fundamentalist" stance begins in the refutation of reconciliation by confirming that "there is a fundamental aversion between the discipline of philosophy and the discipline of faith, between the method of philosophy and that of faith,"[27] and that "philosophy necessarily culminates in complexity, digression, confusion and intellectual sterility, whenever it attempts to deal with issues of faith…and therefore, philosophy never did have an active and initiating role in the lives of people as a multitude, nor did it motivate humanity to advance onwards as has done the path of faith."[28]

This further leads to the opposition of the principle of equivalence reconciliation establishes between inspiration and mind. Sayyid Qutb states:

"Revelation and mind are not equivalent rivals, for the one is larger and more comprehensive than the other, one has come to be the original or primary to which the other relates. It is the balance by which the other tests and measures up its course, definitions and representations, modifying accordingly its own flaws and digressions."[29]

The regression of both Mohammed 'Abduh and Mohammed Aqbal towards the direction of the mind has no justification – from his point of view – except as the burden of the distress *vis à vis* the surpassing of western civilization.[30]

The valid Islamic position, according to Sayyid Qutb's belief, is similar to that decided upon primarily by Ibn Taimaya: "as long as the text is thorough and intact, the deciding factor is the explicit meaning of the text itself without interpretation, and the mind should draw its own conclusions from that explicit text itself."[31]

Upon the basis of this supreme lone parameter is built a comprehensive system, distinct from any other system, not open to other interpretations, nor to be evaluated with its parameters or to be a new product of synthesis with it.

From this same perspective Mohammed Mubarak stated:

"Islam's adequacy does not come from its agreement with democracy, socialism or capitalism…For Islam has its own standards and criteria in differentiating between good and evil, and true and false. We do not mean that these standards have no original rational roots. All we say is those roots extend from its garden and those branches stem from its original tree."[32]

For Islam is a self-contained system in its values and its rules, even in its terms and expressions. Elements from other systems should not be adopted before being scrutinized by the standards of its values and the expressions of its terms. The fact is that "the transfer of expressions from one faith to another and from one disciplinary framework to a different one brings with it discrepancies, including related definitions from its own particular cultural environment. Expressions of democracy, socialism and freedom, for example, emerged and developed within certain atmospheres and environments, and were associated with certain concepts and theories which, if we use in relation to Islam and its concepts, with no regard to accuracy and good Islamic conscience, we would be risking introducing foreign concepts and causing a deviation from the right direction."[33]

These value standards become clear by virtue of their refusing to ascribe phenomena to natural causes. It is a deviation, from our perspective, that we should include within our educational curricula expressions that offend the sanctity of our convictions, such as the expression that *nature* has bestowed us with "a fine climate…and plenty of rain…" because these expressions were conceived of during the 18th century in Europe when nature replaced the role of the creator. Nature was deified and God's existence denied, and this is a clear atheistic perspective. The repetition of these expressions to attentive novices is an implicit teaching of the atheistic theory and resulting in subconsciously spreading it among people. Likewise considered are the expressions that describe the heroism, the outstanding roles and the genius of prophets, for these are normal human attributes. The concept of a prophecy, however, rests upon a communication of a chosen person with the divine power, a communication whose nature and essence we do not know.[34]

This puritan selectivity goes so far as to remind us that the word *aqidah*, belief, is not a proper Islamic term since it did not occur in the Quran or in the tradition of early Muslims, and that it is creation of later theologians.[35] It is therefore necessary to return to the Quranic word *iman*, faith, due to the connotations the word *aqidah* had acquired from philosophy and *Kalām* (theology).

It is evident that no intellectual or cultural reconciliation is possible to this highly self-sufficient "fundamentalism" trying to reach the ultimate puritanism in order to achieve an immunity that makes it appear as the all-comprehensive Islamic system (This is the "fundamentalism" used in its original meaning, not as it is used now).

The strict adherence to the limits of the Islamic term ensues, in a stricter manner, to evaluate accurately the meaning of new upcoming systems and their kind, measured against the particularly distinct Islamic system: "The serious danger occurs when we deal with a well-established school of thought, like socialism, whether we mean what the Marxists called scientific socialism or one particular school of socialist thought, or whether we deal with democracy as a comprehensive school of thought which has its own philosophy, and we claim that this socialism or that democracy is Islamic, or that it is contained in Islam and is part of it.*** It is certainly true that such a declaration is a distortion of Islam and a misrepresentation of its concepts, as well as dissolving it into another system and wasting its identity and individuality."[36]

Democracy, for instance, contradicts Islam in its "equalizing between faith and atheism, between anarchy and restriction." Democracy gives the ruling authority to the people while Islam decrees that "the ultimatum is God's alone. He is the originator of authority, and His will as manifested through the Quran is the ruling authority."[37]

Thereupon is the standard by which we measure all things regarding other human systems.

Even if we find "the impulse of reconciliation with democracy or socialism in Islam, we should not make these slogans the promulgated maxims in our lives by which we summarize our renaissance and describe our civilization.

"We ignore an essential and crucial principle. That is, political and economic systems in every country and culture are built upon the foundations of a belief system, and these are simply the outer face of the creed and philosophy in which the culture believes and upon which it is constructed."[38]

Contemporary fundamentalism is in harmony with its logic and its roots when it calls upon a similar renewal as that of Shaikh Al-Islam Ibn Taimaya, who was "among the finest Islamic intellectuals." "Of his most significant works was the opposition to attacks upon and deviations from the Islamic faith in the face of Greek rationalism and esoteric currents, the correction of concepts, their return to their sources of the Quran and the *Sunna*, as well as to soliciting understanding from the first generation of *Al-Sahaba*, the Prophet's companions, whether in the domain of jurisprudence and beliefs or in terms of divine services."[39]

Thus the required modifications do not only "deal with those aspects influenced by European thinking" alone, but also include rejecting influences that are products of "the Greek, Persian and Indian intellect," the interaction of which with Islam caused "that amalgam which deteriorated into various static and unstable forms."[40] That is to say, the rejection of the heritage of Islamic thought in the disciplines of *Kalām*, philosophy and Sufism (considering the non-Islamic factors combined with it).

Here then is the starting point in the struggle for an authentic and purgative existence: "we are in need of reconstructing our thought afresh and of abandoning much of the thought we took for granted, gave in to, and were brought up with in our primary, secondary and higher education, as in our lives, intellectually, politically and economically. This is a massive yet necessary radical and fundamental undertaking. Upon this, our lives and our effective contribution to the domain of civilization depend."[41]

If, from this perspective, our "contribution to civilization depends" upon our adherence to the fundamentalist system in its all-comprehensive; then, from a secular point of view, this same effective contribution depends upon our taking an altogether antithetical position, as Dr. Constantin Zureiq states: "To become, in deed and in spirit, and not only in name and outer appearance, a part of the world in which we live, progressing alongside it in terms of livelihood and thought, speaking its language, connecting with its principles, and joining our resources to its resources."[42] Or, as previously determined by Taha Hussain: to embrace European civilization, the good and bad of it, what is sweet as well as what is bitter.

In order to achieve this comprehensive identifying presence, we must "adapt the machine and use it in the investment of our resources as extensively as possible," which ensures "the destruction of tribalism, feudalism and other such existing systems that stand in the way of nationalism," as well as the "absolute separation of the state from religious authority," and "the training of the mind to pursue positive and experimental sciences," and generally to be "willing and ready to adopt the best of what human civilizations have achieved regarding mental and spiritual values that have stood the test of time, and of human perseverance, in action as well as thought, to build civilization."[43]

Furthermore, secularism shares with fundamentalism its contradiction of the principle of equivalence with reconciles between *Naqal* (tradition) and *Aqal* (reason); yet opposing it in considering reason alone as top criterion and ultimate value, and appointing it as decisive judge in value judgments and even in sieving tradition itself. This is because "our tradition includes that which is only ephemeral, which will fall willy-nilly and fail in the face of the power of modern civilization. As for what is sound, enduring and compatible with these times, nay with all times, we cannot detect it, or separate it from what is corrupt and evanescent, nor relive it in our modern lives fully and with vitality, except by the means of the orderly free mind which we should adopt from modern civilization as the basis of building our own revelolution."[44]

It is extremely important to notice here that even the "sound and enduring" part of our tradition cannot stand witness to itself, nor will its representation and revival be carried out save by "the means of the orderly free mind which we should adopt from modern civilization" and its approval.

With that, the human mind does not remain merely a parallel power to divine power, balancing and equaling – as with reconciliation – but becomes – itself alone – the antithesis, the reviving, critical, corrective power and constructive force.

The mind and revelation in this secular school of thought are of two different and opposite natures, and when there is "a connection made between human or natural causes with divine will...we sense exaggeration and superficiality, and a lack of harmony between premises and conclusions, and an unsuccessful attempt made to reconcile two doctrines that proceed from different standpoints actually contradicting. It is advantageous therefore, to clarify these preliminary situations, and draw the main differentiating outlines between the various orientations."[45]

This mind is not only the essential means of achieving knowledge but is the most effective driving force behind the course of history and civilization, "since whenever reason finds itself encumbered and limited, the whole dynamics of a civilization weakens. Yet the mind refuses this condition and rebels. If and when elements of limitation and suppression multiply and prevail...it finds itself ways out into other societies, where it constructs, develops and provides grounds for power and prosperity."[46]

The elements of this comprehensive rationalist standpoint come together to become the test of contemporary Arab revolution: "the correct revolutionary mentality is that which takes the mental revolution as its ideal model and guide. We usually consider the mind as the epitome of peace and stability, while in fact, it is a revolutionary force and perhaps even the greatest revolutionary dynamic force in human life and the history of societies."[47]

In the light of this, there remains no significance in the integration of Eastern spiritualism and Western materialism in order to create the ideal order, "for there is no spirituality today in the East or materialism in the West; and as for catalyst for progress, this is spirituality itself and it is present today in the West, its live example being modern Western civilization itself, which should be a model to live by for all those who desire life."[48]

Just as fundamentalists insist that Islam is a comprehensive order that does not allow for divisibility, so secularists insist, by contrast, "that this modern civilization with all it bears of sciences, philosophies, arts, morals, and customs, is an indivisible unity, and so it cannot be adopted in part while other parts are rejected. Ethics should be the primary adaptation, since they are founded upon freedom and responsibility, rather than by enforcement; that is to say, the digestion of values, the true root source of the modern western renaissance…but let's be warned: this civilization should be comprehended in its entirety; in other words, we must reach its spirit and essence before its supplementary parts and superficialities."[49]

In spite of the confirmation of moderates from this school of thought that "this kind of secularism does not mean denial of spiritual motives or being atheistic,"[50] the positivist experimental mentality in particular, if taken to the limit, would eventually reach the refutation of "metaphysical myth" – this implies the "myth" of religion, since if the metaphysician tries to derive "from sensory preliminaries, outcomes of another truth beyond sensory experience," it becomes impossible for him to reach "the existence of something or characteristics that are outside the domain of experience…therefore he does not use synthetical statements as do natural scientists nor analytical statements as those used by mathematicians. So, what kind of statements does he use? The metaphysician talk is void of meaning."[51]

When this positivist experimental standpoint is transferred to Marxism – under the influence of social development – the viewpoint on this issue becomes more explicit. "Religion, as it is involved in the core essentials of our lives and as it has influenced our mental and psychological makeup, conflicts entirely with science and the quest for scientific knowledge."[52] Thus the "radical" standpoint, in brief, constitutes, "the destruction of traditional establishment as a whole, with all its various political, social and conventional set-ups."[53] In accordance with this perspective, the decided priority of matter emerges: "You wonder about the principal cause of the primordial nebula, and answer by saying it is God, and I, in my turn, ask of you what proof is there of God's existence? And you will reply that God's existence is not to be evidenced. Then to this I'll respond: And why suppose that the existence of primal matter is not to be evidenced? Thus, the discussion arrives at an end without recurrence to supernatural beings of whose existence we have no proof."[54] Thus is the issue presented by Sadiq Al-A'thim.

This brief dialogue could symbolize what is at the core of the conflict between intellectual fundamentalism and secularism, and sum up the battle between them, embodying the decisive duel that resulted, as surmised by Hassan Saab, in what he called the "New Revolution Movement" and its expected synthesis, when he first presented this confrontation between whom he names "Marxist" and "Wahhabist" in the following manner: "Revolution is man's movement towards the cancellation of this duality, the starting point towards an order in which everything advances to a new quest or returns to an old quest, whether real or envisioned. The revolutionary personality is like the Marxist who witnessed the death of the old establishment, believed himself a new missionary and emerged in the light of this absolute faith to change all things. Or he is like the Wahhabi who is only able to see the new as a way to go astray and is not able to see anything except his old and esteemed ideal, and thus moves in the light of this faith, to destroy all that is new and resurrect upon its ruination his old and desired ways."

"These two archetypes are extreme, to the right and to the left, to the past and to the future, as presented by Hassan Saab, while modern Arab political thought swings on the spectrum with varying revolutionary standpoints...but the totality of the revolutionary mission that recreates the self, establishing it as an integrated entity...is in the totality of either the Wahhabi or the Marxist revolutions. The former represents the totality of faith in a divine order whose wisdom encompasses everything, and the latter is the totality of faith in a scientific order whose knowledge encompasses everything. The two systems pervade the human self and create the feeling that, by the totality of their orders, cosmic direction is determined, God's will or the destiny of history embodied. All else which goes beyond these two stances...is a fragmentation of both orders, or a rift between past and future, or it is a foreshadowing of a new order that surpasses both orders. It still remains an order whose presence is potential rather than actual. It is the responsibility of the Arab mind to liberate it from the state of potentiality to one that is of actuality."[55]

It is a theoretical assumption that Arab thought should have been occupied by the battle between these two opposites until one integrates the vital elements of the other, and the matter is decided in favor of one of them in a new synthetic form, just as Islam was victorious over *al-jahiliya* (Pre-Islamic beliefs) after having absorbed those factors capable of survival and of adopting new structure.

The prevalence of the reconciliatory tendency in modern Arab thought has transformed this dual conflict, the logical and natural struggle between fundamentalism and secularism (between the Muslim Brotherhood and the Marxists), into an intertwined and more complex tri-dimensional struggle, farther away from the fruitful decisive achievement. Thus, in addition to the struggle between fundamentalism and secularism, another confrontational thought emerges that is intertwined with these two schools of thought on the one hand, and reconciliatory thought on the other.[56] This, in addition to the repulsion between the two elements –

fundamentalist and secularist – within the reconciliatory framework itself. (This accounts for the branching out of the moderate reconciliatory direction itself into "progressive" or conservative branches, *Mu'tazelite* (rationalist) in spirit, or with an *Ash'arite*. (traditionalist) leaning.)

We imagine that this tripartite struggle (fundamentalism – reconciliation – secularism) represents a particular law and a unique phenomenon in Arab thought, essential for its comprehension and evaluation. Arnold Toynbee discussed the emergence of the two types of men in times of conflicting civilizations:

1. The Zealot who, in the face of new confrontation and challenge, adheres to the past and to tradition.
2. The Herodian who opens to the world, encompassing even the challenge itself.[57]

The two types apply to fundamentalism and to secularism in Arab thought. Based on the event of Arab particularity, we should add a third type to these two, namely, the *reconciliatory* who is neither zealot nor Herodian.

This is actually a dual entity and is a strange blend of the two entities. The reconciliatory lives mentally as a Herodian, closer to openness, and lives at heart as a zealot, closer to conservatism. Because of this duality, he fights the secularist Herodians with his pseudo-fundamentalist zealot heart, and he fights the fundamentalist zealots with his pseudo-secularist Herodian mind. For this same reason, the reconciliatory suffers internal strife between the mind's tendency towards liberation, and the heart's tendency towards conservatism, thus living his tragedy behind the mask of reconciliation.

Our account is not an attempt to draw an imaginary abstract model. There is an obscure and dark realistic side in the belief system of leading reconciliators that reveals to us – if we draw its scarce evidence from research sources and examine it carefully – the truth about that disturbed, restrained tension of belief, and that concealed struggle between zealot and Herodian, which the reconciliatory impulse prevented from emerging in a healthy and public manner, to remain a spot of dark shadow, provoking wonder and bewilderment, instead of coming into the light as a legitimate psychological and mental struggle aimed at strengthening faith. "He said, do you not believe? He said, yes, but for my heart to be consoled." (*The Holy Quran*: Surah Al-Baqarah 260)

***

As to Muhammad 'Abduh's creed, "even among those who knew him well and liked him, [there were those] who doubted whether he was himself convinced of the truth of Islam."[58]

Lord Cromer said that he was one of those who tended towards agnosticism,[59] while Blunt, the English liberalist who was sympathetic to him and to the Egyptian cause, said of him, "I fear he has as little faith in Islam…as I have in the Catholic Church."[60]

From the other side, his fundamentalist critics blamed him for his laxity in upholding religious obligations, including that of prayer.[61]

These doubts, notwithstanding its contradiction by his high perseverance and his celebrated efforts for the cause of Islam, both in thought and in action, "were not altogether void of truth."[62]

As for Abbas Mahmud Al-Aqqad, the most prominent of contemporary reconciliationists, he "began his life as if religious belief had no place in his heart, to end up a passionate, courageous and staunch defender of Islam."[63]

There is nothing strange about this development, yet how does the transition happen from indifference – to say the least – to absolute certainty? Where are the steps and phases upon the path of suffering in Al-Aqqad's writings, especially since, "in his beginnings, he often seasoned his speech with blasphemous expressions?"[64]

Despite the highly authentic tone of certainty that prevailed through his Islamic writings, it is Al-Aqqad himself that reveals in a passing glance – of significance, however – the other side of his spiritual crisis. He evokes in the introduction to his book *The Genius of Muhammad* (1943), the first of his Islamic series (*Islamiat*), the phases of spiritual tension he underwent, as if to succinctly make known to those acquainted with him the reasons for his shift towards writings about religion with conviction: "Where have we been these thirty years (1913 – 1943)…expanses in the world of intellect and spirit which, if it appears as a concrete space, would cause one to hold his head in his hands to steady the vertigo from the vast endless expanse: so many opinions, teachings, provocations, crises, revisions…so many earthquakes one's entity has buckled under, the self with its pillars and essential principles having been subjected to ruination. How so very often in these thirty years has the self been churned by persistent experiences and trials without so much as life's rendering a moment's daylight relief? And how very much of this has had to do with the consolidation of opinion, and with the abating of rebellion and of sandstorms?"[65]

This brief and shy reference could be perchance the sole direct confession in al-Aqqad's Islamic writings, of that long and arduous journey full of thorns, that he traversed from doubt to faith over the span of thirty years across "expanses of the worlds of intellect and spirit." It is a reference that is not bigger in size and in generality than the glimpse that Al-Ghazali stated in his *Al-Munqith* (*The Believer*) regarding the psychological aspect of his doubts, though Al-Ghazali is naturally more prolific in the presentation of his intellectual quest.[66]

The emergence of this problem of belief at the heart of Islamic thought is most likely because of the lack of granting a legitimate room for the element of wavering and tension within the spiritual experience, as part of its process and an indispensable agent for its completion and maturity (because there is no concept in Islam of the fall or original sin). Certainly, this questioning evidence does not touch upon the faith of the believers. The matter can be summed up in the lack of legitimate channels to contain the streams of sincere wavering within the sources of the religious experience.

Thus, this element – which expresses human frailty – is suppressed, and its role and effects are covered up; since revealing it in broad daylight would result in a conflict with the exoteric text.[67]

Furthermore, the reconciliatory impulse, in its turn, demands the confining of the effects of this factor of questioning within the narrowest limits, if not having it done away with altogether, for in order to complete reconciliation and establish its structural grounds, all kinds of opposition and duality need to be overcome, especially the duality of wavering and faith. It is our opinion that this is what caused the reconciliators to summarize their principles of faith – mentally – as if they were final and absolute constants or complete given facts, from the start, and not the fruit and outcome of long and arduous search, digging, examination, and questioning.

***

If it is contrary to the spirit of Islam to admit the truth of constant struggle in the cosmos, the Islamic reconciliation's acceptance of the dialectic concept does not mean the abandonment of its idealist concept of unification, since dialectic – especially in its original, spiritual, Hegelian sense – works, in its turn, to create a new unity that is higher and more sublime than the previous unity. And the conflict between opposites is nothing but its destined path towards realizing the pursued total unification, to which reconciliation itself strives, in its search for the "unity of Truth."

Therefore, one of the ways to renew Islamic thought is to allow the freedom of dialectic interaction – natural and inevitable – between the antithesis of this thought, and in particular, between its two main antitheses (*Salafism* and rationalism),[68] so that what is in the first (*Salafism*) of being, stability, and originality intertwines with what is in the second (rationalism) of becoming, change, and innovation, and the reconciliation between them incorporates the two sides of the truth in order to reach "unity of Truth."

It is not, moreover, of our opinion that such incorporation of dialectic necessarily means the ultimate end of reconciliation. The heralding of this struggle – ruled by laws of dialectics – is bound to lead in the end to the creation of the new synthesis between the opposites in a natural way. It is this outcome which will go to form the solid core and strong foundation for the sought progressive reconciliation. This reconciliation would finally be able to, creatively and positively, draw connections between the idea of unification and modern dialectic of this age. It would reinstate the unity of its two factors – heritage and modernity – in a form different than current forms in Arab thought.[69]

(15)

If we examine closely the prominent incoming trends of philosophy with which Arab contemporary thought has interacted, within the last few decades, we find that the concept of dialectics constitutes the milestone of the interaction process. There are a number of intuitions and signs available to us that show that this thought – in its two sides, religious and social – was about to incorporate that concept and apply it to its subjective theses and traditional subjects allowing – finally – for the aspired for reconciliation between the Islamic unifying basis and the dialectical basis of modern time.

The interaction has taken place upon the influence of two philosophies:

- Existentialist philosophy (subjective) in both its branches of atheism and faith.
- Dialectical philosophy (objective) in both its Hegelian and Marxist branches.

Despite the existing struggle between these two philosophies, in their view of existence, mind and between the human being – since Kierkegaard criticized Hegel's objectivism until Sartre criticized Marxist absolutism[70] – a deep and common attribute unites the influence of existentialism and that of dialectic philosophy in Arab thought.

Thus, both philosophies together carry the seed of conflict and contradiction (within the self or existence) in a more dangerous and radical way than did previous European influences which had infiltrated Islamic thought earlier.

Existentialism bears with it a subjective dialectic, of the human self, between elements of doubt and certainty, the void and fulfillment, perdition and salvation, so that tension and strife work within the core of this self, and at the heart of its sufferings, regarding all levels of existential awareness, including the level of religious experience.

As for the Hegelian-Marxist tradition, it bears with it an objective dialectic that involves the cosmos, nature, history, social reality, and intellectual awareness, whether we trace the grounds back to the spirit, as with Hegel, or the matter, as with Marx.

If the believing existentialist subjective dialectic has been comprehended by reconciliatory thought, within the scope of religious experience; and if the objective dialectic has been comprehended by philosophical and social Islamic thought, within the context of existence, history, and society, then this might represent the true entrance to find common ground between the foundation of traditional unification and the foundation of contemporary dialectics.

Here reconciliation reaches a decisive crossroads, represented by its unification principle being inlaid with contemporary dialectic, and its tension between dualities and opposites, which has been suppressed and illegitimate, being transferred to an open and healthy dialectical tension that has its acceptable natural place within the framework of the comprehensive unification perspective. What is significant is that some interaction within this direction has already occurred, even if not within the direct naming of these directions.

With regard to the dialectics of subjective existentialism in its theist side, we find the beginnings of an awareness of its significance and its role in the inner spiritual anguish with the contemporary Islamic thinker, Dr Imad Al-Din Khalil, who conforms to a conception of religion that is comprehensive, and his work is considered an outgrowth of that of Sayyid Qutb.[71]

He says, "Internal tension is one of the dynamic factors that bring about the experience and the desire for self-expression, a tension that comes from the pain of suffering which in its turn has emerged from the disharmony in the interaction between the individual and the world. This tension has presented us with great creative talents...Does this mean then that any system which attempts to alleviate this alienation or discord between the individual and the world will destroy one of the most vital elements of tension...Has Islam, in its ingenious order regarding the relationship between the individual and the world, buried for good the tragedy of the misunderstanding between man and these values, and therein has terminated his pain, tension and suffering?

"The answer is in the negative. Islam has destroyed tension in its primitive and destructive form, but has established deep within the selves of believers an tension of a new kind, profound and unfathomable, the purpose of which he can faithfully and fully comprehend, and which positions before him various aims and goals which stimulate his existence, and provoke tension to the very heart of his existence."[72]

This deep inner tension the author sees in Islam is analogous to the process of existential experience with its ascending levels, as it is an open road, like that of Sufism, towards the infinite: "Some of these aims and goals are quickly reached by those who become easily exhausted, others in the middle of the road would be reached by those who can walk a longer distance; while the rest are in the far distance beyond the fields of direct vision and the movement limited by time and space; if ever, they would be reached breathlessly, by those who have known thorns and the hot desert blaze, as it is a path trodden only by those few who have experienced tension to the end, have willpower to its highest limits, and have reached the deepest depths of passion and faith."[73]

This sensibility towards existential tension in modern theist thought which conforms to religion represents – from our point of view – a sign that interaction between Islam and theist existentialism is possible. This, after atheistic existentialism had been prevalent among Islamic thinkers during preliminary stages of influence, and after the traditional belief remained – from its point of view – wary of attempts which exposed faith to such existential anxieties, the roots of which had no unity with the self-contained sacred text.

Perhaps within the heritage of the Sufis conforming to the general framework of orthodox Islam, is what might initiate an encounter of Islam and theist existentialism. For those have undergone the experience of existential tension – as the writer himself states: After their wearisome journey, they were received in Heaven by the Lord Supreme, with the welcome rendered to heroes, and the Lord bestowed His light and blessings upon them, shading them in His shade and caressing their hearts with the touch of His hand, so that their inner expressions, literary and artistic, became immortal masterpieces, in the foundation of Islamic civilization."[74]

In another manner, we find in the studies of the phenomenon of Man from the Quranic view (1969) by the Quranic researcher, Dr Aisha Abd Al-Rahman (pseudonym *Bint-al-Shata*), a sharp and prevalent awareness of the idea of nihilism and absurdity and of the role of this concept within the human existential experience, along with its antithetical optimistic idea (concerning immortality, resurrection, and salvation). This would demonstrate that true belief cannot be founded upon the absolutism of textual theses, and that veritable belief is an open truth, the other side of which is living tension and questioning in hope of greater faith. This is the essence of theist existentialism.[75]

She says: "Humanity has long striven nobly to escape the idea of nihilism, yet has remained for decades and ages inconsolable by those old efforts with which it supplicated the hope that death would not be the final ending to the story of man."[76]

Heavenly messages did not provide the expected ending to this human living with the worry of nothingness because "doubt and worry remained, haunting her as it listened to the promise of the heavens, depriving it of assurance of the heart and peace of mind."[77]

Until this day, it remained that "the convincing of another life after death is an extremely difficult issue, as it is difficult for man to imagine a return to life after the decomposition of the body. Of those who made it before us to the cemeteries, none returned to talk to us about what is there, and science is incapable, until today, of entering this unknown undisclosed area...."[78]

By looking at the existence of this absurd nihilistic dimension in the human conscious, alongside the higher certain dimension, "the book of Islam made sure to satisfy that which humanity was tracking to reach the possibility that it can achieve its long-sought hopes and goals for reassurance. At the same time, it acknowledged that the nature of the intelligent, aware human had the predilection for debate, and acknowledged his right to ask for whatever would reassure his heart, even if it were a matter dealing with the unknown. Man has an example in the prophet Abraham (peace upon him), and the Quran had recited to us from his speech saying, "When Abraham said to God, 'Show me how you revive the dead,' and God said, 'Didn't you believe?' He said, 'Yes, but for my heart to be reassured.'" And this question did not take away from the faith of Abraham and did not deprive him of the honor of being chosen as a prophet and a companion."[79]

From this Abrahamic anguish, wondering and searching for more reassurance in front of the Divine presence (and it is an anguish that the Abrahamic tradition began) comes the following question: "What did religion, at the end of its messages, present to relieve humanity of its prolonged suffering of worry and doubt as it resisted the idea of nihilism and clung to the hope that our existence in this life would not vainly end in the grave?"[80]

The answer gives legitimacy to this sincere uncertainty: "The book of Islam...appreciates the need of man for proof, convincing him with the other life, and expecting his debate in this unseen matter: And Man was above all dialectical."[81]

We can see in both these references to the legitimacy of the inner tension in the religious experience within the conforming, believing thinking, and in the contemplation of the Quranic verses in light of human anguish in relation to the absurd nihilistic dimension, implicitly accompanying the higher reassuring dimension within the process of theist anguish – in all that, there is what indicates the beginning of the acceptance of a currant of

Islamic thinking for the subjective dialectic (the theist existentialism) by combining the element of uncertainty within the core of the faith procedure, and by freeing faith from the rigid interpretation of the scripture. This is so that the legitimate existential choke which accompanies the faith motivation does not remain outside the circle of faith, but becomes an integral part of it, and an effort for which the wondering faithful are rewarded in their salvation to find their Lord.

The anguish of the sincere search for Truth is the right of Man, leading to the duties of faith and imposing certainty. The true religion – as Pascal noticed – is the one that can contain the two opposing elements of human nature (doubt and certainty) and organizes the relationship between them.[82]

When there is space for this subjective dialectic within religious experience, we find preliminary acceptance of objective dialectic beginning to appear within the scope of renewed religious thought and of sociological thought that is reconciled with the essence of religion.

We can thus see three reasons for Hegelian philosophy to be acceptable and of particular attraction to Arab thought and its reconciliatory impulse. These reasons are:

1. Hegel, even when he called for dialectic or the principle of contradiction inherent in every being, he defined this principle and conditioned it to strive towards a comprehensive unity; that is to say, the struggle is not perpetual, nor is it without purpose. The purpose more precisely necessitates its disintegration and transformation into that which is higher than itself, within the unifying synthesis, in the unity that overcomes the level of struggle that culminates in the process of sublation; sublation in Hegelianism being an important factor parallel to dialectic

and representing its purpose. It is that creative leap which is unifying in dialectic where the encounter between two opposites results in the triumph of the positive element of existence over the negative element of nonexistence, and the emergence of the new unity, surpassing its two constituting factors qualitatively, and is comprehensive of both in a new creation.[83]

This concept of "sublation" can represent common ground between Hegelianism and reconciliation since it resembles, in the second, the decisive transformation from the state of opposition between the two orders, object of reconciliation, towards their merging into the new comprehensive unifying of truth or the new synthesis. In order to be in accord with Hegelianism, reconciliation needs only to admit that what it considers an apparent opposition between orders, is reality a dialectical opposition and a necessary condition for true unification to occur. In any case, it is a radical change.

2. Hegelianism has rationalized existence, on top of that, the Divine existence and the religious phenomenon, so that the phenomenon of religious development for humanity has become an embodiment of the activity of the universal intellect, and the hypostases of creed have become the hypostases of the mind.

This organic unification between revelation and the mind represents the ultimate goal of reconciliatory thought (since ancient times), and Hegel came to go beyond the duality of modern age and its separation between the two elements, Faith and the Mind – with his understanding of the significance of the struggle, which accounts for Hegelianism being the closest of the philosophies of the modern age to religious heritage, and the richest, in reference to its needs in development and renewal.

3. Arab contemporary thought, in its being influenced by material dialectics and its interaction therewith on the level of a socio-political sphere, has to return to the source and origin of dialectic if it is to fathom its philosophy. This also means a return to the Hegelian source to comprehend the active and dynamic elements from which emerged sociological dialectic.

Thus, Hegelianism surrounds Arab thought on both sides. If it returns to its reconciliatory roots which rationalize religion and search for unity over conflict, then Hegel is exemplary of this, and if it tended toward a revolutionary direction, then here again is Hegelianism the source of dialectical heritage.

In a contemporary intellectual attempt (1976) to determine "our standpoint regarding western heritage"[84] and upon an admirable framework of critical approach that is relevant to us alone – us, Arabs – nowadays and in the past, we find the following evaluation of Hegelian elements: "Hegelian philosophy is considered of the most excellent in the history of humanity throughout the various schools of thought if not altogether the most excellent – as seen from Dr. Hassan Hanafi's point of view – for it is Hegel who has divided European philosophy into modern and contemporary; in other words, he constitutes the climatic achievement of European consciousness. It is also Hegel who has divided the world into the two camps of capitalist and socialist, taking into consideration that Marx is one of his students. His school of dialectic, through Marx, is now the dominant one over developing countries where it has proven its dynamic influence and validity in its direct analysis of reality, and its ability to eliminate contrived divisions and artificial boundaries whether of thought or of reality.

"Hegel's philosophy is considered the most outstanding of religious thought that humanity created, for he transformed religion into thought, then transformed thought into existence. It did not suffice him to lay the foundation for belief in God and the immortality of the soul on rational grounds, as Descartes had done, but he spoke of religion as philosophy, and viewed belief as existence itself. He did not pose the mind as contradictory to faith and as destructive of belief, as is the case with the free thinkers of the Enlightenment, but joined mind and spirit, and religion became to him everything and not a special field unrelated to existence."[85]

As a result of this evaluation by Hassan Hanafi, Hegel becomes a familiar and intimate symbol within our own proper heritage, returning to us in the garb of a *Mu'tazilite,* of an Averrosian, or a *Sufi*: "Hegel has been able to overcome the duality of knowledge that up until now still puzzles the human spirit...which means Hegel, in this sense, is a *Mu'tazilite* or an Averrosian philosopher. The *Mu'tazilite* and the philosophers are the closest intellectuals to the standpoint of Hegel regarding religion. Whether we take the lesson from Hegel or delve into our old traditions, we are able to eliminate the source of duality of knowledge and see the revelation in reality, meaning to reach spiritual truths by way of the mind, while the mind is reality and is history also..."[86]

Hegel does not, however, retain this old garb, and quickly we see the heartbeat of his dynamic dialectic touches upon – as Hanafi sees – the understanding the concept of Divinity itself: "In our opinion on religion, which we have inherited from our old heritage, especially from *Kalām* (theology), we preferred its conception of God, i.e., God's transcendence (*tanzih*), which can reach *ta'til* (lit. 'stripping' or 'divesting' God of His attributes)[87] and considered God outside the world and outside of history...whether the people were hungry or full and whether the land were independent or occupied."[88]

Yet there is a conception of God – who is nearer to us than the jugular vein – instated by the Sufis whom "we blamed as blasphemous because they stated the unity of Being and that the history of prophecy was in correlation to the history of human development...and that God was not outside the cosmos but at one with it according to the description of Ibn Al-Arabi."[89] The self-same conception exists in Hegel, that is to say, "God is in history." It is a vision derived by him, among other European romantics, from "Islamic Sufism" and from his concept of "the unity of Being."[90]

Based on that, "It is therefore possible, whether with reference to the Hegelian model or by delving into old Sufi tradition, to imagine God close to us, present at moments of development and perfection, and not separate from the history of people, past or present...for God is closer to the dynamic than the static and a motive for progress...and inside history more than outside it."[91]

In this way, this tendency of thought brings together what we have called the unification foundation in heritage, in the sense of static, transcendent and abstract, and the dialectic foundation of the modern age, in the sense of its being dynamic, active and determined. Thus, God becomes "closer to motion than to stillness."

Alongside this dynamic concept of the 'Divinity,' there is an invitation to adopt the dialectic method which has brought us to the truth of this concept, since this dialectic method – which is the movement of reality itself – is the method before us now, and which could serve sustaining contradictions, for contradiction is the requisite of motion, and negation is the requisite of surpassing. Dialectic here is not an application of a method foreign to reality, but rather the application of reality itself from which all are isolated until now.[92]

As an effect of this method and its consequent dynamic concept regarding the existence of God, it is Dr. Hassan Saab's opinion that the essence of "value modernization" that is desired for the Arab mind is represented in "our re-reading of the Quran" by revealing the "dynamism" in the word of God that is the miracle within the entire cosmos (and he employs the term "dynamism" in the place of dialectic, as illustrated by the following text dating back to 1969: "The miracle of the creative word of God is the miracle of the Quran, and the miracle of true Islam. Perhaps its most miraculous aspect is that it is a divine command of perpetual movement. It takes a person the first reading of the Quran to perceive in each of its verses, that it is the book of motion. It is the marvelous image of the dynamics of divine creation."[93]

The motion becomes eternity, and it is the only constant in the word of God: "The divine command of motion is the sole fixed and unchanging command."[94]

This dynamism manifests through the re-reading of Quranic meanings – upon various cosmic levels of creation: "The Quranic word is a remembrance or an awareness of this cosmic motion, for it is a remembrance the process of creation as one of wholeness...it is a remembrance of the dynamism of the miracle of nature, a remembrance of the dynamism of the creation of man, a remembrance of the dynamism of society...and a remembrance of the dynamism of history.

"The dynamism, which the word of the Quran reminds us of, is a dynamism, which is divine in its beginning and its end, albeit it had changed into a creative human dynamism. Hegel, the philosopher of dynamism in the modern age, was the best of those who noticed this dynamic act of the Quranic word, which he mentioned in his book *The Philosophy of History*, saying that the most important and distinguished factor in Islam is the negation of the "static" in every tangible being."[95]

The purpose of this interpretation of the dynamism of the word of God is to legalize the multiplicity phenomenon within the crucible of unification: "God is one, the Truth is one...but Man's paths towards God are many, and his ways in the universe are forked and, therefore, there are necessarily so many ways towards the one final Truth."[96]

It is an attempt to derive the "becoming" of dialectic from the "being" identity of unification and to transform the one word into a dialectical act that is multiple, and an attempt to see diversity in unity: "The meeting point in religion between what is physical and what is metaphysical; and it is also an encounter between necessity and freedom. It is a dialectical encounter between nature and God...in the degree that the meeting point in religion continues between necessity and freedom, as much as it stays an expression of what is in being without separating from what is becoming, and as long as this meeting in, or through, religion renews itself, the basis remains for the eternal dialogue between God and man."[97]

Under the presence of this dialectical logic, religious thought senses the impending danger that keeps threatening traditional logic, which is the logic of self-harmony upon which the philosophy of religion was originally established. The contemporary Shiite thinker Mohammad Taqi Al-Modarresi (one of the Karbala doctors) attempts to trace the principle of contradiction as propounded by dialectical thought to the principle of change that is brought about by cause and effect (the causality, as decided upon by the Aristotelianism and the Averroism *s*chool). It thus follows that the contradiction of dialectic is the same contradiction occurring between cause and its effect and propagates change and motion. Therefore, there is no need to contradict the formal logic on the pretext of the novelty of dialectical logic, nor is there excuse for replacing metaphysical philosophy with dialectical philosophy, for "dialectical philosophy has changed the term 'cause' to the term 'contradiction'...and it sees that contradiction is the reason for motion; the same view as metaphysical philosophy...although the language differs...and it is evidence that terminology alone was the barrier between the two philosophies."[98]

However, in harmony with formal logic, Al-Modarresi refuses to accept the principle of self-contradiction within the one entity, the idea of the entity being inclusive of its contradiction, and rendering an opposite from its own opposite, as dialectic would in truth have it. For him, it was sufficient to say that contradiction can happen between two different things, which are the cause and the effect. That is, he stopped at the exterior contradiction between things and did not accept the principle of self-contradiction within the same one thing, because this concept includes a contradiction with the principle of self-harmony in formal logic, and furthermore, it touches upon the purity of the idea of unification in religion.

Whatever may be the value of his explanation of dialectical thought, his attempt to reconcile between dialectical logic and Aristotelian logic, between the two philosophies of dialectic and religion, represents a kind of concerned response on the part of contemporary religious thought, as it reacts to the challenge of this axial and highly significant foreign thought.[99]

In Al-Azhar – as in Karbala – we find that the same thought is the object of contemplation and filtering of the contemporary *Salafi* thinker – *Ash'anite* in spirit – Dr. Mohammed Al-Bahi, author of the book *Modern Islamic Thought and its Connection with Western Colonialism*. He sees "that there are three expressions mentioned in the *History of Philosophy* that express the confrontation. These are opposition, duality, and contradiction.

The expression 'opposition' was defined in ancient philosophy, and used by al-Nazzām, the *Mu'tazilite* thinker...in the proof of God's existence. He says that in this world there are naturally opposite things, like heat and cold...but they are united and forced to become other than their nature...so that there must be a force that conquers these opposites and unites them for a higher purpose.

The principle of duality was known in Aristotelian philosophy in terms of the form and matter, as it was known to Plato, his teacher, in terms of the ideal and the shadow of the ideal.

The principle of contradiction is of a deeper level of understanding to the principle of duality and the principle of contradiction...for it is not a 'contradiction' between the parts of the one thing, but in the nature of the thing itself, so that one of its two constituents is actually existing while the other becomes the whole thing, after this first constituent disintegrates and disappears. Hence, the principle of contradiction is based on motion, and requires the 'becoming' aspect in the one entity that is of one particular nature.[100]

Mohammed Al-Bahi does not reject this concept in principle and sees it as true and holding, as long as it is employed to prove "the existence of the general cause of the cosmos," and is not restricted to "deduce what can be perceived by senses." He accepts it in its Hegelian spirit (rejecting its Marxist interpretation) and returns it to the equivalency of reconciliation, where he sees that, in the "contradiction existing within the individual himself" as with society, neither side should overcome the other, since "subsistence of either side is not of the nature of the thing with duality." It is therefore necessary to retain the balance required by religion in the individual's duality, and in society's various classes."[101]

It therefore seems that spiritual Hegelian dialectic is able to be contained within the framework of conventional religious thought, after going through some adaptation and modification, this in order to adapt to the spirit of reconciliation, as was the case with Darwinism and other borrowed philosophies.

However, is it possible to comprehend Marxist material dialectics as well with an equal degree of acceptance? This question represents the last crossroads in the history of neo-reconciliation, yet it may well be the most impending and problematic. If the fall of Marxism, on the one hand, and the rise of fundamentalism, on the other, have blocked the road to these reconciliatory attempts, then it is worth learning from this as an example.

It should be affirmed first and foremost that Islam is a comprehensive divine system, and Marxism, a comprehensive human and materialist system, which is to say that Islam within its own perspective is a self-contained system while Marxism is also self-contained in its own angle. It is therefore exceedingly difficult for them to meet upon common ground, if not, in fact, next to impossible.

This is all in principle and form an abstract perspective. Yet the reality between civilizations does not always fall under such considerations, for there are necessary historic factors and coercive interactions, the equal attraction that transforms into reconciliation, the desires of intellectuals on both sides, and other such factors which make of this in principle impossibility a possibility for reconciliation. (In ancient times, the positive interaction between Semetic heavenly heritage and the Greek heritage did occur, in spite of the fact that the Greek heritage is a totally human intellectual one with roots originally in idolatry and materialism.)

Perhaps the clearest proof of this line of thinking is what we have seen of gradual development in Arab thought, from absolute rejection of Marxism to an attempt its study and contemplation, to the stage of research and investigation on the reconciliatory aspects therein – at least those concerning social Islamic principles.[102]

Arab thought has achieved the reconciliatory stage between Islam and socialism (this being a collective concept and legislation embracing the nationalization of property and general ownership) at the hands of specialized Islamic judiciaries and scholars, qualified to pass Islamic opinions, such as Al-Shaikh Mustafa Al-Sabai (d. 1966), Dean of the Syrian College of Jurisprudence, and Al-Shaikh Mahmud Shaltut (d. 1964), the previous grand Shaikh of Al-Azhar mosque.

Some Marxist concepts wore Islamic garb, like Sayyid Qutb in *The Struggle between Islam and Capitalism*, so that the proletariat was the weaker class of people who are sufferers and are persevering, and are the sole upholders of the entrusted Islamic faith within the Islamic community, while the capitalists became home to "indulgent luxury" and allies of the unjust and abusive rulers, and the spirit of class struggle and strife merged with the dormant spirit of noble religious *jihad* in Islamic movements.[103] Meanwhile, Khalid Mohammed Khalid decided on his part in direct thoughtful clarity: "The spiritualism we proclaim does not begin upon its own initiative, but begins with a full stomach...and the last word we say to people is that their spiritual energy is a result of their economic energy, and that if a person is not fortunate enough in his circumstances to live without need and without poverty, he will live with no soul."[104]

These efforts of thought were completed by and culminated in the Nassarist manifesto proclaiming "scientific socialism," a maxim originally Marxist, with all its reservations and justifications.

This was followed by a new concept for "Islamic materialism" where God's place is secured, while the soul is traced back to material origins.

At this stage of development, it was impossible to avoid confrontation with "material dialectics" itself, or to ignore its dialectical methodology.

In Dr. Ismat Saif Al-Dawla's book, *The Theory of the Arab Revolution* (1972) in which he attempts a total formation of a comprehensive theory of the Nassarist movement, he suggests: "purging the dialectical system of the metaphysical germ."[105] In other words, from Hegel's insistence upon the precedence of the spirit, and the insistence of Marx upon the precedence of matter, it becomes a practical method for the social development which limits its dialectics to the evaluation of the phenomenon of historical class struggle and its socio-political issues. He sees that where this is concerned: "the awkwardness that begins discussion on the issue of social development stating the question of whether it is either material or ideological is nothing but metaphysical sophism."[106]

After the avoidance of this embarrassing "metaphysical sophism," material dialectics is no longer wrong: "Material dialectics is not totally wrong, for it is correct in its being dialectical. Yet it is not correct in its being materialistic, nor does this mean that it must be idealistic to be correct. For the correct solution in terms of dialectic for contradiction between matter and thought is the human being. This is because the human being is unique as a qualitative unit: composed of intelligence and of matter, he is the fundamental factor of development."[107]

The reconciliatory standpoint that oscillates between materialism and idealism still holds true to this kind of thought. Yet we believe that next to this is the search for "the valid dialectical solution to the contradiction between materialism and thought (meaning, the soul)."[108]

Further, the subject of dialectic shifts from objective reality to the human being, who becomes "the fundamental element of development" and not material or economics. This shift reveals the attribute of attraction in this way of thought between materialism of Marxism and the humanism of existentialism (leftist – Sarterian) which accepts the dialectical method without sacrificing the freedom unique to a human being as part of the general framework of determinism.[109]

What crowns the research for a method of thought regarding the theory of Arab revolution is the call for "human dialectic" and this is a concept different from both the dialectics of the soul and of matter, and yet it reconciles them. For the human being is the only creature in the world who can join these two factors, and the invitation to "human dialectic" means sustaining both sides of the equation, and material-spiritualism or *madraheya* (to borrow the Arabic neologism of Anton Saada's term.)

As for the most prominent confrontation in human dialectic, this is between past and present,[110] in other words, between heritage and modernity, and this is the basic reconciliatory confrontation in our contemporary thought. Thus, does human dialectic become "reconciliatory dialectic" and that kind of dialectic that is accepted by Arab reconciliatory thought with no sacrificing of factors of the soul or of matter, nor abandoning aspects of either heritage or modernity. However, the relation between the two parts in human dialectic is not a matter of addition or compromise or borrowing, but – and here is what is new in the matter – is a relation of contradiction and interaction and a new birth. This is because: "The contradictory factors in human dialectic are past and future which succeed one another and each canceling the other, and they never meet, yet the human being combines them placing them face to face within himself. He remembers the past in memory and contemplates the future in his imagination and each is a uniquely human characteristic."[111]

Therefore, "In the human being, the past and the future contradict, and he takes it upon himself to solve the contradiction" with a synthesis "that goes beyond them both towards a new creation."[112]

The various types of contradictions in Arab thought can be summed up in the contradiction between past and future, between heritage and modernity and between Islam and modern civilization.

Here then is the dialectic that still awaits a new synthesis. Here is the significance of the transformation of this dialectic that is idealistic and realistic – at once – to human dialectics in process between two entities that do not meet face to face at all except within the one divided self, longing for a "new creation."

This dialectic between past and future means in one of its aspects – and from the viewpoint of another thinker from the same direction – the emergence of the following kind of new creation: "the birth of scientific socialism with its constituents...does not mean – in spite of its atheistic ideology – the end of the humanistic religious revolution with its natural socialist constituents, but rather means the inevitability of the extension of religion to the scientific socialist revolution, for its integration, to integrate it and expand its range, and support it...and it is indispensable to make a close comparison so as to make sure that they do not contradict, but work in parallel in the great race for the sake of freedom, knowledge, justice, work and the pleonasm populace."[113]

"The inevitability of the extension of religion to the scientific socialist revolution, for its integration...in spite of its atheistic ideology," is a sum-up that expresses the nature of the confrontation between abstract unification and material dialectics in this stage of development in reconciliatory thought.

That which was a timely aid in deepening the discourse was the development on the other side, namely, the aspect of Marxist dialectic. Soviet intellectuals reached the necessity of separating metaphysics from the dialectic methodology. Modern Marxism is no longer concerned with driving its materialism beyond physical existence, searching for the primal being. Thus, materialism is limited to the interpretation of nature, history and society, without metaphysics.[114]

This is what brought the first side, the Islamic side, down to asking "a question about God" and connecting it to the full confidence of the believer, until the future answer comes, without insistence upon an immediate answer, "so as to close the cycle of discussion at the point of making agreement on disagreement possible."[115]

The answer to scientific socialism, from the Islamic side, we summarize by the following: As far as Islamic believers are concerned, they cannot, using evidence that is confined to materialistic scientific tools of experimentation, prove the existence of "God" to those who cannot accept His existence except by using these tools. The materialist socialist Marxists, in their turn, also are not able to use these same tools – used to test scientific material – in order to prove the impossibility of God's existence to those who believe without the use of these tools.

The question then concerning the issue of God is equal in both Islam and scientific socialism, but since scientific knowledge is an established basis in the intellectual structure for each of them, then the expectation of the decree of science upon this matter – and it is an acceptable judge to both of them – does not hamper their common and parallel quest upon the path where there extend many meeting points of agreement.[116]

If the difference between them on the issue of God is delayed waiting for the decree of science, then the revelation will be rationalized so that it reveals those same natural laws that are the foundation of dialectic, just as Al-Farabi 'rationalized' the revelation to disclose the cosmic conception by virtue of prophecy's intuition.

This is because "the revelation in terms of reconciliatory thought is an external influence which transfers to man the will of this ultimate power over cosmic laws, so that man imposes this scientific consistency of these laws over his life, thought, work, relationships and purpose. This influence requires a high mental and psychological sensitivity to the cosmos and its movement. In its highest levels, this sensitivity reaches the degree of prophecy, or direct reception from God of the heard word and the clear sign."[117]

Therefore, it is possible to say that if metaphysical dispute is set aside – the sharpness of which has actually lessened – then Islam could accept historic and social laws of dialectic, since these are considered a mental discovery and part of the general cosmic order which is dominated in the end, in one form or another, by divine will.

"If the Muslim could accept – retaining his fundamental divine creed – the Newtonian laws of gravity and the laws of Darwinian evolution without its atheism, then why would he not be able to accept laws of material dialectics if it has limited itself to the levels of history and sociology as part of the highest law with its broad and diverse framework?"[118]

There is an historic Islamic-Marxist experience which has remained unknown, obscure and distorted in the Arab mind until recently; yet the attempts – within this awareness – begin to clear up its obscurities and to understand it in a way that is closer to acceptance within this type of neo-reconciliation.

In this concern, we have heard that Islamic-Marxist thinkers have begun the adventure of the difficult reconciliation between Islam and Marxism. They did have their intellectual achievements and their scientific influences, from the viewpoint of those concerned with this kind of rapprochement.

In Soviet Islamic Asia, near the home of Avicenna, "it has become clear to the Russian Muslim doctors (meaning the Asian Soviets) that Islam supports Marxism in many aspects and procedures; instances of this are: the elimination of feudalism, the achievement of equality, promoting the value of work, and denying usury...and from here occurred the meeting ground, and upon such occasion appeared Sultan Galiev and Hanafi Mazhar among other Soviet Muslim leaders, who founded the Islamic Communist Party, and who made it a point of policy that wherever there is agreement and Islam accepts Marxist teaching, they seize the opportunity and put their hands with Soviet leaders, and wherever Islam rejects Marxist concepts, they open the door for dialogue with the hope of convincing the Soviet leaders to abandon these concepts and correct the process of the Bolshevik revolution. This policy had its effect at a later stage"[119]

At the beginning of this encounter and at its core is what has been clarified by Sultan Galiev, that "there is no relationship between materialism and socialism, any attempt to tie the materialist interpretation of the cosmos to socialism is redundant and out of place." The atheistic materialist may or may not be a socialist, just as the socialist may or may not be a materialist...and Galiev has confirmed the strength of the relationship between religion and socialism regarding sharing the same essence, for both reject injustice and using others...and the saying that matter is the cause of all existence...and a kind of substitution for a true god, who is God, with another god which is matter. We now find that many Marxists admit this truth.[120]

By virtue of the contributions of those Soviet Muslim intellectuals in "the development of Marxist thinking, and even the correction of many of its concepts," we find today "the socialist applications in some Arab nations meet in accord with the opinions proclaimed by Sultan Galiev, such as the idea of the believing socialism."[121]

Of the same potential we also find the attempt of "an Arab/Muslim who embraces advanced dialectical thought"[122] to research *The Quran in the Light of Material Dialectical Thought*.

(1972)

The supernatural sacred word of God is finally positioned – in this research – under microscopic view of dialectical materialism, but with dignity, care and love, and with consideration for the spirit of both sides: unification that is transcendent and dialectic which is earthly. From this emerges that image: "a cosmic perspective, the earthly and worldly, and the transcendent and sublime – together" in the form of "an interconnected system exchanging ways of connecting life between them."[123]

And it is an image that is a result of "an objective vision of oneness of the whole cosmos, in its multiplicity of beings and phenomena,"[124] a result of "dialectical synthesis" also between two laws: the law of development of life and its diversity, and the law of its sublime comprehensive oneness, so that the two laws become "two faces of one true law becoming more sublime by virtue of the relationship between the two laws. Therefore, what is created spontaneously, and by the same logic, is a more significantly comprehensive law, which can be named dialectical, and which is characterized by multiplicity and oneness at the same time.[125]

"Dialectical law: multiplicity and oneness"??!!

The naming of the term may as yet be crude, and the raw compound of 'oneness – dialectical' be nearer to *syncretism* than *synthesis*, but we do need to understand, however, that a new type of initial thinking has been attempted, in spite of the toughness of the attempt and the difficulties of coordinating between unification and dialectic.

Here then is the crux of the research, to be specific, when we began to investigate the extent to which Arab reconciliation could transfer from its logic of harmony and unification to the dialectic of the contemporary age with its pluralism (while remaining within its framework of unification). Nothing is more revealing of the preliminary understanding of this pressing intellectual requirement than what is similar to the term: monist pluralistic dialectical law (a term with compound formation that could be included in the dictionary of reconciliatory thought: Material-spiritualism – equivalency – Islamic materialism – realistic idealism), regardless of the extent to which we either accept or reject it as such.

Within this line of thought, of searching for an Islamic dialectic, another book came a few years later (1976) that probes the possibilities of the same quest: "Is it possible, regarding this absolute unification, to hold discourse regarding a Quranic dialectic?"[126]

Here the issue has depth that is worth contemplating the case of the dialectic between consciousness and revelation, "if we suppose that consciousness springs from the human mind and senses...and that revelation springs from beyond human power, then the issue of the dialectic between consciousness and revelation is brought to relief with all its complexities and problems. So, is it possible to suppose an internal revelation (individual – social), and an outer revelation (divine – angelic) to the absolute human mind and to the prophetic mind in particular? If this supposition in its two parts does hold, then strife will take place between the two opposite beliefs: the first proclaims the unity of revelation as one of the activities of human consciousness of the world, regardless of the source of revelation. The second proclaims the oneness of revelation (divine message), whether that of its source, which is God, or that of its receptor, which is the prophet. This second opinion is what we encounter in the Quranic dialectic, when we raise the issue of the relationship between 'eternization,' absolute unification separate from all human factors, and the 'divine message,' this special revelation given to the consciousness of the chosen prophet. Then how does the 'eternization' transform into 'divine message?' In other words, how is the connection established between that which is absolute, eternally and perpetually, and that which is relative temporally and consciously?[127]

This problematic issue on the relation between 'eternization' and 'divine inspiration' looks like a contemporary reiteration of the issue between *Mu'tazalites* and *Hanbalites* regarding createdness of the Quran and whether it is created or eternal, for 'eternization' means being eternal while 'divine inspiration' means being created. The connection between them is examined today from the perspective of the dialectic relationship between the absolute and the relative, as it had been examined previously through the logical relationships between the eternal "one" and the created multiple.[128]

***

Did these signs and indications, collectively from "existentialist" subjective dialectic to objective dialectic, contribute in Arab neo-reconciliation overcoming the greatest challenge of its history, the challenge of achieving reconciliation between Semitic Arabic unification and European Germanic dialectic?

Or has this reconciliation with these adventures led in the end – to its final shattering – between tendencies of unification and requirements of dialectic, so that it is substituted by another method that is not reconciliatory, achieving a decisive stance by one side triumphing over the other?

(16)

Starting with the sixties, international conciliatory philosophy brought new hope for Arab neo-reconciliation for the accomplishment of reconciliation between contradictions of the age.

The two striving master philosophies of this age – Liberalism and Marxism – began to relate along reconciliatory lines, after having outdone possibilities of the conflict, which the terror of nuclear power impeded the continuation of violence and confrontation, while the period of open-door-policy led to abandoning the strict dogmatic sectarianism.

Liberalism moved in a direction more towards social justice and collective commitment, while Marxism came to accept little by little the idea of freedom and respect for essential human individuality (until it negated itself); and there could be, in the phenomenon of international 'conciliation,' what bear some resemblance to the coming reconciliatory method between the two philosophies of this age. It is the model upon which the national movement has depended in its bringing together of democracy and socialism, and it was in its core call to moderate thought between the two schools, and for neutrality and non-alliance between both camps.[129]

From a farther-sighted historic perspective, the long-exhausted dialectic, between the age of religion and the age of science, appears to be on the verge of giving birth to a new synthesis.

If we agree – according to the law of dialectic – that the Middle Ages, the ages of religion, represent a *thesis*, and the ages of science since the Renaissance represent an *antithesis*, then the *synthesis* must be a merging of the spirit of both ages into a new age that reconciles religion to science throughout the coming centuries.

This new *synthesis* has become an intellectual quest as it is clear to some thinkers in the West: "The great issue the world faces today" is that of reconciliation between East and West, which requires as a preliminary requisite the correction of the narrow viewpoint of both of these civilized parties towards truth and knowledge, since each of these intuitive and theoretical methods is incomplete in itself, but is liable to be corrected and completed by the other. True knowledge is that which is gained from both methods together or from a method that overcomes their boundaries and combines their better attributes. Here then is the aim which should be followed by the coming generations of both East and West, if they are to resolve the differences of their great civilizations and reconcile between them, and to reach the advent of humanistic understanding, international peace and the establishment of a flourishing, distinguished human civilization."[130]

Perhaps in the call of the Russian intellectual Nikolai Berdyaev (1936) to revive "new Middle Ages," where faith meets with the mind, religion with socialism, and certainty with existentialist suffering, there is an expression of this aspect, through an insight into the nature of the forthcoming historical phase of humanity.[131]

While for Arab thought, this hope represents a return to the original source, to primary reconciliation: "The human being today faces a difficult situation between religion and science...while the antagonism between them is old and ancient, and Islam should have put an end to it...but historical reality confirms that humanity stopped short of what religion expected for it..." Has the situation then reached the edge of despair, where holding on to the belief in the final resolution between science and religion is a kind of naïve daydream and just a barren illusion? Has humanity reached the decisive edge that forces it to return, not believing in science or not believing in religion? Not so...for despair in life's reckoning is failure, and the abandonment of scientific knowledge or of religion is suicide....

"From the achievements of this realistic experience...humanity looks forward to its new age with a higher degree of sensitive awareness and of ambitious hope, to dispense it with suffering the sterile clash between religion and science," as expressed by Bint Al-Shata.[132]

It is an aim of Arab reconciliation to reach beyond preliminary grounds of encounter between the ages of religion and of scientific knowledge so that, in its turn, it can accommodate scientific material socialism, and present religious belief to those peoples who have embraced communism: "What is happening now, in this age, is an important phase in human history, where there is a coming together of both the divine and the human based revolutionary systems, that hope, through science, to build satisfactory and just human societies. In this predestined encounter, hundreds of millions of Muslims and Christians move towards the will of socialist social liberation, but based upon a scientific belief in God, which is an extension of the tribal vision since the dawn of history, of what is metaphysical. While the feelings of hundreds of millions who have in fact established a society of scientific socialism, as in Eastern Europe, China and Cuba, are directed towards the wish of faith, which cannot be a luxury or ignorance in the life of a socialist human who has abandoned his sense of individual self and has formed the peoples' system upon the ruins of the priesthood."[133] What happened in reality is that millions have outgrown Marxism and have regained faith.

(17)

Whatever the direction and fate of reconciliation, we are obliged at this final standpoint to take a critical view regarding the influence of the reconciliatory impulse upon the nature of contemporary Arab identity, and the extent to which this identity has developed a distinctive originality under the influence of this impulse.

In light of the reconciliatory makeup of contemporary Arab character, what remains, in the final analysis, of its true distinctiveness and singular uniqueness?

I mean to say, what can be attributed as authentic to

contemporary Arabs alone, within their own appointed time and place, of their unique cultural character, special historical image, distinctive creativity and unique singularity?

From our studies of contemporary Arab thought, contemporary Arabs are either past-oriented fallen under the pressure of heritage, or scientifically oriented intellectuals fallen under the influence of the West; or reconciliators who are mostly attempting to establish a lost equilibrium, almost impossible, between the West and their heritage.

In these three instances, they are prisoners of that which is external to their present proper identity both in time and place, for the West is external by virtue of place, while the past is external by virtue of time.

They are in a state of limbo between two confining powers, one representing an alienation of place and the other of time, while between them expand distances of history and culture for which the contemporary Arab self become an arena once its main concern became the transformation from strife to reconciliation.

As a result, this identity lost its own particularity, and the possibilities of its independent and individualized growth, while its cultural hopes were confined to becoming an open meeting ground governed by the balancing of two powers and whatever relations and compounds develop between their elements.

This reality is what legitimizes the questioning: Where is the contemporary Arab with his particular identity and unique self after having given back to the past what belongs to the past, and to the West what belongs to the West? Where is his particular creativity, and what has he given of himself in his present time and his actual position, independently from both his ancestral past as well as the offerings of the West? That is to say, by possessing the two factors like a property that he is free to do with as he pleases, and not as conditional inheritance or a permanent loan?

Where is his voice? Not the voice of the distant past, nor that of the foreign West, nor that which is the compound of the two voices?

And where is his own proper willpower? Not the will conditioned to reject one in the interest of the other, nor the will paralyzed by oscillating between two blades?

This internal paralysis between two distant powers in time and space cannot be ignored for the role it plays, in the interdiction of any fixed and final stance of civilization in Arab life since the dawn of the Arab Renaissance.

No one dominant idea prevailed in Arab society or moved it with a persistent ascending trend. The sequence of reconciliatory formations took shape and then were undone, only to be followed by a series of aborted or stumped attempts which did not in their totality arrive at what resembles a true and comprehensive renaissance.

Perhaps this handicap comes as the first of the reasons that made contemporary Arab history devoid of the kind of achievements that are typical of developing eastern nations of this age. Nothing in our contemporary history compares with modern Japanese technology or the rise of communal China, or Indian democracy, or the upright stand of Vietnam in the face of challenge.

The contemporary Arab character has remained suffering the agonizing severance between opposites and contradictions with an awareness that is elitist and reconciliatory, optimistic and deceiving.

The tendency to borrow from western civilization is mainly out of the need for western technology and its progress, more than it is out of belief in humanistic and intellectual values upon which the West is founded. The best proof of this is that borrowing from the civilization's gains is accompanied by attacking it, belittling its importance and predicting its expected decline.[134]

As for heritage, the other factor of reconciliation, the contemporary Arab often adheres to this either by virtue of loyalty to tradition, or by virtue of *taqiyah* (self-protection), lest he be considered infidel or blasphemous, or in order to ensure an integral sense of collective identity which had been threatened by the West in terms of politics and culture; since Islam, at the time of modern national upheaval, represented the final defensive sanctuary for that identity after the fall of imposed modernizing forms.

The contemporary Arab may not have the same faith in Islam as did his forefathers, and he may not be adamant in worship nor in obedience to the God of Islam, but he does adhere to protecting the faith that is threatened and does make a point of announcing his faith, which is in fact national and political Islam more than being that deep-rooted religion which his forefathers believed in with all faith, conviction, and obedience, and were ready to defend and die for.

Here is the hidden truth of a critical duality between actual behavior and theoretical awareness, to no avail regarding equivalency and reconciliation, for while secularism and indulgence increase in Arab society, in both practical life and behavior, so also does the call to hold on to Islam and the revival of Islamic laws and their implementation.

Perhaps it was natural that Arab society should be divided into two clearly defined rival parties, in which one party moves towards secularism and the other wants to return to religion. But the schizophrenic phenomenon comes to light when a rather large section of those who adopt a modern secular lifestyle – and at times with indulgence – whether in public or in private, are those very same who also demand a return to the revival of Islamic law and its application. Yet were this to become a reality, they would certainly be the first to be reprimanded by its laws.

This misleading practiced on the self, the others, the history and the religion is a continuous daily process – in the shade of misleading reconciliation – being practiced by most Islamic societies caught between a modern reality that is separate from religion and a deceiving "awareness" of a dual nature, adhering to religion by utterance and form, but not stopping to question the significance of this duality, and the way to cure it and be free of it; whether it be by a return to the practice of religion with conviction, or by an adherence to explicit secularism, both in action as in thought, or, by determining the field of each factor with the utmost clarity, without trickery, duplicity, or deception.[135]

Thus, the crisis of neo-reconciliation is not limited to being an attempt to bring together two factors different in culture, thought and history; but is also manifested by the fact that those two factors have each lost their authenticity and have entered modern Arab life in two incomplete and distorted forms, to the point that reconciliation becomes one that attempts to conjoin partial modernism and a flawed heritage.

Here then is what draws the difference for us between neo-reconciliation and that authentic reconciliation which was the product of a comprehensive and genuine belief in religion, whence it is a fact of existence and destiny, and of brave, loyal acceptance of wisdom as an absolute truth for which is freely desired for the sake of God, rather than for any gain from inventions, material pleasures, or military power.

Finally, in the light of this truly difficult crisis, what if the contemporary Arab decides to break free from these two overriding powers, and exits from the pitfall of reconciliation between them, and puts an end to his state of alienation by returning to the innocence of the free self, its innate nature, away from the chains of both what was inherited and what was borrowed? And what if he derives from his personal anguish, his being, his tragedies, his passions, his unique position in time and place, one particular fundamental value, through which he sieves what he accepts from both heritage and modern civilization equally, instead of his personality being ruled by the double values of two sources, strange to him by virtue of time or place?

It would be no easy choice. Nothing emerges from the void, and it is impossible for the Arab to start from scratch. His heritage is a standing truth, present in his consciousness whether in a negative or positive way, while modern civilization is the most outstanding of all facts of our age and impossible to ignore. It is therefore difficult to tell what remains of the Arab self if these two powers are uprooted.

It is best for him, after all, to be aware of this personal chasm, reveal it and replenish it with authentic creativity rather than remain within a vicious circle drawn by the two forces *ad infinitum*. What should he have to lose now, after all the breakdowns from which he was unable to be released by his expertise of reconciliation over one and a half centuries?

It is hoped that if he regards his actual state of being as a high value and uses it as a benchmark for all ranks of other values, inherited or acquired, the he would be able to rediscover, after having discovered himself, heritage and modernity, from his individual perspective that is independent, honest and effective.

Endnotes

(1) The word *Tawhid* (unification) in Arabic culture has a unique significance in terms of richness and extent of effectiveness. It has been explained through numerous different schools of thought. After Islam committed itself from the start to a theology of unification, *the Mu'tazilite* were called the people of justice and unification, expressing their focus on the intellectual and philosophic singularity of the divine essence beyond the multiplicity attributes. The opposing *Wahhabi* and *Salafiyya*, were called the unification movement, expressing the purgatorial return to the original belief in unity and the rejection of heresies and the artificial use of an intermediary element in supplication. The Druze, from another perspective, also are called Unitarians, and when the Darwinian Arab scholar, Shibli Shumayyil, embraced the scientific materialist belief that unites all living things and particles within the compass of the one unity of nature, he summarized his belief with that one same and eternal word, *Tawhid*. (Shumayyil, *The Philosophy of Evolution and Progressive Development*, p. 30). These are only four of the many instances that reveal the extent the impulse of unification has upon Arab thought.

(2) See the essay on "Atheism" in the *Encyclopedia of Islam*.

(3) Philip Hitti, *History of the Arabs*, pp. 430-431.

(4) *Ibid*, pp. 310-312.

(5) Kamal Al-Yaziji, *Landmarks of Arab Thought*, third edition, pp. 198-199; (in Arabic) an explication of what Al-Farabi had already established.

(6) Majid Fakhri, *A History of Islamic Philosophy*, pp. 376-377.

(7) *Ibid.*, p. 377.

(8) Al-Shahrastani chose to explain, of the Aristotelian principle of unification, what Thamistius stated which was ascertained by the leader of the later philosophers led by Abu Ali Ibn Sina (Avicenna). It states, "Aristotle began to explain that the first principle is oneness, as the world is oneness." He said, "The many, on the basis of agreement of quantity, is only a many in kind...for the first and primary initiator in articulation as in quantity, that is to say, in name and in self." He said, "For the initiator of the world is one because the world is one." *Kitab al-Milal wa Nihal (the book of sects and creeds)*: 2/180.

(9) Ahmad Amin says, "The logic that reached the Arabs is that of Aristotle in a modified and appended way and explained in the manner of the Stoics (followers of Aristotle) and of the Alexandrians, and the Arabs did not add any significant additions." *The Dawn of Islam*, 1/274-275. See also: Abdulrahman Badawi, *Aristotle and the Arabs: A Study of the Unpublished Texts*: pp. 6-66; (in Arabic)

(10) Nietzsche, *The Birth of Tragedy*, pp. 76-79.

(11) Al-Ghazali wrote *al-Munqith min al-Dalal* (*The Deliverance from Error*) after he had regained his faith. The book includes his stabilized intellectual convictions and the logical proofs for the belief he had reached and had started to preach. Yet one will not find therein that aspect of human psychological suffering which arises from doubt and shows echoes and gives signs only from afar. Al-Ghazali summarized this decisive psychological experience in the following two lines of his book: "This sickness became more complex and lasted nearly two months when I was of the Sophist creed, by virtue of circumstance rather than by virtue of speech and essay, until the Lord cured me of this ailment and my self returned to balance and well-being." It is clear

here that he describes the experience briefly and externally and does not reveal its inner process. Al-Ghazali, *al-Munqith*, p. 13.

(12) *Ibid*: pp. 39-40. As Al-Ghazali explains, "It is a state that cannot be expressed, an attempt for it to be expressed verbally would contain an obvious mistake."

(*) There are certain historical periods where harmony and stability prevail, and others that are overcome with struggle and insecurity. Reconciliation finds factors for thriving within the first kind of these ages, what Hegel calls "periods of harmony, when the antithesis is in abeyance." *Philosophy of History*, p. 27. That is to say, when the negation agent is held still (and in an inoperative mode). This is in total agreement with our describing these periods as being the spirit of reconciliation; for reconciliation is "negation of the negation" and (a unifying) encompassing of antithesis.

(13) See Issawi, *Egypt in Revolution*, p. 15, where he refers to this historical phenomenon, supporting it with modern comparative statistics that illustrate how Islamic nations are different from others of the Third World regarding the low percentage of suicide. See also Sami Al-Jundi, *Arabs and Jews*, p. 180, where he refers to the suicide of General Abdulhakim Amir as an exceptional case and a warning of a mental transformation unprecedented in its nature in this region.

(14) The "unification thesis" of Muhammad 'Abduh began neo-reconciliation upon the principle of non-contradiction and the rejection of opposition or confrontation between positive and negative elements in the one creation. He confirms that "it is impossible, by intuition, that the positive negates itself" which negates the credibility of dialectical opposition

between the positive and the negative in one existence. He sees, on the other hand, that "it is impossible that one entity has various existences," confirming the abstract oneness. This implication of this confirmation – philosophically – prevents finding convincing intellectual form for the relationship between the one and the many, and at the same time, between the oneness of creation and multiplicity. Further, Muhammad 'Abduh was in agreement with *Mu'tazilites* on the issue of the createdness of the Quran and refuted its eternal existence; since "to say otherwise is logically impossible (but which logic?) and an audacity to the eternal Quran by attributing change and transformation to it." Review Muhammad 'Abduh, *The Message of Unification*, pp. 38, 49, and 51. That is how the thought of unification was renewed without confrontation with the contemporary dialectic.

(15) See the sources (in Arabic) on modernist Islamic thought, for instance: Muhammad 'Abduh, *Islam and Christianity between Science and Modernization,* pp. 72-73. Mustafa Al-Ghilayini, *Islam, the Spirit of Modernization* (1908): pp. 73-74. Abdul Qadar Al-Maghrabi, *Jamal Al-Din Al-Afghani*, pp. 98-99.

(16) Bertrand Russel, *History of Western Philosophy.* N.E., p.173, and see the impact of this warning on Murad Wahba, *Philosophical Essays*, p. 256, the writer of which is an Egyptian professor of philosophy. He warns of the difference between the two logics, the formal and the dialectical in general and does not refer to their relationship regarding Arab thought.

(17) This spiritual definition of the mind becomes clear from Averroës statement: "Observe the material world and consider this proof of the maker." Intellectual observation

here is related, naturally, to evidence of the maker. It needs no explanation that the modern mind does not endure this spontaneous definition of faith, for this is a mind that could announce its inability to prove the maker's existence (in terms of the Kantian pure reason) or announce the lack of proof of the maker's existence (the Sensualists).

(18) Rene Descartes, "Discourse on Method." (Arabic trans. Mahmud Al-Kudairi), 2nd ed., p.151. Descartes says, "Since I think and doubt the truth of other things, it follows by deduction to the best of my faith, that I am." And here resides the crisis of the modern mind, for its faith is derived from the fact of its doubt.

(19) Kant has, in the preface to *The Critique of Pure Reason*, explicitly stated: "I had to deny Knowledge in order to make room for Faith," which suggests that the space for sure intellectual Knowledge is not one and the same for Faith. Kant refers to the shortcomings of the pure mind to prove the existence of God, saying "it is essential for man to contemplate God's existence, but it is not essential to prove His existence." See Kant, *The Critique of Pure Reason*, Preface to 2nd. Ed., p. 10.

(20) Hegel, *The Phenomenology of the Mind*, pp. 122-123.

(21) Charles Malik stated that modern logic neither criticized Aristotelian logic nor explained it: "...and regarding the claim some modern logicians make that modern logic abrogates Aristotle's logic and contradicts it is a false claim." Malik, *The Introduction*, p. 236. As for Youssef Karam, he was more in harmony with the spirit of Aristotelian philosophy when he admitted a contradiction between Aristotle's mind concept and that of the modern idealist school. (Karam, *Reason and Being*: p. 6). He was biased to

the former definition in adherence to classical reconciliation. Charles Malik, although he united the two logics, he affirmed his rejection of the "incorrect" metaphysics standpoint which of German idealism. Malik: p. 195.

(22) Gaëtan Picon, ed. *Panorama des idées contemporaines (overview of contemporary ideas)*. Paris: Gallimard, 1957, pp. 608-609.

(23) Abbas Mahmud Al-Aqqad, *The Convictions of Thinkers in the Twentieth Century*. pp. 161-173.

(24) Sadiq Al-Azim, *Criticism of Religious Thought*: pp. 46-51.

(*) Review the definition of *al talfiq* in the section "The Reconciliation Phenomena." Also look in Saliba's *Dictionary of Philosophy*, Vol. 1, pp. 336-337.

(25) Wajdi, *Modernism and Islam*: pp. 34-35, or the generalizing of Khalid Mohammed Khalid: "All that science discovers is willingly accepted by religion," This or *The Flood*: p. 155.

(26) As Dr. Hassan Saab presents the issue, "The modern spirit is the spirit of this change and the Islamic spirit in particular...is the spirit of the unknown which never changes. The Islamic spirit is an entity. The spirit of modernity is that of becoming. This spirit which begins with discovering the rules of becoming and of change, ignores what does not change, not believing in it..."this is the difficult challenge," that Islam is confronting in the modern age. Review Hassan Saab, *Islam and the Challenges of the Modern Age*, p. 19.

(27) Sayyid Qutb, *The Islamic Concept and its Characteristics* (1962). pp.10-11.

(28) Ibid., p. 16.

(29) Ibid., pp. 18-20.

(30) Ibid., pp. 18-21.

(31) Ibid., p. 20.

(32) Mohammed Al-Mubarak, *The Individuality of Islam facing Doctrines and Beliefs* (1962), p. 5. The author is a former Dean of Faculty in the Syrian College of Jurisprudence, and a leader of the Islamic Socialist Front in the Syrian Parliament (1947). His writings include *Modern Islamic Thought, Towards a Happy Life,* and *The State and the System of Al-Hisba as Seen by Ibn Taymaiya.*

(33) Ibid., p. 29.

(34) Ibid., p. 30.

(35) Ibid., pp. 13-14.

(*) It is likely that Al-Mubarak here criticizes the efforts of his two friends, Al-Shaikh Mustafa Al-Sabai in *Islamic Socialism* (1959) and Abbas Mahmud Al-Aqqad in *Democracy in Islam* (1957).

(36) Ibid., pp. 33-4.

(37) Ibid., p. 35.

(38) Ibid., p. 42. A branch of this puritan perspective is the national viewpoint which rejects that our nationalism should have a new "content" imposed upon the devout and intuitive belief that is its original nature, as if to say that it is nationalism inclusive of socialist, revolutionary or rational content. For a defense of the puritan viewpoint on nationalism, see Adib Nassur, *Calamity and Error*, p. 67 and Nazik Al-Malaika, *Fragmentation in Arab Society,* pp. 104-

117, representing an antithetical stance to the definition of rational socialism or intellectualism in any Arab nationalism as it is represented by Michel Aflaq and by Munif Al-Razaz (*Studies in Nationalism*, p. 28) or Constantin Zureiq in *Us and History*, pp. 36-7.

(39) Ibid., p. 46.

(40) Ibid., p. 46

(41) Ibid., p. 47

(42) Constantin Zureiq, *The Significance of the Calamity,* (1948), p. 50.

(43) Ibid. pp. 50-1.

(44) Ibid. p. 52.

(45) Zureiq, *In the Culture Battle* (1964), p. 196.

(46) Ibid., p. 172.

(47) Zureiq, *The Significance of the Calamity Once More* (1967), p. 121.

(48) Mohammed Wahbi, *The Crisis of Arab Modernization* (1956), pp. 86-7.

(49) Ibid., pp. 87-8.

(50) Zureiq, *Us and History* (1959), p. 37.

(51) Zaki Najib Mahmud, *The Myth of Metaphysics* (1953), p. 82.

(52) Sadiq Al-Athum, *Criticism of Religious Thought* (1968), p. 21.

(53) Nadim Al-Bitar, *From Defeat to Revolution* (1968), p. 55.

(54) Al-Athum, p. 28.

(55) Hassan Al-Saab, *Islam and the Challenges of the Age* (1965), pp. 91-2 of the third edition.

(56) In spite of its potentiality, no actual direct and decisive confrontation occurred between the members of the Islamic Brotherhood and the communists/secularists to determine the direction of the nation. The moderate reconciliatory direction appears at the right time and intervenes to prevent the rift and suppress the struggle in its balancing capacity (just as Nassarism appeared in Egypt and the Ba'athists in the East). Reconciliation sides with fundamentalism at times to strike at secularism, and with secularism at other times to restrain fundamentalism, and so on. For this reason, it appears "progressive" one time and "conservative" another. The continuation of this dual type of struggle, however, would lead in the end to the creation of a secular Islamic front on both sides to stand against reconciliation.

(57) See the application of this theory on modern Islam in A. Toynbee, *Civilization on Trial*. New York: Oxford University Press, 1948, pp. 185-212.

* "Because of this duality, the matter gets mixed up between "renewal" and "conservatism," between "progressiveness" and "backwardness," so that it remains unclear whether those innovators are for renewal but appear in conservative cloak, or whether they are conservatives in the veneer of renewal." Constantin Zureiq in *The Battle of Civilizations*, p. 242. The truth is that "progressiveness" attends the reconciliatory movement just as backwardness does, both being from the same source, for in its keenness on rationalism, it was able to put an end to a chain of fixed and barren traditions; and in its upholding of rationalism, it entrusted reason (*Aql*) with a dogmatic theological significance which the age had bypassed and neglected. Khalil Hawi, *The Mind and Faith* (manuscript) p. 112.

(58) Albert Hourani, p.141 (from the English original), pp. 175-6 (from the Arabic translation).

(59) Cromer, *Modern Egypt*, Vol. 2. London, 1908, pp. 179-180.

(60) Blunt, W. S., *Diaries*. London, 1932, p. 346.

(61) Rashid Rida, *Ta'rikh (The History of) al-Ustādh al-Imām al-Shaykh Mohammed 'Abduh*. Cairo, 1921, 1/1042.

(62) Hourani, p. 176 (Arabic translation). It is worth mentioning also that the teacher of Mohammed 'Abduh, Jamal Al-Din Al-Afghani, had a predilection for Freemasonry. It is from this perspective that he called for the unification of Judaism, Christianity and Islam in one religion, and claimed that this was a prophecy which should be written upon the walls of the pyramids and which future generations would discover (a call that is unacceptable in Islam). Al-Afghani used to allow, within his own personal code of behavior, attending bars and talking with European girls there. As for his beer drinking, it is controversial. See 'Abd al-Qādar Al-Maghribi, *Jamal al-Din al-Afghani*. Cairo, 1948, pp. 41-42.

(63) Fathi Rathwan, *An Era and Its Men*, p. 230. It is worth mentioning that Fathi Rathwan is a renowned Egyptian intellectual and political personality. He was the Head of the New National Party, and was responsible for the Ministry of National Guidance during the period of the revolution (1957) and he documents for Al-Aqqad on the merit of their knowing each other, although they did differ upon political

issues.

(64) Ibid. p. 229.

(65) Al-Aqqad, *The Genius of Muhammad*, pp. 10-11.

(66) Mustafa Mahmud represents another contemporary model who shifted from doubt to faith between his atheistic book *God and Man* (1955) and his book on faith *My Journey from Doubt to Faith* (1969). This writer, however, discards any justification of his experience of doubt that led him to faith and denies its role in the process of his spiritual crisis, and attributes it to the vanity of youth and to his showing off of learning and knowledge, as well as his desire to be prominent in rhetoric and intellectually superior, but nothing else.

(67) The lives of Islamic spiritual leaders are never free of profound mystic experiences that include both sides of spiritual crisis. However, custom would have it that those should be extremely cautious in opening the gate of Sufi experience to common Muslims, so that the experience remained confined to a select few. Al-Ghazali regards Sufism as the path to the Truth, yet is extremely wary and cautious, saying, "Assume the best and do not ask for news." (*Deliverance*, pp. 39-40). As for Mohammed 'Abduh, despite his openness to spiritual heritage in Islam and Sufism, he refused to agree to the printing of the book *Meccan Conquests* by Ibn Arabi to avoid noises about faith. *Al-Manar*, Vol. 7 (1904 – 1905), p. 439.

(68) Zureiq thinks that contradiction in Arab thought "will remain alive…at times repelling and clashing, and other times in agreement and in harmony…yet the combat will persist even if it does change form or color." Review *One*

Hundred Years of Arab Thought, p. 644. This means that reconciliatory coordination cannot be successful on its own and the inclusion of dialectic is necessary.

(69) It is useful to notice that Islam, though always aiming towards unification, never loses sight of the necessary intermittent toll to be paid as a part of the vital struggle to achieve his unification aim. Furthermore, he placed the struggle at the heart of jurisprudence (the pillar of *jihad* with its moral and psychological dimensions, intellectual certainty, and political strife).

The struggle between good and evil in Islam is a dialectical phenomenon (the greater *jihad* being that confronting the self, badgering it to do evil). In the encouragement of Islam for direct *jihad* is its acknowledgement of the legitimacy of religious war, and in its requirement to spread the call to Islam around the world, which indicates its belief in the presence of intellectual political confrontation in this world. Similarly, the call of Islam to Muslims to undertake this strife with wisdom and with good preaching sometimes, or as holy war other times, is a practical confession of the reality of conflict inherent in history – in spite of the existence of the one sublime will – and of the idea that the overcoming of this worldly and historic struggle is the way to the omnipresence of this will and its ultimate victory. Hence, Islam is engaged in positive reconciliation with the world and does not act in passive complacency towards its evils. Before the realization of reconciliation, there must come effort and strife.

(70) Review the features of the strife between the two philosophies in Arab intellect:

1. The absurd in existentialism brought to relief from the Marxist viewpoint: Anwar Abdul Malik, *Studies in National Culture*: pp. 105-113, and Salah Mukhtar, *Some Ideological Issues of the Petites Bourgeoisies*, pp. 153-175.
2. The criticism of Marxist materialism and its authoritarianism from the existential viewpoint: Abdullah Abdul Dayyim, *Arab Nations and Revolution*, pp. 43-44.
3. *A Kierkegaard Viewpoint on Perpetual Tension* and his critical work on Hegelian dialectics and its alleviation of tension to unification, in: Abdulrahman Badawi, *The Age of Existentialism*, pp. 28-31.

(71) Imad Al-Din Khalil is a professor at Mosul University in Iraq. Some of his most important writings are *Features of the Islamic Revolution during the Caliphate of Omar Ibn Al-Khattab* (1970) - *On Contemporary Islamic Criticism* (1972) – *The Game of the Right and the Left* (1973) – *The Absurdity of Secularism* (1975). In his vision of a comprehensive Islamic belief, the writer follows the same lines as Sayyid Qutb, although his thought is imbued with modernist influences to a larger extent than that of his predecessor. The above-mentioned citations are from 1972.

(72) Imad Al-Din Khalil, *On Contemporary Islamic Criticism*, pp. 26-27.

(73) Ibid., p. 27

(74) Ibid., p. 27

(75) The author reveals that she returned to contemplate Quranic verses on the issue of Man after a personal calamity about which she does not conceal its existential tone: "The long phase of being suspended between life and death, Man not knowing where his next step will tread, and what all the tortuous struggle to discover the self's secret self was for, if

it is ordained that I should, in a dreadful moment, lose it to wilderness and perdition." *Essay on Man,* p. 7.
(76) Ibid: p. 127.
(77) Ibid. p. 127.
(78) Ibid., p. 124.
(79) Ibid., pp. 127-128.
(80) Ibid., p. 128.
(81) Ibid., p. 124. This Quranic verse on man's dialectics, "And Man above all is dialectical," will be of various connotative value for modern Arab thought in its attempt to comprehend the definition of dialectics. See for example Mohammed Aitani, *The Quran in the Light of Material Dialectical Thought,* p. 30.
(82) Pascal, *Thoughts on Religion and Philosophy,* pp. 93-96, 143-144. He states that "The true religion must instruct man in his grandeur and his misery; it must lead him to esteem and to despise himself – to love and to hate himself."
(83) Review a detailed analysis on Hegel's definition of *Al-Rafa (Elevation)* in Abdulrahman Badawi, *The Age of Existentialism,* pp. 24-30.
(84) Hassan Hanafi, *Contemporary Issues,* 2/3.
(85) Ibid., p. 171.
(86) Ibid., p. 251.
(87) The definition of *Ta'ti* (passiveness) is the opposite of the definition of motion and action. It is therefore against the dialectic concept of Divinity.
(88) *Contemporary Issues,* 2/252-253.
(89) Ibid., p. 253.
(90) Ibid. p. 253.
(91) Ibid. p. 253.
(92) Ibid., p. 251. This invitation to dialectics is not necessarily connected to "the left" since "conservatives can find in Hegel a way to support renewed faith just as those who

refuse established religion can find thought that is objective and dialectical."

(93) Hassan Saab, *The Modernization of the Arab Mind*, p. 87. The Quranic genius presently undergoes reinterpretation in the light of dialectics.

(94) Ibid., p. 87.

(95) Ibid., p. 88. Perhaps Saab refers to the following sentence by Hegel which is given here in the original: "The leading features of Mahometanism involve this – that in actual existence nothing can become fixed, but that everything is destined to expand itself in activity and life in the boundless amplitude of the world." Hegel, *Philosophy of History*, p. 357.

(96) Hassan Saab, p. 93.

(97) Ibid., p. 92.

(98) Mohammad Taqi Al-Modarresi, *Islamic Thought: The Confrontation of Civilization*, pp. 126-127.

(99) In its development, national ideological thought reflects an awareness of the definition of dialectics and its significance for Hegel and Marx. Moreover, it assures that the contradiction of a phase does not mean self-contradiction within the framework of a nation, but rather in the questioning of contradiction and external challenging, and that this includes the rejection of class struggle or civil war…in other words, the freezing of internal dialectics. Munif Al-Razzaz, *The Philosophy of the National Movement: The Background Philosophy*, p. 136.

(100) Mohammed Al-Bahi, *al-Fikr al-Islami al-Hadith (Modern Islamic Thought)*, p. 385. This understanding of the dialectic of negativity and positivity in existence, when compared with Mohammed 'Abduh's maxim in *The Message of Unification*: "Self-negation within one entity is impossible" makes clear the change in thought that is in discussion.

(101) Ibid, pp. 385-386.

(102) It is the French Orientalist and Marxist Maxime Rodinson's opinion that "history reveals to us in a practical manner the merging of ideologies of this kind." Furthermore, based on that, "there is nothing to contradict the Islamic world's adoption of socialist ideology...for if irreligious minds are capable of creating a method and style of life that is based solely on socialist ideology, then we should expect that many others, having other (existential) needs will cherish their religious beliefs or retrieve them." Maxime Rodinson, *Marxism and the Muslim World*, (the Arabic trans.) p. 186.

(103) This meaning has become accepted in national thinking itself: "Islam remains the property of the people...no one thinks of Islam nowadays – in whichever country – but feels that he is dealing with a value discriminated against and thus a revolutionary power." Manh Al-Sulh, *Islam and the Arab Liberation Movement* (1973), p. 67.

(104) Khalid Mohammed Khalid, *From Here We Begin*, pp. 70-72.

(105) Sayf Al-Dawla, *The Theory of the Arab Revolution*, p. 51.

(106) Ibid, p. 51.

(107) Ibid., p. 68.

(108) Ibid., p. 47

(109) Ibid., p. 116.

(110) Ibid., p. 110.

(111) Ibid. p. 110.

(112) Ibid. p. 110.

(113) Ahmad Musa Salim, *Islam and its Contemporary Issues*, p. 184.

(114) A Group of Soviet Intellectuals, *Leninist Marxist Principles* (1962), p. 60.

(115) Ahmad Musa Salim, p. 202.
(116) Ibid., pp. 202-203.
(117) Ibid., p. 135.
(118) The gist of this serious reconciliatory question can be found subject of a rare essay of Islamic thought, published by an Arab journal that is popular among the large majority of educated Arabs; see Mohammed Shawqi Al-Fanjari (Egyptian), "Islamic Thought Develops Marxist Concepts", *Majalat Al-Arabi* (Kuwait), no. 180, November 1973, p. 47-49. The title of the essay, which is formed purposely but wisely in this way, may also be read from another angle, and in an opposite sense, i.e., "Marxist Concepts Develop Islamic Thought." The importance of the essay is in its study of the experience of the communist Islamic thinkers in Soviet Asia – with an unprecedented understanding – and how they reconciled their Islam and their Marxism after overcoming their metaphysical differences, and the significance of this to Arab socialism.
(119) Mohammed Shawqi Al-Fanjari, "Islamic Thought Develops Marxist Concepts," *Al-Arabi,* November 1973, p. 48.
(120) Ibid., p. 48.
(121) Ibid., p. 49.
(122) Mohammed Aitani, *The Quran in the Light of Dialectical Material Thought* (1972), p. 117.
(123) Ibid., p. 112.
(124) Ibid., p. 113.
(125) Ibid., p. 114. In terms of a dialectical interpretation of the Quran, the advent of Islamic religion has been interpreted in terms of class struggle (Abdulrahman Al-Sharkawi, (*Muhammad the Messenger of Freedom*, pp. 32-49), and the war between Ali and Muawiya for leadership following the prophet, as a conflict between the right and the left. While the Shiites became a moderate left, the

Kharijites became an extreme left, and the conflict between them, a schism within the leftist party (Mahmud Ismail, *Issues in Islamic History*, p. 63), and the biography of Ibn Khaldun, the objective thinker of sociology in the history of Islam, has been rewritten, so he became a 'revolutionary' thinker, intending a revolution against the Mamluk feudalism and sharing the Egyptian populace's strenuous suffering through his intellectual struggle for its cause. (Rushdi Salah, *A Man in Cairo: Abdulrahman Ibn Khaldun,* pp. 49-51; 70-71).

(126) Khalil Ahmad Khalil, *Dialectic of the Quran*, p. 89.

(127) Ibid., pp. 95-96. The author criticizes – in a reference that suggests the new direction – the non-dialectical reconciliation which Muhammad 'Abduh has established between the eternal and the created, and he sees that this leads to "erasing the historical positivist connection between revelation and consciousness" – Ibid., pp. 99-100.

(128) Related to this research on 'the eternal' and 'the created' is the *Nasikh* and *Mansukh* (the abrogating and the abrogated) in the Quran. Here, there is a sequence in time between the abrogating text and the abrogated text in the revealed Quran, which may refer to – from *Kalām*'s perspective – 'the created' within the context of the 'eternal.'

(129) The idea of neutrality and non-alliance constitutes the way in which Arab reconciliation expresses itself in international politics. It is an idea that originally springs from the moderation of this reconciliation between liberal capitalism and communist socialism and its preference for the idea of reconciliation – rather than the conflict between them. In 1957, Michel Aflaq wrote, "This positive neutrality does not find its justification within political and economic needs alone, but is also justified by our civilized stance, our stance regarding freedom in doctrinal,

religious, and political international strife that surrounds us, just as its influence reverberates through interactive relations between our regions, and upon the relations of various classes within these regions individually, so that it is possible to say that the aim of neutrality is international peace as well as internal peace." *On Methods of Al-Ba'ath*, p. 216.

In the final analysis therefore, neutrality is "a new standing of civilization that is creative between two civilizations at strife, not adopting in total commitment either Eastern or Western values." *On Methods of Al-Ba'ath*, p. 218.

As for the ultimate and more sublime aim, it is a reconciliatory compatibility aim to "develop the camp of capitalism towards socialism...and to develop the socialist camp towards freedom" by means of preventing the explosion of strife between democracy in its deeper and comprehensive sense and social justice in its complete socialist form." *On Methods of Al-Ba'ath*, p. 219.

This Arab reconciliatory vision of 1957 represents a sign of present compatibility. See also the call for philosophical neutrality to moderate between materialism and idealism, and Marxism and existentialism in *Neutrality in Philosophy* by Yahia Huwidi.

(130) F.S.C. Northrop, *The Meeting of East and West*. See also Constantin Zureiq, *The Battle of Civilizations*, pp. 133-134.

(131) Ibid. pp. 133-134.

(132) Aisha Abd Al-Rahman, *Essay on Man*, pp. 165-174.

(133) Ahmad Salim, *Islam and Our Causes*, p. 207. This thought is present in Arab Christian thought also. "We must look towards the most unusual and courageous of

extreme social revolutions, upon the condition that we begin contemplating the truths of the Bible and the Quran." This is from one point of view. From another point of view, "the resemblance between the true revelation and revolution is so deep that if the revelation stops its revolutionary act...it would be untrue to itself." Rene Habashi, *Our Civilization at the Crossroads*, pp. 106; 217.

(134)   Sayyid Qutb attempts to create a semblance of *fatwa* (legislative explanation) to define what is allowed and forbidden (religiously) in the process of cultural interaction or acquisition from modern civilization. He assigns as allowed and possible for the Muslim to learn abstract sciences, such as chemistry, physics, biology, astronomy, medicine, industry, agriculture; methods of management – in terms of purely technical and administrative functions – as well as technical methods of work, methods of war and battle – in terms of the technical – and other such activities. As for what concerns the forbidden, this includes "all philosophical directions, all interpretations of human history, all psychology – except fieldwork and its recordings – all the sciences concerned with ethics, all studies of comparative religion..." – Sayyid Qutb, *Milestones on the Path* (1962), pp. 169-171. He is also certain of the collapse of modern civilization and its bankruptcy (pp. 3-5), without explaining how a civilization so bankrupt in values would bring about all these achievements. See also Mohammed Qutb, *Suspicions Surrounding Islam* (1953), *Man between Materialism and Islam* (196?), and *The Changing and the Constant in Human Life* (1964).

(135)   This phenomenon was a point of scrutiny with the conservative Salafi intellectuals and with the liberal intellectuals, for both sides agreed – each from its own standpoint – on the falsity of this camouflaged

reconciliation. Sayyid Qutb says, criticizing the "Islam" of modern Muslims, "The issue at its core is a matter of disbelief or belief...this must be clear. Those people are not Muslims as they claim – while they live a life of *al-Jahiliya* (pre-Islamic) nonbelievers. If there is among them one who wishes to deceive himself or deceive others and reckons that Islam can flourish amidst such disbelief, then he can do so, but neither his self-deception nor his deception of others will bring about any change of the truth." ("This is Not Islam" in *Milestones on the Path*, p. 213) Abdullah Al-Kusaymi – from a liberal viewpoint – defines this phenomenon under the satirical title *True Belief and the Clandestine Behavior of the Disbeliever* and says, "Backward thought focuses on theory rather than application, for great value is given to belief rather than behavior; so that whoever deviates in his behavior from all known conventionalities would be forgiven and become a good citizen if he is quite conservative in his thinking. As for whoever deviates in thought from what is accepted, he becomes a despised clandestine disbeliever, however upright his behavioral, social, or psychological attributes." Abdullah Al-Kusaymi, *The World is Not the Mind*, pp. 349-350. It is the opinion of Ehsan Abbas that "I know of none calling for the sufficiency of heritage alone and deriving all modes of life and thought from therein, for this is contrary to the nature of development; and supposing there were someone calling for this, he would not have any intellectual support, let alone that his practical behavior in life is the clearest proof against call." (See Ehsan Abbas, "The New Arab and his Ancient Heritage," in *The Arab Cultural Journal*, Beirut, Nissan 1973, p. 103.

The Contemporary Political Significance of the Historic Viewpoint in Question

In: *Political Crisis for the Arabs and the Position of Islam: Ingredients of the Chronic Condition.* Beirut: Arabic Institute for Studies and Publishing, 1995, pp. 187-197.

The interpretations and analyses presented throughout this text, with their various subjects and angles of approach to those objective factors that have shaped Arab political formation, have led towards a number of findings and conclusions concerning the nature of the present Arab political crisis in the modern age. These should be taken into serious consideration when contemplating – objectively – the reasons for "inadequacies" in Arab politics through the many experiences and trials during recent decades, having resulted in catastrophes, defeats, and awkward retreats in more than one domain. These findings go beyond individual interpretations and ethical judgments, or local "selfishness" and external "conspiracies."

In short, the core findings and fundamental conclusions that are the focus of our studies can be summed up in the following points:

First: The Arabs – throughout their long history and until recent times – have not experienced life within an organized state, stable and stationary, in the classical sense of statehood and by traditional definition of the term. It is their historic experience that a state is prone to an abortive process and to a continuum of interruptions between the consecutive states of "state" and "non-state." While the Arabs have lived within a "unified" society in terms of civilization, religion, legislation and culture within the Arab Islamic civilization, or *Dar-Al-Islam*, they did not experience this same principle of a unified society in the political sense. This was because the "political society" of Arabs did not always coincide with the overall and comprehensive "civilized society," as it did for instance with the coordination of the course of Chinese civilization and the course of a Chinese unified nation throughout most ages of history.

On the one hand the Arab "political society," in its capacity as symbolic of the state's foundation, was prone to fragmentation between numerous entities, as history will bear witness even since the early centuries of Islam. It was exposed, on the other hand – whether in a state of fragmentation or unification – to being overpowered by nomadic forces – foreign, internal, and external invasions – which had a great deal to do with the breaking of any possible continuity of the state and its foundation as settled upon stationary ground within a specific regional area, a matter which became a stalemate and hindered the growth of an accumulation of associations and organizations upon a fixed, stable, and unchanging foundation. This, given that the most important requisite for establishing a state and for its survival is its settling in a particular place and its durability for an extended length of time "upon a particular section of land…for many centuries."[1]

This did not occur – not sufficiently – for the Arab Islamic state (which had in fact, from the outset, been a flexible union between tribes), nor did it occur for its branching political entities. It is remarkable how often the capital of a state was uprooted to be centralized as a new capital, and there are instances of the whole state as such "moving" to a different region. If we wish to contemplate the extent of fragmentation to which the organizational and institutional entity of the Arab Islamic state was subjected over the ages, the capital city of the state shifted from Medina to Kufa to Damascus to Baghdad to Cairo…to Istanbul(!) not to mention repeated moves and journeys of regional capitals, their government bodies and organizations.

This is a phenomenon of rare occurrence in the experiences of other established states who might have shifted capital location once or twice in the course of their history, but not in such a way that was deterrent to the accumulated gradual growth process of its institutions and organizations, for which stability is a vital necessity so that it is able to become a permanent and secure organic entity founded upon stable and secure grounds.

This is certainly not to say that Arabs have not known authority and government. They have established various patterns of this, as well as having been exposed to other forms of rule. The term "state" in the Arabic language signifies "government" and "existing authority" liable to "become a state" in any case.

However, establishing authority is one thing while the building up of the comprehensive government establishments of a state is quite another. As George Bordeaux, in his research on the concept of a state has remarked, "not every political organized society is a state…and many are the types of authority that are unrelated to the idea of a state."[2]

In addition to the factor of political fragmentation, which was originally brought about by the desert's vast distances between the inhabited and prospering centers, and to the factor of overpowering nomadic invasions that fall under the categorical concept of the dialectical struggle between Nomad livelihood and civilization in the Arab region and its surrounding desert areas, it is the factor of "tribal entity" that figures as the core social structure and as a perpetual antithesis and alternative to the entity of a state. The tribe is in antithetical opposition to the state and replaces it in terms of gaining the Arab individual's primary allegiance and securing his loyalty and the expression of his communal identity. As the individual is primarily bound to the tribal entity and its values, it is almost impossible for him to contribute positively to the state or abide by its rules, simultaneously. As Ibn Khaldun remarked, "Homelands of numerous tribes and lineages rarely become a state,"[3] whether because of repeated strife internally between the tribes within the state or regarding their substitute set-up for a state.

If a "state" is built upon tribal grounds, and this is the historical norm for the founding of "states" and their political entities – according to Ibn Khaldun's theory and as a fact of history – it will only become a "tribe-state" or a "higher ruling system" for the tribe, as Yves Lacoste has noted.[4] If some prosperous Arab coastal city locations have experienced the "city-state" phenomenon, as Greek cities of old have done, it is the "tribe-state" principle that has decided the political fate of Arabs through most historic ages with the force of its overpowering lineage loyalty, imposing its authority upon the cities as well. Given that, the Arab city itself in many instances was actually none other than "a settled tribe." In the event that the tribe remains unsettled, however, and in a state of free nomadic shifting with no rooting in a fixed place, then it embodies the absolute contrary of a state and the total impossibility of its existence in any form whatsoever (since the only authority is that of the tribal shaikh and tribal tradition). Thus, as Philip Salzman points out, "True Nomads do not establish states."[5]

In this way, the Arab political experience has been diffused throughout history between a "temporary" state, hardly achieving statehood for one or another reason, or a "tribe-state" closer to the antithesis of the true definition of a state, or a "non-state" in a state of complete Nomad release. It is difficult to say that, given these conditions, the Arabs have experienced, experimented and managed life – in any constant, consistent way – within the framework of a state, its establishments, organizations, and traditions, or that they endured responsibility for this through which they gained the experience of "state" political practice, cooperation, administration, leadership and discipline.

If we take into consideration that the state is a "political school" and is the focus of its dynamics, activities, thought and organization, and no other school can provide for political practice and achievement common to all its persons, then it becomes clear that historical Arab experience in the school of politics is, the least to say, fragmented, disjointed and unstable. It is more of significance than of coincidence perhaps, that the term state (*dawla*) in Arabic semantics, from the roots of *dal – yadul – dawla*, signifies having a temporary upper hand and authority in the transformation from one condition to another, as opposed to the foreign static significance of being fixed, state – static – statique. Thus, the Arab state is one of transforming temporary authority. As far as the definition of a state as an organized comprehensive, and permanent entity, this was quite unknown to the Arabs except through the experiences of the neighboring countries, which they called "kingdoms" or *mamalik*, of the foreigners that were ruled by "tyrants."

These were unsuited to the free Arab – even if it were within an organized political entity, Arabs would not be subordinate to this. As for themselves – that is to say, the Arabs and Quraish – they were a people who were "proud and virile, owing no debt to any king while no Sultan owns them."[6] Furthermore, Arabs were "reluctant to render each other allegiance to leadership" as Al-Shafai has said, and which Ibn Khaldun explained some centuries afterwards in his famous statement, which usually stirs up anger in many Arabs without instigating their objectivity or a calm approach in order to consider what is revealed of facts concerning Arab political experience. Ibn Khaldun says – and perhaps the recent bitter political trials that the Arabs have been through will call for a reevaluation of what he stated with a more objective reading of the matter:

"It is within Arab character to diverge from the grip of the establishment and to avoid being led into politics…for they are rivals over leadership, and it is seldom that one of them passes authority to another even if father or brother…thus there are numerous rulers and princes…and the mass remain in their own world as if it were an anarchy without leadership. Thus, Arab character distances itself from ruling politics."[7] Ibn Khaldun, with the realism of a sociologist, accounts for this objectively with reasons from Arab geographical, societal and historical life. He does not pass personal or ethical judgment as many assume.

In the light of all this, the Arabs as a whole, in their various zones, regions and fringe areas, of which some, until recently, shared land with no borders and with neither power nor authority, nor development there of any state, never had any direct experience of a direct state, organized and secure, other than their individual said "nation-states" or "regional states," as known in terms of national ideology in the modern age. While the oldest of these modern "states" – that of modern Egypt – is only two centuries old, since Mohammed Ali founded it, others have not even completed a quarter of a century, and yet others remain prone to internal fragmentation because of the numerous lineage loyalties which threaten the foundation of any possible "experience as a state."

Thus, if we consider the "sum total" of the Arab state format in the various regions of the Arab World, we find that it is still torn between the struggle of being a state and a non-state and that its history in state formation in some regions is diminished by its non-state elements in other areas. The Arabs must now win the time race regarding their founding the state and its consolidation in the various regions, and to become aware of the historic significance of this needed and expected process. It is a process that does not seem to correspond to "skipping steps," with leaps up from the basis of a solid national foundation, and by triggering projects either "revolutionary" or "unificationist" which cannot be sustained by the present stage of development of their "state frameworks" and establishments.

Second: As far as authority in power existing in some civilized settlements of ancient Arabia, no sooner had this authority had presence than it was removed from local Arab hands at all levels into the hands of foreign and imposing nomadic forces, so that it can be said of some Arab countries that their people neither ruled their countries nor themselves for thousands of years. This resulted in the development of a clear historic contradiction between the structure of national local "civilization" and the superimposed "authority" structure, which placed civilization and authority – as a principle and in practice – at opposite ends in the gamut of the genius of the people with its various effects that go to characterize the present condition, political, mental, sociological, psychological and cultural.

These effects can be summed up in the following four aspects:

1. Military: Internal and external military matters of defense and security became the exclusive responsibility of foreign forces while civilians knew nothing of armament or self defense. They became "a burden upon others in terms of self defense and fortification" as they were described by Ibn Khaldun.

2. Politics: Military and security defense dependency soon gave way to a new political reality. This led to the limiting of power, with its various levels, to the foreign military forces, while the nationals no longer had any connection to authority in power, so that the best learned Muslims and their men of letters considered any connection to the Sultan "a great malady" (Al-Ghazali).

This phenomenon extended up until the onset of the modern age, when Napoleon was surprised to find how far the Turkish

Mamluks had been empowered with various levels of authority and administration in Egypt, and he tried to hand over responsibility to local powers in order to gain their favor for his own purposes and benefit. He was advised by men of opinion in Egyptian society at that time not to do so, since society would only be subordinate to the royal Mamluks, as Al-Jabarti said. Napoleon was convinced and halted these efforts, especially after an unsuccessful experience which did not last long because of a lack of efficiency in the native elements he had appointed to management. Furthermore, in another Arab society of ancient culture, Iraq's cities (such as Najaf) were not able to establish self-rule and administration after the Ottoman power left and remained in a condition nearer to a non-state until British rule took over the situation.

3. Economy: This military structure, an inverted politics, led to an inverted economic structure whereby the true productive force (tradesmen, city bourgeoisie, townsmen professionals, skilled labor, craftsmen) had no representation on effectiveness at any level of government over which foreign forces had total power, a matter which impaired – historically – political self-development enabling self-representation or contract through constitutional law or judiciary processes. This, according to what was decreed by the enforced feudal system as well as by the European bourgeoisie. This has led to discrepancy and conflicting interests in political development between the productive force and the ruling authority in Arab societies, where the inverted form became "those who produce do not rule and those who rule are not involved in production."

4. Thought and Culture: What prevailed was the conventional and one-sided viewpoint, while the intellectual stance on religion, thought and life weakened and thus prevailed a sharp contradiction between the nature of the extremely conventional nomadic authority in power and the broad-minded nature of the city center. "There can be no culture without cities."[8]

This long historical process, which developed the network of reversed relationships in the general Arab structure (and which started wavering only at the close of the Ottoman reign) began, in fact, when the Turkish authority in power took over during the age of Mu'tasim (218 H) when Samara became a symbol of the external overpowering tribal force, while Baghdad became the symbol of the distressed and helpless national civilized homestead society. It is a discrepancy and irony that has control over the Arab scene everywhere and will remain one of its most vital political and cultural features. We can find further forms and styles of this same discrepancy even today, for the Arab city will remain, according to Ibn Khaldun, "a burden upon others for self-defense and fortification."

Modern urban Arab power will not be able, whether old or new, to reinstate its dynamics and its own individual sense of unity and lineage loyalty which expresses its needs and political ambitions, and will remain subordinate in one way or another to a force foreign to its civilization, just as it was subordinate for years to the horsemanship of the Nomad (nomadic overpowering) until the end of the Ottoman period, with Turkish rule being the last of the nomadic invasions of civilized regions of the area. Subordination then shifted to the presence of European imperialism, from which the Arab city adopted aspects of what was known as "the modern renaissance."

Once the modern age of national independence emerged and forced them towards self-rule, the historical hollowness was discovered because of its limited ability to recreate the necessary political and administrative strengths for self-rule, including the surrounding society. As soon as the long-deprived rural populace grew in power, they invaded the city just as the nomadic forces had done long before – its invasion taking at first the form of armed military uprising through the rural populace that overtook the army, then by means of direct peoples' movements of rural origins with its declared genuine ideology. It is as yet uncertain as to whether the

Arab civilized society – which represents the middle class, its cultured people, its businessmen as well as skilled professionals – will be able to recreate a unified and dynamic political power with "progressive" political parties that express their ambitions, whether with the aim of an Islamic civilization or of radical modernization.

In addition, a further significant dimension of this historical crisis is in the fact that "a city society" is the necessary condition requisite for a "civil society," for there is no civil society beyond the city – in rural or in Nomad areas. In turn, the "civil" society is the necessary requisite for establishing the foundations of democracy, its systems, its practice and its traditions. In the light of this historical crisis of the Arab city society, the question remains valid as to the extent that it is possible to create an Arab "civil" society with a democratic system in accordance. It remains that unless the Arab civil society is able to restore its own cultural strengths, its values and intellectual thought, becoming able to recreate its unified and dynamic political strength, and completing the urbanization of rural life rather than "ruralizing" the city, then this historical crisis will remain at a stalemate.

Third: Arab ideological thought has ignored, especially that of Eastern nationalism, the organic relationship between the national state – which represents the container and political framework that is fundamental and realistic, and in which crucible all Arabs as individuals and Arab societies live – and its historic roots. These are sociological in terms of general Arab political formation, and this has been used against them from a stance of refusal and blame with no objective in-depth study or analysis of the roots and significance, the reason being considered merely a conspiratorial fracturing that developed out of imperial schemes and the "selfishness" of the ruling authorities, while ignoring the historical background of the Arab social structure itself which had produced the "national" phenomenon ages before the advent of "imperial fragmentation."

Any solution to the general political problem the Arabs have and to the chronic political strife they suffer does not begin with the national state, its nature, historical significance (modern, post-modern and futurist), and only presents an escape from facing the political issue seriously, whether it takes an Arab nationalistic, religious Islamic or liberal democratic direction. Nor will it achieve anything, as is the case at present, other than to construct ideal possibilities, and a topography that is isolated from the present political environment as it is veritably and tangibly lived by the Arab individual everywhere, and will determine, in return, his formation, destiny and the future of his forthcoming generations in terms of livelihood and politics. This is the true national state, which represents the only political society for the Arab wherever he be and whether he accepts or refuses it.[9]

It must be absolutely clear – and with decisive determination of thought – that the solution to the Arab political problem, without approaching it from the viewpoint of the national state which represents the only political scope for every Arab, is one of the most important problems of contemporary Arab political thought and one of its most dangerous drawbacks and crises. Such idealistic, topographical and sought-after solutions deal with anything and everything but the actual reality of politics which the Arab individual and the Arab community live on a daily basis and as thriving within the framework of the national state. The political situation will remain at odds and in a state of emergency as long as there is a lack of realization in the Arab (and) Islamic mind and conscience of the lawful "analysis" for natural interaction – without a sense of guilt or original sin – with the actuality of the national state and its reality and requirements, its historical past, as well as its future.

Once there is this awareness and understanding, it becomes possible for whoever wishes to present ideological advice beyond the national state. However, we should begin from the tangible ground upon which we stand and not any other political ground – or leaping up high in the air (as has been and is done at present, with many of the subjective prevailing approaches which reap, for themselves, their slogans – and for all Arabs – nothing but the current bitter harvest spanning the breadth of the Arab World).

It is an astonishing matter from any logical viewpoint that Arab political thought should take its starting point, questioning and aspirations with an almost complete denial of the necessary and most important logical step that should be its point of departure, namely, through information as to the grounds upon which he stands within his national framework of a state. How did this happen? And how has it continued to be so for this long, until a grave series of events came pouring down over the "heads" of these ideological approaches as upon the heads of all Arabs? Yet some still insist that we achieve "results" without having departed from logical and realistic preliminary requisites!

From our point of view, in understanding the issue of the national state, the following points must be taken into consideration:

1. The phenomenon of the national state was not the result of imperialism and its fragmentation alone, but for the most part, it is the result of Arab historical, social and geographic development long ago. How else can we explain the numerous political entities since the early centuries of Islam after establishing the first unified state at the beginning? The struggle between Iraq and Phoenicia had been a chronic historic event since the Rashidi rule and after (for over 1,000 years before Sykes–Picot). Morocco and Egypt were distinguished in their independent political entities from the early centuries.

Throughout Ottoman rule, Morocco, Yemen, Oman, and Nejd were never part of the Ottoman state framework.

It is true that this political enumeration remained within the limits of a unified culture and belief of *Dar Al Islam* of the Islamic world, but it was politically a clear reality. This reality deserves to be studied in greater depth within the scope of contemporary Arabic and Islamic scholarship and thought.

2. Since the Arab Islamic world experienced no veritable stage of true feudal growth, as opposed to popular assumption, and since this historical stage is a necessary turning point for those areas nationally affiliated but politically at differences between themselves, how could it develop and resume the organic growth of a unified national entity – as has been the case in western Europe and Japan – for the national state occurred during the age of world capitalism and international powers – with its own particular logic and form, to compensate for the lack of the feudal development stage in Arab history? Feudal development, that is, in its essential significance as a completely integrated and organic national fabric.

This was compensated for by a stage of national development within modern circumstances – naturally – and its various factors and influences. These are passive and negative in terms of the process of national development in the Arab regions in comparison to the circumstances of the "feudal" development which other states had experienced in past decades. Thus the present national Arab state represents a delayed stage of feudal development in an age of international capitalist state domination.

We have discussed and explained in detail this assumption within the scope of a different subject elsewhere for whoever wishes to follow this research.[10]

3. The fundamental misunderstanding in Arab Islamic awareness, in our opinion, is the obscure and confusing relation between unity on the one hand and diversity on the other, which can be accounted for mainly by the existing discrepancy between the strength of moral ties in religion, language, and sentiments between the Arabs and the great weakness in realistic "material ties" among them, in terms of livelihood and practicality in the various parts of the state, its economics and shared associations. The Arabs suffer from an exaggeration of moral interest and a great lack of material

interest that could unite them, and this is a grave matter; yet another among the issues of shortcomings in contemporary Arab life.

In the past, the flow of interaction, taking place in terms of group immigration and trade and culture exchange through a network of caravans crossing the Arabian deserts that joined the Arab regions, fulfilled a great part of the need for material ties. However, established borders and barriers and the increase of Arab differences in the modern age put a stop to this interaction. This linking has not been compensated for with a new form in any practical way. If in fact the balance between moral unity and material diversity is not reestablished in Arab life, then the general state of Arab schizophrenia will prevail.

4. With the analysis of the facts of the present situation regarding the small units and the fragmented social structures within the general flexible framework of the Ottoman Empire, it becomes clear that the national state is the first Arab experience of a state. A state, that is to say, in the direct and organic sense, realistic and practical. It is also the first experience of Arab unity – yes, of unity! – the true social unity of their many small and scattered local and sectarian tribes, in whose limited frameworks they had lived for long centuries.

5. Therefore, this impending historical stage of Arab development is one of constructing and bringing to maturation this vital and significant experience of a state and of unity. If the Arab national state does not mature, nor transform into a truly well-built state, with one true organic entity of the smaller structure within, then there can be no way towards Arab unity. Unity develops through the growth and maturation of the national state and not its destruction and obliteration by the bulldozer! Unity will be none other than the sum total of the national states. Zeroes do not transform into one whole number. It is only the true numbers, intact

and whole in themselves, that can produce a true number greater than themselves.

This elementary process of mathematics seems to have escaped Arab ideological thought.

6. The issue of founding democracy will be intricately bound with the matter of the maturation of the regional Arab state and the completion of its development and transformation – through strengthening civil society – to a civil society where the old diversities have merged, for there is no democracy without a well-integrated state that can support itself and its outcomes, and that is based on the concept of a civil society. Whenever the integrated state wavers and its foundations sway, then democracy becomes delayed. Whenever the state's construction is given room for growth, its structure reinforced and its construction consolidated, then there is more possibility for democracy.[11] Naturally, there are other conditions for the growth of democracy, of which this is not the place to elaborate, but the one most essential condition is that it find a "womb" in an upright and integrated state in which to thrive. Otherwise, there would be repeated abortions.

If these considerations regarding the regional state are valid, then it is clear that any political research or political documenting of the Arab outside its reality or its historical and future significance will not go beyond the vicious circle that controls the Arab political situation during the present stage.

In conclusion, the awareness of the reality of Arab politics and its analysis and evaluation must be channeled through historical principles, those sociological ones which the Arab World has experienced during recent centuries of its history…those that present Arab awareness names as the "fallen ages" then drops it out of practical calculation.

As for measuring up against the imagined and long past golden age of Islam or measuring up against – reversed – modern foreign political examples, these two measures can only result – in terms of understanding the present reality, at least – in more far-fetched idealisms. The Arab golden age is too far off in time, while external examples are too far away in place, and there is no escaping their harvest in the present reality.

If it is the right of intellectual human endeavor to search for an ideal wherever he will, then it is his duty to be in touch with the true reality upon which he stands, for the ideal will not rescue his fall into the void if he loses grip of the solid ground beneath his feet.

Endnotes

[1] Joseph Strayer, *On the Medieval Origins of the Modern State*, pp 8-22.

[2] George Bordeaux, *The State*. Translation by Selim Haddad, p.17.

[3] Ibn Khaldun, *The Muqaddimah*, Dar Al-Hilal edition, p.105.

[4] Yves Lacoste, *Al-Alama Ibn Khaldun*, Translated by Michel Suleiman, Beirut: Lebanon. Dar Ibn Khaldun, 1982, p. 3.

[5] Philip C. Salzman, *Political Organization among Nomadic Peoples*, in: *Proceedings of the American Philosophical Society*. Vol. 111, No. 2, April 1967.

[6] Mohammed Jaber AL-Ansari, *Political Arab Makeup and the Signification of the Nation-State*, p.83. See also: Dr Radwan Al-Sayyid, "Authority in Islam" in *Islamic Studies* (Beirut 1984), p.15.

[7] Ibid, Chapter I.

[8] Ibid, pp.77-78.

[9] As Mohammed Abd Al-Jabri has expressed recently (1992): "The Arab regional state...is a standing fact of Arab and national life, socially, economically and psychologically. It is no longer possible to leap beyond it... Thus, all thought of Arab unity which does not begin from the present reality of the Arab regional state is thought that pertains to a stage long past and gone." Al-Jabri; *A Point of*

View: Towards Reconstructing Fundamental Issues of Arab Contemporary Thought, Center for Arab Unity Studies, Beirut, p. 206.

[10] Mohammed Jaber AL-Ansari, *Political Arab Makeup and the Signification of the Nation-State,* Beirut: Center for Arab Unity Studies, 1994, Chapters 6 & 7.

[11] Ibid, Chapter entitled "Is It Possible to Establish a Standing Democracy before Establishing a Fully Developed State?"

Towards a Sociological Approach that Views the Crisis at Its Roots

In: *The Renewal of the Renaissance by Self Discovery and Criticism*. Beirut: Arabic Institute for Studies and Publishing, 1992, pp 105-110.

If there is a pressing need today for prolonged contemplation concerning the sociological historical roots of the Arab crises from the Dark Ages up until the present moment, then the science capable of dealing with this is sociology, or analytical and critical sociological thought which is armed with various social sciences such as history, economics, politics and collective psychology.

It is such thought that is capable of viewing the sociological historical factors that have branded Arab existence with their features.

Much has been said, and much written, about the reasons for the current deterioration in Arab life.

Methods of interpreting the problem have varied and been discrepant. There are those who have said it is because of a shortcoming in disciplines of education, and those who believe it goes back to the political system and its methods of organization. Others propose it returns to the Arab socio-economic set-up and the relationship between the social classes of such a structure. Yet others believe that it is all because of the inability to attain Arab unity, which they see as the key to any qualitative change in Arab life.

In addition, there are those who claim that the problems begin in the Arabs abandoning their authentic heritage and traditional values, while those in opposition reply that the problem originates in the Arab inability to absorb this age's modernism while exaggerating, in their pertinence, old goals and loyalty to the authority of ancestry.

Then there are those who say that the Arabs need one solution only and none other, which is democracy, and the respect for freedom of expression and the opposite opinion, while those in opposition reply, it is a just dictatorship of which the Arabs are in great need and which will realize, for us, in a matter of years, that which we have failed to achieve in centuries (according to the expression of Sheikh Mohammed 'Abduh).

Also, there are those who are certain that there is no escape from backwardness except through modern industrialization in order to change the mind and behavior together, as in the line taken by Salama Musa, and as the current Arab developmental school ascertain today in many Arab oil and non-oil countries, and for which many conferences and seminars are held and many researches and studies published.

Because calamities and deterioration continue to occur, while dangers increase day after day, it becomes impossible to find any one of those many and conflicting interpretations credibly worthwhile. Nevertheless, each in its own right has a viewpoint worthy of attention, and some at least build towards an overall larger interpretation and a more encompassing and complementary solution for the whole crisis.

The issue has become so dangerous that some Arabs have come close to accepting the often repeated tenet of imperialism and Zionism, which developed in British and French cycles of imperialism, then was adopted by Jewish circles that worked towards its realization, claiming the Arabs suffer from a major flaw in their construct, involving the Arab mentality, psychology and behavior; it is their makeup that is incapable of organized scientific thinking, and incapable of effective planning because of their disdain for vocational teamwork and because of their exaggerated individualism and self-importance, as well as inherent discord between themselves – the matter which has helped and continues to help divide the Arab World into small conflicting entities dependant on the West and consequently obliged to accept Israeli ascendancy, which is a continuum, according to this theoretical assumption of the advancement of western civilization in this backward and belligerent area.

During the past few years, certain Israeli and Western studies and documents have come to light that confirm the above-mentioned attitude and call for its intensification and its transformation into a final reality that the Arabs cannot overcome. It is possible for those who wish to research further to refer back to these documents and see word by word what we have delivered modified and abridged herein, for some of the Israeli documents go so far as to instigate doubt upon the unity of the Egyptian entity, which in the past and the present has been the most integrated and harmonious of Arab societies, discrediting it in order to dismantle Egyptian social unity like in other Arab societies which have been conquered by the attack of partition. (This is because of Israel's awareness that as long as Egypt remains at the heart of the Arab World, united and integrated, the day will come, sooner or later, when the Arab parts will gather around her anew. Thus, the Israeli plan is to reach the last hope and most enduring capital and safeguard for the advent of Arab unity).

In any case, the successive tragic events led to the confusion in the Arab vision to the extent of coming close, as mentioned before, to accepting this hostile and degrading theory, or what resembles it and moves within the compass of its mental and psychological sphere. And this is the ultimate defeat by which the aim is to have it pervade Arab existence to the core, for when any Arab comes to accepting the inferiority imposed upon him by the enemy within his mind and soul, there remains no space for any rescue or salvation.

What should be clarified in this respect and seen with total lucidity is that the enemy has taken advantage of mistakes and flaws and conditions present in the Arab constitution, because the Arabs did not confront these problems and have been delaying their solutions since the beginning of the renaissance. Imperialism has helped distract them from determining and solving these conditions, and thus they have remained within the Arab body, decreasing its immunity and weakening its ability to fight off challenges, the matter which opened the door for hostile germs to enter, infiltrate, inhabit and fragment this body, as is occurring today.

The roots of the problem, therefore, are not in the power of the savage and offensive attack, notwithstanding its offensiveness, savagery and danger. You do not expect a brutal, harmful, and treacherous enemy to send you bouquets of flowers. It is just natural that finding his opponent feeble, frail, and breakable, the enemy will be offensive and brutal.

The fact is that, in reality, the feeble immunity coexisted with the Arab entity before the establishment of Israel and its wars, and prior to the arrival of imperialists and their times. Furthermore, the distortion present in the Arab vision regarding determining the reasons for the destined existential crisis, and determining its effective remedy, has also been established in one way or another, and in a masked manner, since the beginning of the renaissance. Defeats and calamities caused it to become unmasked now, since it is no longer possible to hide national disasters of this scale and vastness. But the distortion in determining the remedy has been established from the start, before the sequence of events of recent years.

When the Palestinian calamity of 1948 occurred, many Arabs imagined that certain Arab regimes existing at that time were to blame, and a large movement began to change these regimes. This is, in fact, what took place.

When the second calamity occurred in 1967, it became clear that the question was not so simple, for these were regimes of a different kind, facing a similar defeat, if not greater, and thus began a search for different mistakes and causes.

When the Arab calamity occurred where Beirut was besieged and Palestinians slaughtered at Sabra and Shatila, in the light of conditions differing from those of both 1948 and 1967, there began yet another search for a third kind of theorizing and interpretation for the causes of the calamity. Thus, we arrive at the unholy Gulf war of 1990.

The fault in all this is that we contemplate the event in itself, separate from its historical background and the 'fallen age' when the Arab nation at large suffered during the time of the Mamluks, Turks and others, regarding the event as if it were a stone boulder fallen upon us from the sky, and not emerging and originating from the reality of backwardness that we have lived, and still live with now. This is a reality that we inherited from the 'fallen age' that spreads over several centuries, ever since the creativity of Arab civilization stopped in the fourth century *hijri* and the Arab region fell prey to foreign tidal waves of attack, encounters that took the form of invasions since the Turks took over the caliphate, from the time of Mu'tasim, until the Mongol invasion of eastern Arabia led by Hulagu, until the destruction of centers of civilization in Arab Morocco at the hands of waves of assaults from desert nomads, as Ibn Khaldun has noted, and from which he drew his theory of interpreting Arab history on the basis of a tragic discourse between the Nomad and civilization.

These fabricated fragments take up the specific event as the crux of the calamity. It is analyzed and researched as if it had no relation to preceding historical events, while the true reality which gave it birth is ignored by the propagation of daily newspapers and modern journalistic writings and political books that attempt to publicize and create noise. In addition to this, successive news bulletins and television coverage deliver events and actualities in part as matters unrelated, with no common bonds.

This media flood of any one event leads the Arab mind astray in the maze of successive daily events, and if ever a political analysis appears, it would not span more than one week; and whenever a political book is published, it would cover a limited period of time and embarks on elaborations which cut it off from earlier historical periods resulting in this period.

Our own journalism and media, therefore, needs to publish sociological historical studies dealing with the roots of the Arab problem starting with the 'fallen age' until contemporary times, on the condition that these studies are clear in style as well as in content for the ease of awareness and comprehension of the Arab citizen.

The intellectuals, universities, research circles and study centers should confront this essential issue. It should be open to question and discussed in all its proper dimensions and from various angles. It is the role of cultural journals in particular, and newspapers, radio and television in general, to spread these researches once they have been simplified, but without altering significance, or abridged without being superficial, in order to instigate a new cultural awakening concerning the sociological historical roots of the chronic Arab crisis; these same roots that gave rise to various national calamities, and from which branched out different facets of backwardness, all in order to avoid misleading fragmented dissipation in the effort toward finding a solution to the crisis.

In reality, the Arab cultural journal bears the most significant and subtle aspect in this mission, for it bridges – or should do so – thinkers, universities and research centers on the one hand, and journalism, radio, television and the masses on the other. It has the responsibility of delivering thought to the public media. Both sides should cooperate to realize fully this task.

It is my belief that sociology, as a live thinking and not as a descriptive and academic discipline, is the science of the present stage in history of Arab thought and culture.

It was the literature that prevailed at the outset of the renaissance with the revival of language and literary styles at the hands of Al-Yaziji, Al-Barudi and Al-Muwaylihi.

Then came the focus on narrative history and historical fiction, which became the prevailing impulse in the following period with the Georgi Zeidan series and others on the history of Arabs and Islam.

In the 1940's and 1950's, the focus became political science and its ideologies, because of the advancement of national politics as Arabism flourished.

These disciplines contributed in one way or another to the renaissance, yet these efforts proved insufficient in the light of Arab defeats and withdrawals.

If today the need is great, as we have shown, for prolonged contemplation concerning the roots of the Arab sociological historical crisis, then the science capable of coping with this is sociology or social, analytical and critical thought that is armed with all the varied social and human sciences such as history, economics, political science, and collective psychology.

It is such thinking that is capable of envisaging those sociological historical factors which have marked Arab existence; like the age old dialectic between nomadism and civilization, and like the vulnerable Arab centers of civilizations being exposed to successive waves of invasions from the nomads coming from the Asiatic and African deserts, which led to the stunting and fragmentation of civilization in Arab history.

Add to this the presence of the desert as a separating factor between most of the Arab countries, and the influence of tribal and sectarian systems and the communal relations between Arab entities, which contributed to the unhealthy fragmentation and assisted foreign schemes of division and partition to be implemented.

Discussion of these sociological historical factors and other modern strategic factors will take much time. It is sufficient to point out the main points mentioned in brief in the hope of researching it again in another essay, but the invitation is extended to all Arab thinkers and intelligentsia to participate in such research, for the task is greater than can be dealt with by one individual or one particular front.

If, however, the Arab intelligentsia is not able to influence fateful events, then at least they can attempt to draw the proper big picture to the Arab nation concerning what touches the core of its existence.

Western Civilization in Her Confusing Mirrors

In: *The Renewal of the Renaissance by Self Discovery and Criticism*. Beirut: Arabic Institute for Studies and Publishing, 1992, pp. 316-329.

1. The Fragmented Mirror:

Once the Fig-leaf Was Removed! (*)

It was by coincidence that, as I was passing by a hotel, I overheard the router's teleprinter announce a breaking news bulletin entitled "New York under the Siege of Darkness."

"New York in Darkness?" Incredible! Is this the threat of nuclear power closing in? Or has the event actually taken place and catastrophe befallen the largest city in the west?

News reports succeeded each other speedily and elaborating in detail. Reading them I wished that each person interested in the affairs of our contemporary world and its fate would read and analyze these from various angles in order to become aware of the conflict of civilizations and the recent historic trend in face of which humanity stands in much confusion and anxious concerning its fate. These news reports, although seemingly but passing facts in daily events, are valid examples and documentary evidence that predict

---

(*) In this article the negative image of western civilization is exaggerated and is seen by the author through a fragmented mirror.

what will happen in the various courses of life once the material industrial civilization of the west confronts a test of fate, one which her destiny had in store for her, once the choice had been made and its direction set with deliberation.

Our story begins as would an obscure Greek myth when the wrath of the skies sets out to destroy a city gone astray, so total destruction by volcanoes and by thunderbolts prevails.

A thunderbolt hits a New York nuclear electric power station, the power supply is cut and emergency measures are announced; thousands of people fall trapped as mice, suspended between heaven and earth in the electrical elevators that stopped still among the iron and the hot cement awaiting the arrival of ambulance teams presuming they could arrive before oxygen ran out. The traffic stops dead: mounds of iron under the heat of the sun, and entrapped are those people of this civilization who had imagined they had Nature under control and had mastered iron. Yet here they have become its helpless victims. The trains have stopped and thus all related activities, and the mayor has asked the city population to stay within their darkened homes.

So far all is calm and quite normal, for this is the expected fate for every accumulated overgrowth of materialism where iron overpowers man.

But the strange thing which bears more than a meaning is that this civilization's "citizens" in the city of New York, charged together in a grand attack to burn their shops with the intention of plundering. Huge shopping centers were crushed to the ground in the blazing fire, the easier to plunder the contents. The city police force was obliged to arrest thousands of these "citizens of civilization" to stop this great premeditated group burglary.

If the truth about civilization is exposed in times of crises which need everyone's co-operation and dedication to help overcome the catastrophe, then this "truth" that was brought to relief concerning the civilized residents of New York, under the shadow of the grand Statue of Liberty at the city entrance– and which for these dark hours had lost the significance of its existence when the concept of freedom became free plundering under cover of darkness and by any methods even burning and destroying – we say that, in our opinion, this truth having taken place gives further evidence that all the western civilized man has left of civilization are these heaps of iron machinery that will one day devour him. And that his civilization was exposed: the leaf that had covered its nudity has fallen to reveal an ugliness.

I remember the words of our Arab poet and literary figure Mïchaèl Nuaima when he decided to leave New York and return to Lebanon after the great economic crisis of 1929: "I left New York with the cry-of-despair of all humanity in my ears. A cry you'd believe to be the soul's departing gasp. The only word heard through the cry being: Crisis. Crisis." If Nuaima advised his homeland Lebanon not to ape the mercantile civilization at that time, then perhaps Lebanon realized the value of his advice only a few years ago when it was beset with the sickness of destruction, plundering and hatred. He'd discovered that adopting New York values, if we can so call them, was the shortest route to catastrophe.

There remains one question we must confront in all honesty: Is that same civilization whose inner truth was revealed upon the day New York went dark, capable of realizing peace upon our land? Is it valid to expect of her a mission of peace while the only attributes inside her figure destruction, plundering and hate?

Further, do we in fact need ask this question while we know that Israel is none other than another New York upon the Arab shoreline awaiting the moment when the electrical power of Arab life is cut in order to burn, plunder and destroy?

2. The Brilliant Mirror:

Is It the West Alone that is Decadent?

There is not an issue that the Arab intelligentsia find more enjoyable and which they follow up more readily and are glad to confirm, than the idea that the west is in a decadent condition.

No sooner does a European, American or Russian thinker come up with a point of view that criticizes western civilization or its modern society and predicting its decadence, than you find echoes of such opinions reflected as soon as can be, and in the variety of approaches and creative styles available to the Arabic language...and so sleep the Arab thinkers and citizens heavy-eyed in restful slumber in the belief that the west is decadent and on the verge of collapse or even worse.

This is why Arabs have heard more of the decadence of the west than of its renaissance and inventions, sciences, achievements and cultural innovations...for all this is heavy upon the heart of the Arab thinker and unwelcome to the ear of the Arab citizen. None discusses this nor does anyone listen to this...but on the issue of decadence, there is much brash talk.

These inventions the west has created and is still creating and which we observe as on-lookers...do they represent decadence?

Does western determination to go on progressing in various fields, from the transplanting of live cells to the exploration of Mercury and Mars...does this not suggest significance to Arab thinkers? Anything other than decadence?

This ability of the west to overcome social, economic and spiritual crises, generation after generation, and to renew man, society and culture: does this suggest to us nothing at all but decadence? And is this total conquering of our homes by the power of technology evidence of decadence?

Goodness gracious!

We come to the west as tourists, and we only interact with that superficial sector of commercial tourism and touristy temptations that attract us, and it satisfies our wealthy tourists' impulses and tempts us and not the westerners, then we return to gossip about the western women's looseness!

We forget the millions of western women workers' long day in the factories because we do not meet them upon our nightly tourist sprees!

We forget the western working woman.

We forget the western educated and intellectual woman.

We forget the western woman who is devoted to her children's upbringing.

We forget this type of woman because our tourists unfortunately do not encounter her; this type of woman who works more than the men of our society do; then we return to thank God for our virtues...and the decadence of the west and its immorality! We forget that the west believes in directness of behavior rather than indirectness, and places even its smallest problems under scrutiny and practices this publicly without embarrassment; nor are they interested in acting "appearances" of a virtuous life to others, whereas we are still leading a schizophrenic mode of existence.

We have a daytime lifestyle...and another by night...one in broad daylight and the other in the dark where we take whisky hidden in teacups...then we talk of western decadence! We deny our own women productive work and import foreigners to fill the gap...and accuse the west of decadence!

Of the most significant proofs of western progress – and by the west here, I mean modern civilization at large in Europe, Russia and America – is that thinkers are allowed to discuss and question aspects of decadence in all frankness and to diagnose its weaknesses and so, to remedy and to deal with them. Thus has the west been able to resume its progress, since mentality possesses the ability of self-criticism and of being objective, and of self-encounter; of listening to opposite opinions, the opposing opinion expressed frankly and in a constructive way, so that the frame of civilization regains a healthy breathing space, dismissing corrupted air. The blood is revived, and strength returns...and the west is figured as decadent!

Do our societies permit their thinkers discourse concerning its weaknesses as do the thinkers of the west? Or do they practice decadence without discussing it?

One of the most fatal mistakes of our mentality is in our inability to differentiate between two disparate entities: western imperialism and western civilization – we imagine them to be one and the same, despite the great difference – so we have lost the civilization...yet have not conquered the imperialism!

This in spite of the fact that acquiring modern civilization is an essential condition to overcoming imperialism. Japan acquired the civilization and conquered western imperial forces. China acquired modernism and conquered imperialism. We, however, fought imperialism without the weapon of 'civilization' so we lost both battles, the national battle...and the battle of civilization, and there is no way to win the former without succeeding in the latter first. This requires the lightening up of our definition of western decadence and the modest enrollment in the school of civilization.

3. The Analytical Mirror

A. Dissecting Western Civilization

The Arab thinkers' standpoint on western civilization is varied and even contradictory.

From Taha Hussain, who invites us to take on western civilization, its good and bad, both its positive and negative sides, if we wish – as far as he's concerned – to enter the modern age and adopt its progress...to Sayyid Qutb who warns against the founding principles of western civilization and its deviating origins and invites us to minimize our adaptation of it to bare necessities and to stern practical limits, dispensing of theory and moral values.

Between Taha Hussain and Sayyid Qutb, the many rainbow colors spread out in a fan where each Arab thinker takes on whichever color tends towards this or that direction over the broad range of possibilities between the "rationality" of Taha Hussain and the "fundamentalism" of Sayyid Qutb.

Amidst the noise of the various opinions, tendencies and contradictions on this momentous subject, I read a brief article, subtle and serious, entitled "Western Civilization and Us" and find it beneficial to sum up its contents for its clarity of vision regarding this issue for which no solutions have as yet come to light.

The article begins by stating that the suggested severance from western civilization and its refusal is neither practical nor applicable. "If we were invited to rebuff a tribal civilization from the Eskimo it would not have raised our concern." When, however, the issue involves western civilization, which has played a decisive role in human development and has achieved unprecedented scientific and material progress and has in her grasp the keys of peace and of war...then we must make a halt, discuss objectively the invitation, then transfer our attention to western civilization and the question of which stance we should be taking.

The writer states that, "Those most adverse to western civilization are dressed in clothes made in their western factories, they come and go in cars manufactured in Detroit and London. Even those pens that shape the finest poems of attack on the west are made in the west!" Moreover, those viewpoints inviting us to refuse western civilization are in most cases based upon superficial understanding or upon total ignorance.

Given that "western civilization, unlike what readers of either eastern or western action magazines believe, does not begin and end with long hair and drug and sex parties."

Thus, western civilization is a phenomenon we cannot ignore and it is essential that we confront and understand it, sift through and comprehend it through criticism and analysis in order to decide what to select, what to understand, and what to ignore and refuse according to our Islamic civilization, national heritage, values and traditions.

The writer thinks we should dissect western civilization in our analytical approach and should analyze the various angles according to the following gradation:

1. Aspects necessary to adopt if we want to overcome our present backwardness. These include technology, natural and social sciences, management, methodologies and scientific methods of planning. In these fields, it is western civilization that leads the world unrivalled. All that is improved upon in space engineering, in heart surgery, economic theory, and increase of production, happens in the west by western efforts of western scientists speaking western languages.

2. Aspects of western civilization which we would do better to be informed of without necessarily adoption or application. This constitutes western heritage, its politics and philosophies, literature and law...here we should have a medium stance. We should not conform to those inviting us to transfer from the west its political, intellectual and legal heritage, nor should we agree with those who wish to deny us even the study of this heritage, in order to be informed about it.
3. There are aspects of this civilization we name 'neutral aspects" which will not be relevant to us whether we have knowledge of them or not, such as ways of eating and dressing and morés of communication and visiting.
4. There are aspects we need to be cautious of while we benefit from them; such as the philosophy of commercial advertising for instance – which system has pervaded the western world – and such as the phenomenon of ruthless competition, which has the effect of tension and psychological tension.
5. Finally, there are aspects we must absolutely refuse, not only because it is discrepant to our eastern environment as such, but because it is at variance with any code of ethics. Of these aspects is the area of dress and fashion...and unfortunately it is in this aspect that we have excelled in transferring from the west.

This graded analysis of the elements of western society, analytical and critical, is without a doubt an independent and objective effort, aiming equally at the stimulation of those who are in refusal and the attraction of those in favor.

It only remains to mention the undertaker of a thoughtful and intellectual effort, a literary man from the Arab Peninsula, Dr Ghazi Abdulrahman Al- Qusaibi from his book "On This and That." His is a voice that has become one of the most prominent marks of intellectual thought in the Arab Peninsula and in the Arab World at large.

B. The First Encounter of the Arab Mind with European Knowledge

The History of Al-Jabarti is considered one of the most enthralling books, rich in information and one of the most accurately documented in its portrayal of the social, political, economic and religious conditions in Egypt preceding the modern renaissance and during its early decades. This Egyptian historian is known for his prolific reading and his keen as well as comprehensive observation. Al-Jabarti was, in fact, able to record daily historic memoirs of this especially rich and subtle transitional period which Egypt experienced in the last phase of the Ottoman era, during the French Napoleonic invasion of Egypt, and in the beginning of the age of Mohammed Ali, who established the foundation of the modern Egyptian nation.

Al-Jabarti did not limit the work to significant political events. Instead, he delivers live telling portraits of Cairo scenes and depictions from Upper Egypt representing "town folk" in the city and the toil of the peasantry in the countryside, and how both the latter and the former joined up readily in armed uprisings. It is probably the first record of its kind in the Arab Middle East, against Ottoman tyranny and against both British and French aggression. It describes how they celebrated public religious occasions held in the Hussain and Azhar districts, and how later, they would go to public cafés and bars for entertainment and games in an ambience of merriment and the long-known Egyptian sense of humor.

However, *The History of Al-Jabarti* is written in seven volumes, and the reader must approach the text with scrutiny to select from among the many sequences of events these social portraits which are today considered highly valuable documentation of the depiction of this historic period.

Perhaps among the most outstanding, rare and exciting of these portraits which Al-Jabarti depicted, is the first "European cultural caravan" entering the Arab World with new goods unknown to the Arabs, especially during the decadent ages where Ottoman rule veiled from the Arabs the fruits of civilization.

This caravan of knowledge is one Napoleon brought in with him when he conquered Egypt in 1798. He had enriched it with knowledgeable and capable people in different fields capable of investigating all kinds of modern knowledge. Thus the French leader embodied the strong French principle that French culture walks hand in hand with French politics wherever it goes.

Those professionals accompanying Napoleon founded a "cultural center" in one of the elegant quarters of Cairo. The French administration took over the grandest Mamluk palace for this purpose.

The opening of this center took place, with its libraries, laboratories and museums welcoming all, whether Egyptian people or the French army. The learned personnel would welcome the visitors, introduce them to the items exhibited, and perform experiments in chemistry and in physics. These seemed extremely original and interesting to an eastern society never before exposed to such strange experiments – it seems that the purpose of this was to display how far advanced French civilization was. Nevertheless, this work was not without absolute intellectual benefit to those enlightened minds in Egyptian society at that time. Al-Jabarti himself became aware of two kinds of ways of 'propagandizing' civilization during the brief French rule in Egypt.

The first way aimed at influencing the common people with more interest in pursuing entertainment than in having cultural interests. The French did not expect the common people to come to this cultural center, so they set up performances in streets and in public squares.

Al-Jabarti tells us *"The French books are printed papers glued together and marketed; they include: we mean to attempt a French feat of aviation of a boat from the Azbekia pond. On the appointed day people gathered, many of whom were foreigners to see the tour-de-force; being among them* (thus Al-Jabarti himself attended this performance) *I saw a length of fabric hanging from a pole colored red, white and blue* (the French flag) *in the roundness of a sieve, and amidst which a lamp with a wick soaked in grease...when it was afternoon they lit the wick and its smoke filled this fabric and swelled into the shape of a ball; the ball rose from the ground, rose up with the wind and went off a short while and with ease."*

It is clear from Al-Jabarti's description that the French set off a balloon flying the French flag. It is possible they were that day celebrating a national occasion which we imagine must have seemed to them to shine more brightly for being under the brilliant African sun.

This performance, however, meant to display an outstanding French talent, resulted in the unexpected and was contrary to the desired effect.

We leave the story to Al-Jabarti *"...then the balloon fell with its wick and its fabric* (the flag)*...and when this happened their true worth was revealed; none of what they had said would happen did: a boat flying in the air, carrying passengers traveling to far off countries to discover news and send letters. Rather, it seemed to be a flight much like that which the servants create upon feasts and weddings!"*

It seems that the balloon fell speedily and did not fly high enough to go beyond the viewers' sight, which caused some embarrassment to the French who had wanted to impress the Egyptians with their talents...and it is clear from the tone of the above text that Al-Jabarti was glad that the "colonialist trick" became a flop!

The second way of French cultural activity was aimed at the elite among men of knowledge and culture, and this was a serious French academic endeavor by which they meant to investigate the Egyptian environment from its various angles in the fields of antiquities, geography, history and social life.

Al-Jabarti tells us of the "cultural center" they established in the following text, which is considered a valuable historical document of that age: "they placed all at the disposal of managers, astrologists, men of knowledge in branches of science and of mathematics such as geometry, designing, engraving and illustration, clerical workers, accountants and constructors of Al-Nassariya alley in the area of Al-Darb Al-Jadid and the surrounding houses. They placed a large number of books in the charge of a keeper and supervisors for maintenance who made them available for students, or whoever wishes to find references, where they can revise all they desire. They used to meet two hours before noon, seated upon chairs set along a broad rectangular table, where the books were stored, and whoever desires asks for references, which the keeper brings and they can browse, taking notes, even those of the lowliest ranks (referring to soldiers) and if some Moslems come (meaning from the public) from those who wish to observe, they are not prevented access to even the most precious spots, but are greeted pleasantly with courteous greetings and welcome. They express gladness to the visitor especially if they see a positive attitude or that he is knowledgeable or hoping to search the sources; they serve him with kindness, bringing him various references with pictorial depictions of various countries, regions, animals, birds and plants, and the history of ancients, the lives of nations and biographies of prophets and the events of their nations, all of which amazes."

We should remember that Al-Jabarti wrote this description of the French cultural institution in Egypt precisely 195 years ago (or about two centuries) when intellectual rigidity prevailed over our eastern Arab World after the flourish of eastern scientific knowledge came to an end and the following generations did not pursue development. Further, the Turks had secluded the Arab World from new international developments that had started to increase with the winds of change from Europe...and herein lies the significance of this new scientific event that inspires Al-Jabarti to elaborate in description with something of a surprise. However, it is not the surprise of someone who does not know, but the surprise of a scientist who has much of his own heritage and culture, yet discovers what is new with others, and different, and so has the innate desire to resume discovery.

We leave Al-Jabarti to talk of his visit to this place and of his impressions and personal observations which were the result of the interaction between the Arab mind, desirous of scientific knowledge, coming from abroad and revealing its rich secret unto each mind alert to them: "I have been to them time after time and have been shown all this...among everything I have seen I remember a large book inclusive of the biography of the prophet (pbuh) as far as their knowledge and efforts could encompass, the biography is of the Rashidi Caliphate as well as the Imams and the rest of the Caliphs and Sultans. (I also saw in this book) pictures of countries, coasts, seas; the pyramids, the shorelines of Upper Egypt, pictorials and figures drawn and each country's particular types of animal, bird, plant, herb; medical sciences and surgical dissection; engineering and weight-lifting (mechanics). In addition, many of the Islamic books are translated into their language; I saw they had *Al-Shifa'* (*The Cures*) by Al-Qadi Ayyadh and *Al-Burda* by Al-Bousiri from which they memorized verses as well as translated into their language, and I saw some of them reciting surahs from the Quran; and they are anxious to research extensively in specializations, mostly mathematics and languages, and go to great lengths to acquire knowledge of the language: they are dedicated night and day to this end."

"They have rare books in various languages, their grammar and its branches so that it becomes easier for them to transfer all they require from any language at all into their own language in the shortest span of time (meaning the modern dictionaries)... For astrologists and their followers there are special areas where there are specialized strange and perfectly wrought instruments. Of these are eyeglasses used for planet observation, for recording information, knowing their features, their circuits, heights and distances. Of these rarities are photographs which portray persons who you would think were standing out of the picture, so real they seemed you'd think they were about to speak...Yet others depict animals, insects, fish and whales in their various kinds and names. They preserve animal or fish, in kind and name, and a whale that is strange in a substance so that it remains intact and unchanged in appearance, even if for a long time. Thus they specified certain areas for engineers and 'time' specialists and other medical professionals, surgeons and medical chemists."

"Of the strangest I have seen in this place was once when some scientists took a bottle and poured a substance into a glass, then poured another liquid over this; smoke then was rising from the glass until what was inside became quite solid and of a yellow color; then we passed it round holding it in our hands to examine. Then once, some white powder was taken and placed on an anvil, then hit gently with a hammer; it produced a very loud sound, surprising us" (see v.4 of Al-Jabarti's *History*, pp.348-351, new edition).

This text brings to light several facts, the most significant of which is Al-Jabarti's admiration for the European's zest for knowledge (even the least ranked soldiers), their consistent reading in their spare time, and it is truly a matter for admiration, especially that these soldiers at Al-Jabarti's time and in his country were "Mamluks and Sharkases" who were adverse by nature to any kind of learning.

More significantly, Al-Jabarti as a learned man, Islamic and religious, does not shun or avoid any new kind of western knowledge but rather describes for us the various tones of it with interest and in earnest

To the extent that his observation on the biography of the prophet written in French was appreciated "...as far as their effort and culture could..." rather than rebuked, while his own belief, theory and effort remain reserved and private.

Finally, is it too much to ask these learned men of religion in our present times to enrich their cultural outlook and develop it to maturity by reading contemporary and international cultural achievements...as Abdulrahman Al-Jabarti did 195 years ago?

It not only concerns the learned men of religion. Each and every Arab person is today required, as he is in need of, to take this direction, so that we may truly be "actively present" and "actively participant" in this challenging final decade of the twentieth century.

The Only Issue We Do Not Research

In: *The Renewal of the Renaissance by Self Discovery and Criticism.* Beirut: Arabic Institute for Studies and Publishing, 1992, pp 87-88.

In the midst of our Arab problems, crises, and retreats, our writers and Arab intellectuals talked about everything except one thing!

They talked about imperialism, Zionism, and communism. In addition, they talked about oil, space sciences, and the computer revolution. They ignored one thing, something primary, vital, fundamental, and central in our sociological, historical Arab formation, and that, in reality – as events unveil everyday – is the main cause of our problems, retreats, failure, fighting, and destruction in modern life…and in the extent of our respect for work values, production, and order, or, in other words, our disrespect for them!

This main thing is the characteristics of our social and historic Arab self, in its tribal, sectarian, and regional formations. What are the laws and phenomena that govern the behavior of this collective self, and what are the ways and means required to successfully rectify this makeup, which is debilitating and obstructive, and not palliative?

In every period of modern Arab history, or what is called the modern Arabic renaissance, a shiny modernizing ideological cover appears on the surface and the skin – whether its name is liberalism,

The Only Issue We Do Not Research

secularism, Marxism, development, or democracy – and we busy ourselves with the new makeup on our skin for some time...then suddenly, the inherited and genetic blisters and tumors of the old skins appear on the surface...only to find out that democracy is an ugly sectarianism, as in Lebanon, and Marxism is a scary tribalism, as in South Yemen, and the socialist liberating revolution is a return to "village morals," as in the common law of Anwar Sadat!

And there are many examples that we have not mentioned.

So what is this awesome force inherent in the depths of our societal self and our collective formation, that defies all efforts of reform and insists upon appearing in the course of events, in all times, to prove its tragic fragmented bloody existence?

Mut'a Safadi wrote, after the events of Aden, 1986, saying, "...to see the ideological conflicts displaced in a blink of an eye, to be replaced by all primitive tribal rituals. The Marxist dictionaries collapse under the blows of domination and the drives of collective revenge and counter-revenge, meaning that that historical model emerges into existence, and that is the descent of the bloody kin *Asabiyyah*, to rule and to destroy all the new ideological affiliations affixed onto the forehead of man and his body from the outside!"

This historical model, therefore, is it not time to study it objectively and with courage and draw the necessary conclusions from it? And to study it according to its particularity and not according to what others think?

This requires, before anything, freeing Arab thought from the claim of Marxists that they are the only ones that own the methods of sociological scientific analysis. It has been proven that they, in regard to Arab societies, do not own anything except how to transcribe letter by letter from traditional Marxism, which died and failed even in its own birthplace. The Arab particularity needs scientific sociological laws derived from its reality and its historical development, where the creative Arab intellectual Ibn Khaldun began his *Muqaddimah*, and not in the talk of the ambiguous and contradictory Karl Marx on "the pattern of Asian production," derived from the partial and misleading observations of Western travelers.

What is required – therefore – is an Islamic Arab sociology derived from the reality of our history, to understand that history and to attempt to return it to the correct path…starting with Ibn Khaldun….

Before that, the courage of revelation of the reality of the Arab collective self in its historical, sociological reality is required, without accessories…without makeup…without masks…without illusions of self-grandeur. In ancient times, Socrates said, "Know yourself

II. SOCIAL DIMENSIONS OF ARAB-ISLAMIC CIVILIZATION

An Insight into the Roots:
The Responsibility of the Past towards the Crisis of the Present

In: *The Renewal of the Renaissance by Self Discovery and Criticism*. Beirut: Arabic Institute for Studies and Publishing, 1992, pp 111-119.

In order to avoid exaggerated self-flagellation regarding the enormity of Arab backwardness, and so as not to limit present interpretations of our deeply rooted complex problem to tentative and partial undertakings that alter with circumstantial alteration, there has to be a pause for a serious look at the sociological historical roots behind the Arab entity crisis, the crisis of the Arab mind and the Arab individual.

The monitoring of present events is, of course, worth pursuing, but now, more than ever before, the Arab mind is required to go further than this monitoring of the flux of events to achieve a sociological, historical, cultural and dynamic perspective on these factors that have shaped the Arab entity into what it is now. It is these factors that have caused most of the backwardness and defeats in contemporary Arab life.

What we present here is simply an intellectual effort, that is open to discourse, in an attempt to interpret Arab internal conflict, the weakness in productivity and cultural aptitude in Arab societies and their vulnerability to external influences and challenges.

If we return to deep social roots that are deep-seated and

profound and have influenced the makeup of Arab society, the first point we encounter is that the Arab region is characterized by geographic and demographic features that are singular and unique worldwide. It is a region that includes the oldest centers of civilization in human history, such as the Rafidin Valley, the Nile Valley, the Yemeni region, the cities of the Syrian and Tunisian coasts, as well as including one of the vastest and most arid deserts in the world, the Arabian Peninsula desert, the Levantine desert between Syria and Iraq, the Sinai desert that separates Egypt from the Arab East, the Egyptian western desert that separates Egypt from Libya, and the North African region as a whole. The large African desert extends to divide Libya and the Sudan, reaching southern Algeria to draw its borders there, with desert areas and semi-desert areas between western regions and Mauritania to Tunisia and Libya, as if the Arab centers of civilization were islands separated from each other and surrounded by waves of desert sand on every side threatening desertification, not only climatic but cultural and intellectual as well.

These geographic differences have created a cultural paradox of historic persistence, namely, the conflicting relationship between the nomadic and the urban areas, their encounter, attraction and conflict, or, between the nature of the growth of civilization in these centers of agriculture and commercial civilization and the phenomenon of nomadic movement across these deserts and their valleys, so that the history of the Arab region from ancient times falls under the reign of this law of attraction and repulsion between the power of urban civilization and nomadic power. The former prevails for a period of time, short or long, depending on the strength of the ruling power. Then comes another nomadic wave to rule the urban areas for another period, to change the structural nature of the populace, values, politics, culture and economics according to what suits the oncoming nomadic wave...and so on.

Arab Distinctiveness

This law of history was discovered and analyzed in depth by the philosopher of Arab history, Abdulrahman Ibn Khaldun, from whose *Muqaddimah,* discipline and viewpoint, begin all analyses of the roots of the Arab historical societal makeup before leaping to adopt the methodologies of foreign sociology that are materialistic, liberal or otherwise. As Ibn Khaldun's methodology is derived from Arab distinctiveness itself, and his laws are derived from the reality of this particularity and its singular features; while foreign methodologies, in spite of their being modern in analysis and theory, are derived from other particularities and various environments and societies, in many of their aspects, so that their theories and laws do not suit the essential nature of Arab society and may even conflict with it. This explains the failure of many contemporary Arab ideologies which have attempted to solve Arab crises from a European viewpoint, Eastern and Western. But those were in one world and the Arab crisis in quite another, waiting for the arrival of somebody to diagnose it from within.

We talk with pride about Ibn Khaldun for decades now, we profess the intention of reviving his studies, and we celebrate his dates of birth and death; yet, there has not been a single researcher in the domain of sociological, critical and analytical thought to follow up Ibn Khaldun's path in diagnosing Arab society and to attempt to develop it in accordance with the modern age, creating a vision to comprehend the actual Arab impasse, regarding the efforts of development, unity and stability, or to define the qualitative and successful methods to deal with this problematic condition and find the long-awaited solution to the deeply embedded extending problem.

In spite of Arab thinkers like Taha Hussain and Sata Al-Husri, researching Ibn Khaldun and pointing out his importance, there was no Arab independent movement in sociological thought to follow up this direction and develop its much-needed outcomes. For a time, Arab thinkers concerned with Ibn Khaldun and Arab distinctiveness were faced with intellectual terrorism, foremost among which were those who were followers of Auguste Comte, Karl Marx and Durkheim. Those did not recognize Ibn Khaldun as a remarkable sociologist until after his official baptizing as an instigator of material economic theory in institutes of Oriental Studies in Moscow and Paris...the Lord has His ways!

Between Stability and Nomadic Movement

After this introduction, which we found necessary to establish the sociological thinking rooted within our scientific intellectual and historical heritage, we return to the phenomenon of conflict inherent in the Arab makeup between the impulse towards settlement and the impulse towards nomadic movement. In other words, the dialectic phenomenon between the urban and nomadic which constitutes, in our opinion, the most critical dialectic in the future of Arab history, one which is particular to the Arab region and is not recognized by Western European dialectics which focus on the importance of class struggle within the stable and civilized European society, both agricultural and industrial, and is not aware of the possibility of a different kind of sociological historical discourse in the struggle between civilized society as a whole, with all its classes, and the structure of the nomadic society as a whole, with all its factors.

This historical societal fact is not merely due to the existence of desert spaces, Nomad or nomadic, within the Arab region, separating its civilized centers; but it is also due to a more grave fact, that of the Arab region being surrounded by Asiatic vast deserts and steppes, extending from the wall of China to the plains of Persia and constituting rich historical reservoirs for the sweeping waves of invading nomads, of which the Tatar wave under the leadership of Hulagu was only one. In addition, there is the overlap of Arab Africa with nomad black Africa, which made Egypt and North African countries exposed to waves of attack from the South. Also included are the waves of Arab nomads themselves which traversed the Sinai and the eastern Egyptian deserts, then settled in Upper Egypt, and thus overtook centers of Moroccan civilization, as did the Arabs of the Beni Helal with the city of Kairouan and other urban centers in Tunisia and along the Maghreb coast. This also occurred on the other side, when the African nomadic powers organized themselves in the two movements of the Almoravids and the Almohads in the Maghreb, overpowered the Arab-Andalusian modern civilized centers of culture, and subordinated them to the nomadic mental, political and social character.

From the coastal side, Egypt and the Levant were exposed to waves of barbaric Franks during the Crusades, as well as both before and after them, which also led to the destruction of Arab centers of civilization that, if spared the onslaught on land, were not spared the onslaught from the sea, because of their geographic nature, having open plains which lack those geographic barriers and obstacles as defense against conquering offensives and against infiltrating or migrating western elements continuously seeping into the Arab World, if not through invasions then through continuous immigration for living, work and refuge, and then control!

Factors of Destruction and Delay

The exposure of the Arab city as the center of civilization to the consistent flux of nomadic waves of assault has left within the makeup and structure of Arab society the following effects:

First: The tribe as a social unity factor of nomadic waves was transferred to the core of urban society as well as in the countryside, bringing along its conflicts, rigidity and point of view on technical, professional and other urban work. In addition, the tribe, unlike agricultural feudalism in European, Japanese or Chinese societies, tends by nature towards increased fragmentation where the tribe develops into clans divided into rival segments, whereas agricultural feudalism merges with other kinds of feudalism to form the nucleus of a united state, as occurred in Europe, Japan, China and India.

Second: This tribal and clan multiplicity makes up the core fabric of Arab society and caused the multiplicity of other unhealthy sectarian and religious fragmentation. If we return to the root causes of most religious divisions in our Arab countries, we find they are a result of social and political conflict between tribes, clans and families of Quaisiya and Yemeniya, Umayyad and Hashemite, etc. Afterwards the conflict grew with the advent of non-Arab nations within the Islamic state so that when the Turks would follow a particular religious sect, the Persians would respond by following a different sect. This happened at the beginning when the Umayyads tended towards one political direction, and their rivals responded by following the opposite direction. Both directions appeared in a sectarian religious garb.

Thus, the social makeup in the Arab World was not only hit by multiplicity of tribes, clans and other segments, or by multiplicity of belonging and loyalties seeping in from Turkey, Persia, Circassia and Armenia, but also multiplicity of religious sects, so that if tribal differences and loyalties diminished by virtue of intermarriage and historical cohabitation, the differences of sectarian politics remained, provoking prejudice and reminding people of their historical origins.

This has become the tool by which hostile forces are able to fragment the Arab region, and the rebirth of this phenomenon of splintered or mosaic multiplicity does not allow for any real bonding towards a united, solid, stable and civilized entity able to face up to external challenge and focus on work productivity and achieving internal development.

It is worth remarking that Islam, since the beginning, has always fought against tribal multiplicity in Arab society and warned against surrendering to negative nomadic values. The reverent Arab prophet described the tendency for tribal pride: "Let it aside for it is rotten," meaning it is abhorrent. However, throughout the Islamic eras, these unhealthy tribal and ethnic conflicts reoccurred as a part of Arab social constituency. In fact, all the planning of Israel and the covetous foreign powers can be summarized as a revival of this pre-Islamic multiplicity in the Arab region.

Third: The most important outcome of the subordination of centers of civilization to nomadic invasions is the lack of continuity in the development of Arab civilization. It is a fact that the most flourishing Arab progress had been stopped short in its path by invading nomadic powers which left no room for natural growth or maturation, and the transformation from one civilized stage to a higher one, as occurred in Europe and Japan with the transformation from an agricultural-based feudal civilization to industrial capitalism. This is, from my point of view, the reason why the commercially prosperous Abbasid society did not develop into an industrial capitalist one. Maxime Rodinson, the French Orientalist, as well as others, interpreted this strange phenomenon in various unconvincing and inconclusive ways, and it remains a controversial issue among historical sociological thinkers.

Extraordinary Withering

Our possible interpretation in view of the dialectic between civilized society and Nomadic powers is that the Abbasid society, which had been intellectually and socially advanced and prosperous professionally, economically and commercially, was not allowed its natural development and growth by the backwardness of nomadic forces surrounding it in Arab, Asiatic and African deserts. They did not allow for capital accumulation which would lead to an industrial revolution. In fact, they interrupted the commercial routes of supplies, then became aggressive towards civilized centers by political and religious infiltration into the ruling establishment and finally, by the offensive of open war once the internal structure was weakened.

Scholars agree that the era of the caliph Al-Ma'mun represents the peak of prosperity in Arab Islamic civilization intellectually, in economics, and in urbanization. This prosperity would have developed into more advanced stages had the Abbasid society preserved its unity and internal integrity. Then what actually happened that could explain why all the cultural and political intellectual backwardness occurred during the reigns of Al-Mu'tasim and Al-Mutawakil and those who came after?

Is it at all possible that the Abbasid era, which had reached its peak of prosperity during the rule of Al-Ma'mun, had digressed in a natural way towards withering and ageing? This is contrary to the natural flow of events. The natural withering of culture requires long successive periods, just the same as its gradual growth in the beginning. Therefore, it must have been an external and forced element that prevailed over the expected Abbasid development and growth and made it regress many steps backwards.

This is quite clear with the domination of the nomadic Turkish wave over Abbasid society and its government during the rule of Al-Mu'tasim, who was pro-Turkish, due to the fact that his mother was a Turk, which signifies that the Arab loyalty was weakened, even on the caliphate level, by the infiltration of non-Arab elements to the core fabric of its highest social nuclei. (Such dual loyalties will be among the major causes of calamities in the history of the Arabs.)

What happened during the rule of Al-Ma'mun was that it faced up to challenges from Arab nomads in the Levant and the Arab Peninsula and Asian challenges from Khurasan and the outskirts of Persia; while Al-Mu'tasim imagined that once he was in power, the support of Turkish forces would defend his nation, unaware that their power would not only damage his rule and political authority, but would lead eventually to the downfall of cultural structure and the political and economic advancement which had begun at the dawn of Islam. This was due to the backward nomadic element within the Turkish fighting forces.

Nomadic Rebellions

The great Abbasid thinker and writer Al-Jahiz left us an important historical document on the nature of this nomadic wave of attack which prevailed over the capital as well as other governorates, in which he said, in his famous letter on the Turks, "The Turks are owners of tents, dwellers of the deserts and owners of cattle. They are, in fact, non-Arab nomads...When they are not busied with manufacturing and commerce, medicine, farming, and engineering, neither planting nor building, nor digging dams nor collecting taxes, nothing other than conquering, raiding, fishing and horse riding would be their concern, searching for booty and upsetting towns, and this has become their action and their trade, their pleasure and pride, their favorite topic and entertainment."

The uncivilized, combative nature of these people and their lack of productivity are quite clear in the letter of Al-Jahiz, who was their contemporary. In his book *The Second Abbasid Period*, Dr. Shawqi Dayf mentioned this event of the nomadic rebellion and its features in Abbasid society, saying, "The majority of these slaves (the Turks) are harsh nomads. They were used to horse-riding and galloping through the streets, so some of the elderly, children, and women were run over, which obliged Al-Mu'tasim to build the city of Samara north of Baghdad."

It is possible to add to Dr. Shawqi Dayf's description, with no exaggeration, that what the horses of the Turks had stomped over was not just the people of Baghdad, but the level of Arab Islamic civilization and the degree of growth, whether economic, commercial or professional, in the Abbasid nation.

Any social historian trying to study the reasons behind the lack of development in the Abbasid society from a prosperous commercial society to a capitalist industrial one (in the economic sense of capitalism, and not the ideological sense prevailing today), has to pause a long time before such an intermittence in civilization and production caused by waves of nomadic intrusion upon Arab societies which left its marks and sedimentations upon its social and productive constitution for a long time.

In a similar historical experience, Arab society in the Levant and in Egypt had reached an advanced level of civilization and commercial and technological production towards the end of the Mamluk era, when it absorbed the Mamluk wave and Arabized it to a certain extent, and civilized its elements to a remarkable degree. It had been possible for the Arab society in Egypt and the Levant at that time to witness an important economic and cultural transformation by moving from the stage of the flourishing commerce with Italian cities such as Genoa and Venice, to the industrialized stage about to begin in Europe.

However, a wave of Ottoman nomadic attack coming from the plains of Asia Minor seized this civilized Arab society with direct invasions, interrupting cultural and economic productivity, as had occurred previously in the Iraqi Arab society and the east with the first Turkish wave of assault during the age of Al-Mu'tasim. The incident of the Turkish sultan, Suleiman the Great, who forced the best Levantine and Egyptian craftsmen to abandon work in the Arab cities and leave with him to Istanbul, is a well-known story. He took the most valuable tools, artifacts, and antiquities from Cairo,

Damascus, and Aleppo to his capital.

This human and cultural intermittence in Arab societies is no simple matter. Its reverberations are yet to be overcome.

The duality in loyalties, the multiplicity of elements, the recession in production levels in labor and urbanization, and the paradoxes in the Arab social fabric between the highest level of the culture and the lowest unharmonious levels of retardation…all this remains true and still has its impact today, with respect to the coherence of Arab societies against the threats they face, as well as the extent of the efficiency of its production and its cultural abilities regarding the internal structure and the challenge of development.

The Arabs and Progress: Where is the Flaw? In Diagnosing the Phenomenon of the Repeated Schizophrenia between the Situation of Arabs and their Aborted Attempts towards Progress

In: *The Suicide of Arab Intellectuals and Contemporary Issues in Arab Culture*. Beirut: Arabic Institute for Studies and Publishing, 1998, pp. 249-267.

Originally given as a lecture in Bahrain at the *Al-Ayam* Annual Cultural Festival for Writers, 1995

There is a basic question that forces itself strongly upon the Arab every time he contemplates modern Arabic life. At the end of each period of the modern history of Arabs, the same question appears and draws a puzzling question mark because it is not specific for that period alone.

The question, in brief, is: Why did the Arab nation not realize its destiny and finish its renaissance and achieve its goals and unity as did several oriental nations like Japan, China, and India, despite the Arab nation having started its modern renaissance before or around the same time as these nations?

These nations went through experiences and aborted attempts similarly to the Arabs, or even more. However, these nations emerged from their suffering resurrected, productive, and united, knowing their ways and positions in the world, practicing their roles in self-confidence, and working diligently…while the Arab nations emerge from one experience to enter another, emerging from one aborted attempt to fall into the next, without achieving any results.

Why? How?

In a conference about the crisis of cultural progress held by Arab intellectuals in Kuwait in 1974…this question was the dark cloud that resided over that conference. The scholar Dr. Shakir Mustafa was the most precise participant expressing the tragedy of this question when he said, "Why did it take so long for the Arabs to be in accordance with the times, and with no significant results? If this question is still, day after day, taking increasingly tragic dimensions, it is because this nation met modern civilization many years back and yet nothing is happening. There has been enough time for the masses of the Arab regions to reach the level of modern times, its technology and its wide cultural possibilities. Most of them started before China, which only started half a century ago…and some started even before Japan, which started a hundred years ago. Yet these nations reached their objectives – all of them – while none of the Arab regions, even the pioneering ones, reached anything. The tragedy of the question springs from the possibilities of the answers. Did this nation reach old age? Or did it lose the way? Or are there some complicated diseases in its general configuration that paralyzes its joints? That is the issue!"

Yes, this is the issue.

After the collapse of the renaissance of the great Mohammed Ali, this question emerged. After the wilting of the time of Ismail and the failure of the Urabi revolution, this question came back. After the failure of the first Arabic revolution to unify the East at the time of the Anglo-French partition, this question was repeated. After the failure of the Arabs in stopping the establishment of Israel in 1948 and the collapse of the semi-liberal regimes, this question was repeated. After the defeat of 1967, we had to ask this question. And after the calamity of August, 1990, the question is the same. Today, it still remains the issue of all issues.

I am afraid that our children will find themselves, generation after generation, confronting the same question, unless we learn and teach our children how to convert the question mark into a sentence with the correct answer and a mark of calculated act. What I mean by "a sentence with the correct answer" is a complete sentence that has a subject and a predicate, not an open sentence with unspecified words calling for modernization and change, just like that, with ambiguity and cloudiness, hanging in a vacuum like a verbal amulet that sedates more than it treats.

I do not claim that the answer is easy, as no one has ready solutions. However, we must try to be equipped before we begin by informed awareness about the truth of our previous experiences and their lessons.

I am going to present here several informed concepts that I see are basic, as an independent scholar concerned as much as I can be about the truth. I am not going seeking approval in this from any ideology, authority, or opposition in our Arab World, as the truth governs all and should be above all. In the end, only what is correct will remain.

Since the European countries were capable of tilting the balances of power in the world to their advantage three centuries ago by their cultural progress in the different fields of society – intellect, invention, and production – and were able to take out the Chinese and Islamic powers from the circle of leaders of the world, the factor of modern cultural progress became the decisive factor in domination over the capabilities of the world and nations. Progress became the issue of existence and an issue of life and death, if not for people in themselves as individuals, then for civilized nations and groups.

It is no longer possible for any young nation, owning physical fighting power and splendid horsemanship, to dominate with its reborn power any other nation if it does not own the requirements for modern cultural power. In addition, it is not possible for such a nation to defend its existence in front of an invading power with modern technology.

This is in contrast to ancient and medieval history where it was possible for physically strong people with reborn powers to invade civilized nations and dominate them as did the Romans in Greece and the Germanic tribes to the Romans after they were civilized, and as the Arabs did with powers that were more advanced than them in Persia and Byzantium at the beginning of their conquests. This phenomenon was repeated in a different form when the nomadic Asian power invaded the societies of the Arabic Islamic civilizations after they became advanced.

If there has not been an organic relationship established between the old civilizations and the decisive military power as there was between modern civilization and its military means based upon technology, research, and scientific order – meaning cultural progress in the first place – it becomes impossible to repeat these historical phenomena in modern times. What the European immigrants did to Native Americans and their culture is a clear example of this new fact that had been repeated until that time. (The Native Americans did not lack courage and sacrifice, but they were defeated by modern technology.)

The French army entered Cairo at the end of the eighteenth century and eliminated Mamluk power. Western armies entered Beijing at the end of the nineteenth century and eliminated the Chinese empire and entered Istanbul after a few decades and eliminated Ottoman power. It became a fact that there was no way to establish any level of power and any military achievement, offensively or defensively, without modern cultural advancement.

This is what was realized by Mohammed Ali's Egypt and the Mejji's Japan. The difference is that the Mejji's Japan began to gradually adopt this comprehensive cultural advancement, while Mohammed Ali in Egypt only adopted the military side of this advancement very quickly without the proper establishment of comprehensive advancement for the basis of society. When Ismail came, he adopted the same lesson in reverse, where he was concerned with culture and education but not with military, economic, and administrative reforms. This led to the stumbling of the Egyptian renaissance in the long run while the Japanese renaissance continued because of its comprehensive approach to reform, avoiding becoming involved in battles, especially at the beginning of its renaissance.

Therefore, the first lesson that must be comprehended in the issue of progress is that there has to be a comprehensive project for cultural renaissance. There cannot be educational or intellectual reform in isolation from the reality of the society and the nature of its sociological powers. There cannot be economic or developmental reforms without political reform. There cannot be reform or political change that does not have the educational, sociological, and economic requirements to back it up.

The cultural project must either be comprehensive or nothing. Naturally, it is acceptable to prioritize and to plan, but only within a complete vision from the beginning. Futile debates have occupied modern Arab intellect for a long time. For example, should the reform be educational or political? Should it be intellectual or social? Is our battle with Israel a military or cultural one? Etc. And other debates that divided the awareness of the nation into contradicting dualities that never end. Arabism or Islam? National or nationalist? Heritage or modernization? Etc. And other debates that are Byzantine in nature.

These debates prevent us from reaching a comprehensive cultural renaissance which could contain the different aspects and elements, like the European and Japanese renaissances. Even closer and earlier than these is the comprehensive Islamic renaissance during the early Islamic era. The most distinguished elements for its success and establishment was that the renaissance was comprehensive for all aspects of society and man, intellect and life, education and economy, and politics and law.

Naturally, these dualities and contradictions exist in society and life. We cannot jump over them spontaneously. But this is the responsibility of whoever calls for the cultural project. He must contain it and work with it in his vision in a scientific way. There are no magic solutions, neither in the slogans of Arab unity, the slogan of democracy by itself, nor in the slogan that Islam is the solution. Islam is the solution only when the people who are preaching it will extract the characteristics of the aspired comprehensive cultural project and its principles and values, and the project is able to conduct dialogue, evaluation, and debate.

The democratic slogan has to be a comprehensive project for society, family, education, treatment of people, and values. No democracy without democrats, and without true democratic power within society. That is especially true for those who are calling for democracy now. Democracy is not just a ballot box polled by the zealotry of the tribes, sectors, militants, and undemocratic powers. This is a truth that has to be realized by those who call for democracy so that they do not plow the sea.

Maybe there is not enough room to focus on this, but I have treated this matter in a lecture that I presented lately in Beirut and published by the journal *Al-Mustakbil Al-Arabi*, published by the Center for Arab Unity Studies in January 1996, entitled "Democracy and Obstacles of Arab Political Configuration," to whom it may concern.

If we agree on the necessity of having a comprehensive

cultural project, then what is the next step? The next step cannot be conducted by one party or one government by itself. The next step requires having a mature, informed vision among all parties concerned with the project – knowledge of the current realities of the nation, the realities of its history and itself as a whole, and the reality of the world around us. These three dimensions are vast and intertwined, and we must comprehend them with knowledge before taking the risk of drafting the solution and the remedy for a nation that is living in the heart of the world and its crosscurrents.

The ideological projects that have been presented in the past, either by nationalists, religious, liberals, or leftists, lacked the awareness of the facts of this comprehensive reality with its different dimensions. The informed, scientific, and objective awareness for these dimensions was poor, cloudy, or generally superficial. It depended on thinking by wishing and on grand objectives without searching the means of achieving them in reality. That is why the fall [of these ideologies] made a crashing noise when they hit the ground of the reality that they were ignorant of or had overlooked or ignored.

One excuse that was once presented by a progressive Arab public relations man, after the defeat of 1967, was that "we waited for them in the East and they came to us from the West." This statement is symbolic of this overlooking of different dimensions and possibilities of reality, not in its military sense alone, but in its comprehensive way, a statement that reflects the mocking of Arab awareness with itself and reveals its poverty and shallowness.

After the calamity of August 1992, it was said in Iraq, after the completion of the disaster that, "We entered the war with tourist information." The *battle of all battles*… with tourist information?

Between these two events, the only exception is what was described by Mohammed Hassanin Hekal [modern Egyptian scholar and historian inside the close circle of Jamal Abdul Nassar] about the October War/the Tenth of Ramadan War, 1973, and what happened in the Egyptian military headquarters after the "crossing" of the canal. With all its electronic monitors and digital maps, he said the headquarters "represent the comprehension of the facts of science and the world by the Arab military mind."

It was not by accident that this was the only time that the vision fit the reality and the awareness fit the facts, so the "crossing" was across the terrain of reality itself, the reality of solid ground...that is why the awareness of reality is the way to conquer it. There is no other choice, and there will not be any more crossings for the nations except with the accuracy of the comprehension.

If this informed comprehension with all its dimensions with the efforts of the common Arab mind in the different fields of knowledge is not achieved, then the ideological and self-oriented illusion will be the master of judgment. That is because doubts do not change the truth.

"And it is not with your wishes and with the wishes of the People of the Book."

In this current historical moment, because of the huge imbalance in the balance of powers, the Arab cannot achieve any qualitative, political, military, or economic breakthrough on the map of reality. Of course, things to be done have to be done, but we should not delude ourselves with false wishes.

The only possible qualitative breakthrough in this moment is the breakthrough of knowledge by true scientific awareness of the dimensions of the self and the world. This is what no power can prevent the Arabs from achieving unless they allow their illusions and bad mental habits to continue to control them.

Other powers are able to establish a Middle Eastern common

market and to force any strategic conditions they want...the only thing that this power cannot stop is the revolution of knowledge and culture if the Arab mind is determined. Even if it were stopped from one way, it will come from another, as we are in the age of a knowledge revolution and cyberspace.

The danger in this intellectual revolution of knowledge comes from the power of the self and from internal power, not from outside and conspiracies of imperialism and Zionism, as we say.

So can we conquer the self? This is the great *jihad*.

"God does not change what is in people until they change themselves."

We should not have any illusions in this regard. It is the duty of every Arab intellectual and all Arabs in general who wish to own the correct informed awareness to depend upon themselves and sacrifice in order to tread this path. No one is going to send them bouquets of flowers so they can own this correct informed awareness.

The important thing is that the Arabs realize the fateful necessity of owning this awareness and having the determination and freedom of choice to own it. Knowledge is power, or at least, the path to power.

This confrontation must be achieved through knowledge in order to dismantle these two basic infrastructures – the mental infrastructure (upper level) of the Arab mind and the sociological infrastructure (lower level) of Arab society – or, in modern terms, the level of ideology and the level of sociology – or, in even simpler terms, the intellect and reality.

In regard to the general Arab mental infrastructure, meaning the intellectual or ideological level, we have to solve the following dilemmas:

1. The Arab mind tends to deny facts and realities that do not conform to his imaginings and wishes. Not only that, he insists that he is right even if denying leads to calamities. There is always a continuous mix between what is "opinion" and what is "reality." Usually, reminding others of reality leads to confrontation with the others, who consider just the mention of reality as an expression of opinion or private tendency, and they pass judgment over whoever is mentioning it from that angle. If you say that Arab unity is not going to be achieved for the objective reason so and so, they reply to you that you are against unification. And if you say that democracy requires these or those conditions, they say to you that you are against democracy...and so on. It is just like when a doctor tells his patient that he has an ulcer in the stomach, and the patient accuses the doctor of wishing him to get an ulcer and to continue having it. No, brother, I am telling you that, according to the diagnosis, you have an ulcer, so let's work together to treat it. I do not wish for you to get it because you already have it, and if I hide that from you, then I am deceiving you.

   But deceiving is something comfortable and requested among the Arab authorities and Arab masses equally. The authorities want praise – without details of reality and fact – to help them be strong and successful. The masses want intellectuals that praise them and transform their backwardness into revolutionary progressiveness and praise change and mutiny in any form. But whenever reminded of their shortcomings and the requirements for success in any change, they want to silence the voices that do not lull them and tickle their repressed instincts. The Arab masses and opposition are no less dictators than their governments.

"As you are, you will have people who govern you."

The Arab mind will not be able to take the important step in the informed revolution as long as it is not in the habit of accepting facts and realities without sensitivity on any level – living, religious, political, or scientific – and as long as it does not distinguish in a decisive way between what is a description of reality and an expression of opinion.

2. The Arab mind tends towards generalities and abstracts, liking only the grand goals and great objectives, without stopping in front of the details, parts, and minute issues that are connected in the core of any idea, subject or issue. In addition, it gets impatient with searching for specific means and tools leading to the achievement of those ideas and objectives. This explains the failure of several of the general objectives, even by those who called for it and led it.

The core of modern progress in particular can only be achieved by taking care of the details, parts, and minute issues. This is what modern technology and computers that run the world are based upon. If a small wire is cut on any huge equipment, this might lead to its malfunction. This is true for the biggest strategic plans in the world.

We notice that the detailed maintenance services, no matter how simple, are carried out by foreign laborers in Arab societies filled with Ph.D.'s, because the majority of these are filled with philosophers, intellectuals, and people of great ideologies and objectives that do not concern themselves with insignificant – in their opinion – details and parts.

For this reason, their ideas remain hanging in a vacuum. Mr. Adonis said, in my debate with him that took place in Bahrain, that I gave a lot of concern to some details and minute issues, and that this takes us away from the basic ideas.

I say, on the contrary, that details and minute issues are what proves or demolishes the concept. Any huge construction is nothing but these small blocks that make it up. Otherwise, the whole construction might be in danger. On purpose, I chose these details and minute issues to test his ideas. Otherwise, how do the great ideas form in the first place? Doesn't it form from putting it together with the pieces and parts that make it up? If these details are correct, the general concept is. You find this is the basis of logic, mathematics, and the scientific rationale of modern science.

A few days back, I listened at the Beit-al-Quran [a museum dedicated to Quranic manuscripts] in Bahrain to a lecture by [renowned Islamic scholar] Dr. Shaikh Yusuf Al-Qaradhawi, entitled "The Signs of the Victory of Islam." His Excellency presented, in this lecture, signs from the Quran, the Sunna, and history predicting the victory of Islam.

Shaikh Al-Qaradhawi is a man of enlightened intellect. I went to that lecture intentionally, looking forward for him to specify the scientific means leading to this victory, but that is what I did not find in that lecture. Although he fulfilled his identification of these signs, we did not notice specifically how they could be achieved in reality. The other publications of Shaikh Al-Qaradhawi may contain such identification of these means, but to mention these signs at this level, in a reality as bad as the Arab reality, without attaching to it, at the same time, the scientific means to achieve it, may have led to calming the worries of the souls – and that might have been the intention of the lecturer – but did not calm the worries of the minds.

That is why details, parts, and minute issues on one hand, and on the other hand means and tools, are very important elements that we must be careful to not overlook in the core of our thinking.

3. In connection to the common belief that the Muslim mind ignored the divine universal laws and the direct natural cause and effect for things to happen and reach results, he does not bother himself with following the specific requirements for what he wants to achieve because he deludes himself into thinking God will achieve for him anything He wishes, and he sits in his laziness just because he is a Muslim. This is a misunderstanding of the essence of religion.

Al-tawakul (dependence on God) does not mean *al-tawaakul* (lazy dependence and blind reliance on destiny) without contemplating, thinking, or working with the reasons and causes that were created by divine will in the order of the world. [A man left his camel outside and started to enter the mosque, saying he depended upon God to prevent his camel from wandering away. The Prophet saw him and told him no.] The honorable Prophet (pbuh) said to the man, "Tie the knot and then depend upon God," meaning, tie the knot of the camel's rope tightly around the tree so it will not

The Arabs and Progress: Where is the Flaw?

wander away, then depend upon God to make sure it will not get lost. This means, do your duty first, and then depend upon God to grant you your wish. Believing in divine will does not cancel the order of cause and effect which is detailed and accurate, made by God, and which the early Muslims and the great Islamic intellect believed in. The sky does not rain gold or silver.

In reality, in the attack of Abu Hamid Al-Ghazali [early Islamic philosopher] on the order of cause and effect and his attempts to cancel it with the intention of ridiculing the opinions of his counterpart philosophers, while he thought he was defending the act of divine will in the world, this had the worst effect, that of creating a mental infrastructure of lazy dependence on God which was one of the reasons for the downfall of Muslims, misdirecting them from following the reasoning that leads to productivity and progress.

What is dangerous is that the phenomenon of bypassing the law, maneuvering around it, and walking away from the true, direct natural cause and effect that leads to its results by using means that are above law, order, and reason, is becoming a common phenomenon in the downfallen mind dominating the Islamic world in issues regarding this life and the afterlife. In this life, the phenomenon of "intermediary," which is maneuvering around and canceling the social laws and logical natural means in order to achieve different objectives in an unlawful unnatural way, is common and spreading. In the afterlife, there is a dominating idea of waiting for *al-shafi'a* [an intermediary to testify on your behalf and ask God's forgiveness] to avoid proper punishment, while *al-shafi'a* in the correct Islamic understanding means *except by the will of God and His permission.* "Who is there that can intercede in His presence except as He permitteth?" (Surah *Al Buqarah* 2:255) But this backward mentality, with lazy dependence, converted *al-shafi'a* in its specific divine concept to this type of intermediary and did not respect divine will, bringing in a different type of intermediary: *uliyah* [people they think highly of and consider to be true followers of God. When these have died, some people began the practice of calling upon the spirits of these dead to intercede for them with God, like praying to them.], and graves, amulets, cemeteries, etc.

It should be clear and without beating around the bush that this type of mentality is still common in the Islamic world, and that the continuation of the concept of an intermediary in this life and wishing for it in the afterlife in the wrong way is one of the obstacles of progress in any field. Like we said earlier, the sky does not rain gold or silver. It does not rain free progress for anyone. The non-religious West followed the natural laws of God in power and productivity in this life, so they progressed. But it diverted from the laws of God in faith, worship, and morality, so its soul – as we see it! – was filled with emptiness and misery. The Muslims diverted from the natural laws of God in life and they remained backwards. But they continued to follow some of the laws of God in faith and worship, which might be protective as strongly as they are holding to it. These are the laws of God that govern His creation. "You will not find change in the laws of God." These laws are not just for some people. There is no preference for a Muslim over anyone else in the laws and accurate causes except in the strength of his respect for them, Muslim or non-

The Arabs and Progress: Where is the Flaw?

Muslim, especially in this life. In the afterlife, God makes His judgment between people as He wishes.

4. Some of the negativity of the common way of thinking with this mind is the fatal gap between objectives, declared grand desires in Arab life – like unity, modernization, the confrontation of imperialism, Zionism, *al-jihad*, and leading the world – and the tangible daily conduct of the Arab masses and elite in their practical lives. This conduct is very far away from the possibility of progress towards those objectives. This conduct is reflected in the low level of the order, productivity, work, respect of time, necessary daily duties, and the values of civil society in all aspects. What is strange is that the Arab and the Muslim do not get enthusiastic except when they are provoked with grand slogans, but the necessary daily duties for every modern society in this world do not provoke their enthusiasm.

In the conference entitled "The Iraqi Invasion of Kuwait" which was organized by the Arab Thought Forum in Amman recently, I was trying to point out to the participants that "the Arab and the Muslim do not feel enthusiasm or moral responsibility unless they are called for under national or religious banners and loud speeches to wipe out imperialism, but if called upon under a quiet, modest campaign for health, for example, to wipe out all the dirt and garbage surrounding their houses, I am not sure that their enthusiasm will be moved."

How can a nation that cannot organize traffic in its cities and cannot stand in line to conduct its business, stand between the powers of this era and fight its battles?

We cannot escape from stating that progress is not the verbal declaration of grand objectives while giving up on the smaller duties.

"Grievously odious is it in the sight of God that ye say that which you do not." (Surah *Al Saff* 61:3) This is what the new movement of Islamic renaissance and movements of national renaissance should be frank to its masses about instead of sedating it.

This is what leads us in the end to the necessity of cautioning that progress in the end is daily conduct. Moving forward is the life that we live everyday, or don't. Progress is when we leave our homes to work on time, without wasting the time of the country and its productivity. Progress, before anything else, is respecting the order and law above everything, without exception, in the order of traffic, by the basic laws of cleanliness and the polite civil values in dealing with everyone. Progress is the administrator doing his duty and rejecting corruption and bribery. Progress is in the citizen playing his role and doing his job…the advanced nations, through its experiences, reached true national struggle in the capability of development, developing every neighborhood and street, not breaking and destroying it. The two great peoples, the Japanese and the Germans, succeeded in the test of impossible rebuilding while they were under foreign occupation. They resisted this occupation with more work and progress until they conquered it in the battle of civilization and productivity, which is the true "battle of all battles."

Maybe it requires many generations to achieve comprehensive Arab progress. History is a long process, conditioned with its causes. It does not fall under the concept of "Be, and it is."

Does that mean we have to be wondering and incapable, waiting for things to come...and they do not come?

No, there is an appropriate and honorable solution for every Arab Muslim who is suffering from his reality and the reality of his nation. From this moment, if he faces himself with the following fact: "I, as an individual cannot fix the world. I cannot fix the whole nation and the whole country. That is beyond my capabilities. But I, as an individual, am capable of educating myself and reforming myself and my family and children, and can contribute in the reform of my circle and my institute as much as I can. I will reform wherever my hand can reach and no less, so you should reform wherever your hand can reach."

Let every individual reform wherever his hand can reach. From here, true reform begins, and the will of reform is tested for every individual. Let's imagine if every hand reformed what it could reach in its natural position, at home, work, and in society. The big waves in life are the products of small drops and small streams and small steps. It does not come from emptiness or bubbles.

This adherence would enable us to live in dignity and there will be no meaning in all this talk if every one of us goes to his work on time with a true desire for small, modest reform.

The Problem of the Arab Social Makeup: Minorities…or Multiple Majorities?

In: *Local Conflicts: The Internal and External Elements*, Center for Arab Unity Studies, pp. 17-45.

To resolve whatever deep-rooted internal conflicts exist within Arab societal formation, I have found it best to begin where I should, methodologically, to present the essential summary of my own perspective on this problematic issue with its various dimensions as a whole, and in order to avoid any misunderstanding that could possibly occur from starting directly dismantling the elements of the problem one after the other – before clarifying the comprehensive perspective, which could lead to the suggestion that I give one factor precedence over the other or I give another aspect priority, especially in regards to comparing the two sides of 'pluralism' and 'unity' in the Arab makeup, and in the Arab character in general, and especially when comparing the anxious, intertwined, minute chronic attraction – in Arab 'reality' and Arab 'awareness' – between these two sides or these two poles (pluralism/unity), which leads to an uneasy ambiguity in understanding this dualistic phenomenon and comprehending it intellectually, emotionally, and describing it in a clear and accurate scientific manner, and then in how it should be dealt with in Arab life: nationally and nationalistically, politically and intellectually.

First: Between Awareness and Reality

The essential summary of this perspective in its

comprehensive dialectical viewpoint (between the two poles, pluralism and unity) is that the Arab nation is a united nation in its morals such as values, feelings and culture – but is fragmented in terms of its material reality – regarding the connecting foundation of geography and economic establishment, the sociological structure, and the numerous heavily-calloused sedimented makeups from recent and distant historical periods that still remain today. If a primary condition for a united national life of any nation is the presence of true interaction in the cycle of livelihood – economy, growth, daily life, common organization – then this cycle, on the level of essential 'material necessities' between the multiple Arab units, is not complete nor yet mature and is beset with serious shortcomings. In fact, it could almost be said to be lacking altogether in many aspects of Arab 'real' life (as measured against the reality of any other national entity in modern times).

1. The Dialectic of Pluralism and Unity

In another simpler expression, the Arabs are a united nation in terms of 'awareness' – that is to say, where they differentiate themselves from the 'other' and in their sharing of common culture and feelings regarding many things – but they are a divided nation among themselves in terms of 'reality,' material, sociological, economic and institutional organization. This is how the higher level of Arab awareness is therefore connected by values, language, culture and emotions, creating this overwhelming and living feeling of nationalism that we have witnessed in many stages of modern Arab history and until now. However, the deeper Arab level is fragmented within itself, creating, on the other hand, this pluralism, estrangement, and Arab conflict which counterparts that unifying feeling, enclosing it, and resulting in its despair or abortion. This is especially true where there are confrontations and decisive national battles, when moral nationalist feeling rises up in defense, reacting and acting so that the deeper level of pluralism fails – whether official or unofficial, in authority or in opposition – in practical response to that challenge. And Arabs consequently fall into what they are feeling today, overwhelming emotional provocation to confront the humiliation, defeat, loss, and explicit incompetence – at the same time – of the practical realistic levels: political, military, economic, institutional organizational, official and unofficial, in achieving the minimal requirement required for that common direction of shared national feeling.

Having been neither sufficiently diagnosed nor resolved as it should be in its obvious double duality, this dangerous contradiction in Arab lives and their character, in what is being reflected in current lamenting Arab rhetoric, is getting closer to Greek tragedy which is founded upon the conflict of the antagonists (one half being for, the other half against), for we are nationalist and state-nationalist equally and at the same time. We have to codify this double duality in our Arab character to 'naturalize' it before any other naturalization, and to deal with it in order to overcome this condition of unadmitted 'schizophrenia' of nationalist identity which, in each of us, lives its idealist unification in utopia, and its nation-state personality and what is lower than the nation-state in each one of us, too, living its daily reality in a growing and continuing association…but with a sinful conscience…so until when?

In fact, this 'tragi-dramatic' anxiety between the two dimensions and two poles of Arab life and in the makeup of the Arab character is not an analogy nor is it figurative description. It is rather a true reality which we must confront, understand and resolve instead of escaping from it, either by going forward with exaggerated reiteration of nationalist slogans ignoring the objective reality of pluralism, or by retreating to the rear considering state pluralism and what is lower than state level pluralism to be the reality to which we must submit, and stop at that. This did not materialize, in return, as a permanent condition, even in the most isolated conditions and of nation-state conflicts, whether with the separatists in Syria, after 28th September 1961, or with the supporters of Camp David in Egypt since 1977/1979, or with some of the Gulf Arabs in their resistance of Iraq's invasion of Kuwait 1990/1991. In all of these cases, given their different types, natures and legitimacy, we find that a return to nationalism is the determining reference, in one way or another, which stays in the basis of these standings and cases, which was surpassed anyway after not too long a time, towards returning to the nationalist contact, if not in its first form, then in a modified form substituting for it. On the other hand, and from a further-sighted historical perspective, we find that the states and sultanates that fragmented in Islamic history do not remain stable in their fragmentation but return in another cycle unified within a larger entity to which it continued to aspire, even in its fragmentation.

2. The Perception of Agreement

But the realization of this truth – phenomenon – does not exempt the callers for nationalist unity from renewing their thinking, their methodology, and their presentations regarding diagnosing the regional and nation-state pluralism, and what is below the nation-state, and how to deal with it, and finding the practical suitable formats – and this is the most important – for the adaptation and suitability between the source of the inclination for unity and the source of the inclination for pluralism, and between the dimension of the nation-state/national and what is below it…and the nationalist dimension on the other side of this Arab dialectics or Arab tragedy that cannot be avoided, which will remain with the Arabs for a long time, and perhaps all the time, as it was represented in their long history despite the strength of the source of the inclination for unity in Islam. (If the political fragmentation has been succeeded by projects of unity, these projects also have been succeeded by cases of fragmentation, one after the other.) What we can do is to transform this dialectics from its level that is antagonistic, conflicting, unhealthy, and threatening to energies...to its level that is practical, health, and agreeing by transforming the Arab national pluralism into agreeing, positive structures within a national framework capable of movement and action, with the dissolution of the clannish structures, and what is below the nation-state, in the crucible of a modern civil society that establishes first one national space, then contributes to the closeness of these mature and complete national units in one national conglomeration, compatible to all its members, in a free and equal balanced partnership .

Therefore, it is not possible to describe Arab reality by the national dimension alone or the pluralism dimension, alone. The Arabs are unified and similar in a primary part of their makeup, and different in other parts. It is not possible to abolish the national for the sake of the nationalist, or vice versa. And if Arab awareness and action did not reach these two realities – together – in a flexible dialectics format, bringing together positively the requirements of both dimensions, then the roots of conflict and its causes will continue in the Arab makeup, and in Arab life in general, for a long time. The flaw was, and still is, in our evasion from this dual objective reality, and the attempt of its concealment with the exaggeration of the nationalist, unificationist mask sometimes, or with the shy surrender to the inevitabilities of the nation-state reality sometimes.[1]

There is no escape, and this is the case, from a dialectic consideration and a liberated political mind, working in two directions, and possessing the ability of comprehending the phenomenon of duality and pluralism, that means a political mind liberated from the one dominant point of view in Arab awareness, which does not stop placing choices in the place of antagonism and contradictions and does not see the reality of things except their black or white color and with a sharp contradiction between them....

With the historical and current differences between Europe and the Arab World, the methodology that the nation-state and nationalist European pluralism undertook for the long-term towards a common European space (then the unified), remains one of the models worthy of study and comparative contemplation – Arabwise – where modern times surpassed the bygone historical formats and methodologies in national unification, such as the Bismarckian style and others which ended up accomplishing the opposite of what they intended.

From another perspective, if the studies and Arab researches should be directed accordingly to the surpassing and refutation of the "mosaic model" and the inevitable fragmenting interpretation of the Arab makeup,[2] then this cannot be achieved by just saying that these are Orientalist perspectives or colonial – Zionist – (and it is), but by approaching the pluralism of this makeup objectively and in light of national unification in its structure, at the same time, and the diligence with intellectual and organizational creativity in how to make it suitable among the multiplicities under the umbrella of the common Arab space, and not to leave these "realistic" studies to the exclusivity of those suspicious groups. The accomplishment of Arab research and thought for this task, in theory and practice, will be the practical response to those "Orientalist" perspectives, or those hostile to the Arabs in general, that aim towards the fixation of this "mosaic" or fragmented format for the Arabs, its consolidation and codification permanent and absolute.

3. Deep-seated Pluralism

To approach this problem from its harsher and more difficult side, we have to decide first that the multiplicities and incompatible structures in the Arab makeup are not exclusive or a monopoly for the ethnic, religious, or sectarian minorities (as that is the easy side of pluralism in the Arab region!) – but it is a phenomenon whose roots, effects, and divisions reach the Arab body in its totality and in its predominant base, which is assumed to be "harmonious" and devoid of pluralism.

It is common when presenting the problem of Arab civil conflicts that minds turn to the phenomenon of minorities in the Arab World of ethnic-national, or religious-sectarian, then turn towards interpretation of the conflict as a competition between the rulers, systems, parties, and nation-state interests. Before that, or after it, is the common traditional interpretation in Arab political rhetoric, which attributes these conflicts primarily to the colonial, imperialist conspiracies – Zionism….

All of these interpretations are possible in one degree or another, and true in their objective limits and specific cases, but we do not see that they – alone – represent the total final or exclusive interpretations that would interpret the different aspects of long-term Arab civil conflicts – in the past or in modern times – which draw their roots from another level of pluralism and the different, clannish, traditional structures strongly deep-seated in the Arab makeup and the general Arab social fabric, reaching its bottom and its sociological extension – the historical one that deserves from us a moment of comprehension – not idealized, as much as possible – that tries to penetrate the objective reality of this Arab social pluralism that outweighs the contradiction and conflict in its relationships and behaviors – among them and within themselves, too – over reconciliation and peaceful civil coexistence, especially in the times of crises and decisive transformations, although they coexisted peacefully in other times. If the phenomenon of pluralism and multiplicities were a natural phenomenon in human societies, then the problem that deserves study and resolution – Arabwise – is the swerve of these multiplicities towards the behavior of violence and counter-violence, i.e., to the logic of "civil conflicts" in a frequent manner, especially when the central authority weakens or collapses for one reason or another. These "structures" then pounce upon the remains of that authority, then enter into a conflict between themselves, then each structure disintegrates from the inside and is no longer safe from conflict even within its own shell. When Ibn Khaldun summarized this historical observation, his phrase filled with the dimensions of this chronic conflict in Arab life by saying: "In countries with many clans, rarely is a state in control,"[3] he was not pointing out only the matter of the absence of statehood as much as he was pointing out, at the same time, the absence of "civil peace" resulting from voluntary coexistence that cannot be substituted in Arab life except with the statehood as a central authority deterrent to the unruliness of multiplicities in conflict who cannot live together companionably except with the authority of compulsion and, rarely, they showed their ability for harmony and voluntary coalition in a format of political dealing based upon the logic of mutual partnership, giving and taking, in the context of a common civil society based on the logic of free coexistence.

This "fragmented" image in the sociological base of each Arab society, specifically, and of the Arab social makeup, in general, is the one that must be approached, diagnosed, and resolved before moving on to looking into the competitions and the current general nation-state disputes between the Arab countries and Arab regimes on the obvious political surface or the reference to the problems of ethnic, religious, and sectarian minorities – despite the importance of that – when looking at the totality of the comprehensive picture in the Arab World for this problem, naturally.

The sensitive nerve of this disputed problem, in my best estimation, is what the Arab social body suffers from unmelted or coalesced multiplicities in their most harmonious makeup if we assumed, by the logic of the prominent minorities, that is not expected, in its Arabic Sunnite base, to include more ethnic, religious, or sectarian divisions between the Arabs themselves.

But the most dangerous problems are the ones that appear when we exceed the customary pluralism of minorities – ethnic (Kurdish/Black), religious (Christian) and sectarian (Shiite/Druz…etc.) – reaching the main societal base, assumed to be harmonious due to its lack of those multiplicities, which is the Arabic Sunnite base, where we find that this base, in spite of its extension in the Arab World and in most Arab societies, includes multiplicities of another kind that is not less dangerous than the dividing effect of the apparent multiplicities/minorities.

When we attempt to approach these other multiplicities within the framework of the Arab Sunnite majorities – in particular – we limit the problem within its minimal boundaries, scientifically and in research, after excluding different or changing factors (variants) in our research approach to them, in order to reach a knowledgeable scientific understanding of them, as much as is allowed by the nature of the methodology of social sciences. If the Arabic body, in its majority, were a melted and coalesced body, it would have been able to form a decisive power or a critical mass capable of pulling its ends and gathering its own power first in an effective cohesion, then attracting the other structures and minorities towards it in a greater cohesive entity and a national and political coalition capable of forming, acting, and continuing. In the phenomenon of building national entities and the unification of its fabric: either the national fabric is a melted sum, as in Japan where there is no role mentioned by multiplicities and minorities, or there is to be an effective unifying force leading to the attraction of other multiplicities and minorities, as in the role of the Hindu majority within the Indian national fabric, the role of the English majority in the British national structure, and the role of the while European Protestants – historically – in building the American federal fabric.[4] This is a realistic historical role necessary in the beginning of national and state establishment, even if it later takes – and it should take – the format of complete equality between all (that is, individuals, majorities, and minorities).

Such a role was taken historically in the Arab collective structure by a group of northern Hijazi tribes led by the Quraish in the early period of Islam upon the crystallization of the Arabic character and the establishment of the Islamic state. Also Egypt, in coalition with Syria, undertook such a role for some time – during the period of the modern nationalist tide – where there must be an "outweighing force" in any coalition or national formation with the side of unification objectively outweighing the side of pluralism, if there is a desire for this collecting entity to be established, regardless of the nature of this "outweighing force" or the extent of accepting or rejecting of it by some of them for any ideological, emotional, or interest-based reason, or other than that.

As long as the Arab historical sociological information, whether we like it or not, goes back in its initial analysis to its known traditional clannish structures of clans, tribes, areas, and regions, or to the millet system according to another term used by a "collecting" state that ruled the Arabs, i.e., the Ottoman Empire, which had its outweighing central authority of political unity coming from outside the Arab body in the first place, which, until now, has not been replaced by any outweighing Arab force for unification within the Arab body itself, then it is a matter of rational mental curiosity (before any other consideration) that the Arab body is not able to manage, even with its Sunnite framework without considering any other multiplicities of any kind, to play its role as the attracting and outweighing force for Arab sociological and political coalition, which indicates that this body in its predominant makeup suffers, too, from different multiplicities inside itself (that are not connected to sectarian and religious multiplicities), and it has not been easy to establish its coalition until now, even within the dominant millet system itself.

We must study rationally and penetrate this phenomenon in

order for the Arab majorities (Sunnite) not to have the illusion that the solution for the civil, sectarian dispute will be achieved through its consolidation of a greater clanship, fighting the other clanships using its own clannish logic. The logic of clannish disputes will quickly penetrate inside every clan itself, whether majorities or minorities, as the Arab Islamic arena is currently filled with such divisions...

I hope to be totally clear that when I use the expression of Arab Sunnite majority here – from the logic and the term of structural-clanship pluralism in the general Arab makeup – what matters to me in this analytic context in fact is the mechanism of majority as the outweighing force for coalition – regardless of its sect or nature – and it does not concern me as a researcher that it is Sunnite, except in terms of its being a sociological and historical reality in the Arab condition...and it is a reality that I hope we comprehend well in order to surpass it – in the end – towards a more coalesced and harmonious Arab civil society, whose members deal and compete on the basis of citizenship and service to the common good, regardless of their religions, sects, or tribal or ethnic origins.

4. From Pluralism to Conflict

What I want to make specifically clear – objectively and informatively – is that the Arab 'majority' itself – a 'majority' in the criteria and the logic of the ethnic religious or sectarian 'minorities' that causes of conflict are usually ascribed to – this Arab 'majority' which is presumed harmonious in ethnicity, religion and sect, in comparison with the other pluralism, is actually inclusive in its fabric of another level of pluralism and division of no less gravity than the apparent and customary level of minority conflict regarding this 'majority' that we find does not interact internally as a harmonious whole.

The Arab western [North African] region, for example, is

primarily of the Sunnite sector, Malikite to be precise. There are no non-Muslim or non-Sunnite Arab 'minorities' of consequence to which causes for conflict can be attributed.

All regimes and governing authorities in the Arab western countries belong to this Malikite/Arab/Sunnite majority.

If this logic of the majority is the basis upon which the process of unification and unity depends, then what prevents the Arab western union from proving itself as a real "union"...?! And under what heading does the chronic Moroccan-Algerian conflict fall in light of the assumption of this 'harmonious' majority?

This observation and query itself applies to the regimes and countries of the Gulf Cooperation Council of the Arab Countries where the leaders are presumed to be in harmony regarding this perspective so that its regimes cannot be divided upon the criteria of the common minorities.

In spite of this, however, where is the "Cooperation Council" in terms of true cooperation, leave alone unification and unity? On the other hand, if some analysts interpreted the first Gulf war as a reflection of the historical conflict between Arab Sunnite and Persian Shiite, how then can we interpret the Gulf Cooperation Council? Does it not seem that this war – in at least one of its aspects – is a war of Arab Sunnite against Arab Sunnite and one which has broken all their backs at "the Eastern Gate" of the Arab World?!!

I am fully aware and appreciate that this bold and realistic presentation of issues that attempt to diagnose Arab sectarian pluralism in their 'naked' truth alarms many Arabs – intellectuals, officials, and citizens – and causes temporary embarrassment to their sensibilities for reasons that can be nationalist, emotional, religious or political. It is immediately connected in their minds to foreign plans and conspiracies to divide the Arab World, and they are not to blame for this because these plans (and studies that follow suit) do make, in point of fact, this pluralism prominent and use it in ripping apart the Arab Islamic front as much as possible. However, in response to this same consideration, the time has now come for our earnest, objective and nationalist studies to initiate the understanding and explication of the affairs of these emergent pluralism, that have retarded, and still handicap, tendencies towards unification and unity – state-nationalist, nationalist, or Islamic – this, to diagnose and resolve it for the sake of the general Arab good, which takes the lead initiative out of the hands of Western and Israeli research centers and studies that are working in the opposite direction.[5]

This is one point of view. Another point of view is where recent Arab and Islamic experiences have shown – from the Lebanese experience to that of the Somali and the Afghani as well as, even more serious, probable Arab experiences of no less gravity in terms of possible diffraction and misdirection – that these pluralism and sectarian prejudices are able to "reveal" the "naked" truth about themselves, and the transformation into real, natural and spontaneous civil conflict in our socio-political reality, however much we raise the banners of our ideal nationalist or religious slogans above it, or however much we avoid presenting it or talking about it, and however we may face it with preaching on state-nationalist, nationalist, or Islamic unity.

It has become necessary therefore to call things by their proper names in order to diagnose and resolve the matter. Maybe starting from the reality of these pluralism, understanding its mechanisms and development will be of assistance to us, and may be the most successful way of finally arriving at that aim towards which we aspire, a harmonious society that depends on its natural pluralism in a healthy, practical and realistic manner, leading them towards development, advancement, and true change, instead of trying to suppress, frustrate and deny them with no real gain.

If we consider the case of non-Arab national ethnicities in the Arab World (Kurds, Armenians, the black Africans of southern Sudan), it is possible to understand the causes of its current and possible conflicts with Arab authorities and civil powers in the countries and societies in which they exist. It is quite clear – at least in principle and theoretically – that the problem in this instance has to do primarily with nationalist, linguistic, and cultural distinctions and differences – (in addition, of course, to factors and variants in internal and external political strife according to the circumstances of the said Arab countries, their conditions of rule, the system of each government and its domestic and governmental interrelations).

It is necessary to deal with these non-Arab ethnic nationals primarily in terms of the national legal perspective on the rights of all such ethnic groups and their counterparts; that is, if the Arab World is to sustain and confirm its humanistic and tolerant nature from which it originally sprang in light of the Islamic message and its sublime values. Any attempt at denying any of these groups this basic national right on the part of Arab regimes (official or domestic) and resolving the problem by means of force and suppression, and attributing the whole issue from its roots to international conspiracies, will not lead to solving the problem; but rather will increase it gravity, as has been observed in the continuing problems of the ethnic nationals in the Arab World for decades, in addition to the falling of these narrow minded directions into the snare of enclosed national chauvinism, which is not far from Zionist chauvinism denying the rights of the Palestinian people (and until recently, its existence). A position that is neither appropriate to the fundamentals of authentic Arab principles nor to the open and positive human future to which we aspire as Arabs living in coexistence with the non-Arabs destined partners here in the Arab

World, whatever their difference of language, culture or ethnic makeup (historical-sociological).

That is regarding the primary perspective. As concerns practical political problem solving in these cases (like the reformation of establishing autonomous self-rule in its different models and other such political and administrative solutions), this is a matter to be decided upon by each Arab country according to its circumstances and situations. It suffices us here to recall that, in the seventies, when Iraq headed towards the application of autonomous self-rule in its Kurdish region – initially – it was a valid and progressive direction – essentially and in theory – in comparison to the Turkish and Iranian positions regarding the Kurdish problem itself, since both countries deny – especially Turkey – the actual existence of Kurds – considering them "mountain Turks," and they are confronted with incomparable violence, a fact which is strange coming from a country that is 'democratic' and 'liberal,' and with the Western ignoring of it which is not less strange than the Turkish behavior itself, which cannot continue forever.

However, it must also be noticed that the Iraqi directions regarding giving the Kurds self-ruling autonomy fell to drastic distortions upon application which weakened its value, essentially and theoretically, perhaps because of the implications of the two big wars into which this country dragged itself, in addition to the nature of its political regime, which is not in accord with the pluralism phenomena, whatever they may be.

On the other hand, at the other end of the Arab World, we find the reconciliation of King Al-Hassan II – in particular – to the Berber phenomenon (*Al-Amazighia*) in the Kingdom of Morocco has the attribute of an outstanding degree of flexibility and realism to lead to the establishment of practical grounds for co-existence between ethnic pluralism in the greater Arab Moroccan region, if in fact this Moroccan direction transforms itself into a tangible model for the greater western Arab region. Perhaps the contemplation, in turn, of a noted statement by one of the Berber personalities in Morocco (Al-Mahjubi Ahradan) will reflect this shared and well-balanced atmosphere: "We consider Arabic our language, just as *Al-Amazighia* is also each Moroccan's language. Since Arabic is everyone's language, so *Al-Amazighia* should be the same."[6] This is a phrase that meets in its 'logic' with that of a preliminary position declared by King Al-Hassan II regarding the linguistic/ethnic duality in Morocco.

Whatever the matter, the problem of minorities remains, insofar as it is a problem unique in itself, thoroughly dealt with in another chapter of this book, while this present chapter focuses on research into the elements of Arab socio-makeup itself. I nevertheless include it here it within this framework as an introduction and as a different example of what, in my view, works in regard to resolving the Arab pluralism question which needs a very different presentation of thought, another practical method in its approach developed from the line of thought that is the basis of this chapter.

If the consideration of the problem of ethnic minorities in the Arab World ought to start in this case with the criteria of clear nationalist distinctiveness, which is our right as Arabs as it is the right of the non-Arab groups at the same time, and without double standards (of which we complain when its application is not to our advantage), then the consideration of religious and sectarian distinctiveness between Arabs themselves (Muslims/Christians... Sunnite/Shiite) should not stop at what is "apparent" in this religious and sectarian distinctiveness in its ideological or theological or jurisprudence [*fiqh*] or "rhetorical" as related to the science of rhetoric; rather, it should be examined from its socio-historical roots, especially in its organic relationship to sociology and the history of groups that it has embraced, developed, and matured with,

5. Confusion between Absolute and Relative

If the heavenly messages have their source and origin in divine inspiration based upon religious faith and believing, the different sects that have branched from religions throughout historical human development after the divine inspiration had ceased (Sunnite/Shiite/Ibadi/Zaidi... Orthodox/Catholic/Protestant...etc.) are a result of socio-historic environments that have particular circumstances and positions in time and place, while the sects in terms of theological decree or rhetoric or jurisprudence came as the ideological expression and higher level of its reality in society and history (while we should remind ourselves here that what is agreed upon in Islam is that its jurisdiction is from God Almighty; as for "jurisprudence" – especially sectarian – this is human creative effort being vulnerable to wrong and right, and most Muslims and their scholars do not differ on this.)

In other words, if religions have come from the heavens, then sects have appeared on earth from history and society, and the Arab religious sects are obliged to embrace relative historical truth and to halt sectarian strife on the level of the "absolute"... absolute believing/atheism. Religious belief is the absolute, while sectarian opinion only carries relative significance...'the relativity' of human perspective on the "absolute" within the limitations of its possibility: "or knowledge it is only a little that is communicated to you,"[7] for even if we were to argue the "absolute," each of our human perspectives on this absolute would necessarily be a relative perspective that will not rise – religiously or scientifically – to the level of absolute in any way, shape, or form. For God Almighty is the sole absolute in the universe and what is beyond the universe as required by the oneness of God. All else, human and all other creatures and existing entities, are relative phenomena, limited and vulnerable to transformation and mortality. Thus, giving the attribute of absolute, its validity, truth, or immortal continuity to anything else is blatant blasphemy regarding God the Absolute. This is what can befall the sectarian relative position when it presents itself in absolute terms.

This is an intellectual glimpse where we think that our religious thought is called upon to approach the line of thought touched upon here in order to overcome confusion between absolute and relative, and not only for theoretical concerns or "rhetorical" concerns that have been mentioned, but because civil conflict can neither be enflamed nor deepened - ideologically then realistically – except when each side imagines that it represents the 'absolute truth' while the other represents atheism or heresy. This became evident since [the time of] the "Kharijites" labeling as infidels those Muslims who opposed them, and the resulting slaughters, bloodshed, and rulings from this...up until the new wars of elimination between sects and factions of Islam at the present time (the Pakistani state of affairs, the Afghani, the Algerian, etc.).

If this kind of perspective is necessary intellectually and theoretically –that is to say, on the level of awareness – to establish the "relative" degree of interaction between the different sects and parties, then the realistic historical perspective is no less important in looking at the formation of these sectors and groups in the reality of history and society, and the change from 'deifying' these sectors. The fact is that the call to re-write Arab Islamic history will not be effective if it does not take into consideration, basically, the shedding of light upon sociological, economic, and political roots in the formation of these sectors and groups in Islamic history by becoming independent from closed and absolute sectarian ideological theorizing. This is what provides the modern scientific researcher with sample observations, once these sample observations have researchers and thinkers intent upon their reading, interpretation, and deducing their general meanings.

According to what has been reached by the writer of this research – in another study as yet unpublished – there are researched historical testaments that show that the growth and human geographical spreading of all Islamic sects have been due to specific cultural, sociological and environmental considerations, and this is why each has been distinct from the other in the way it responds to the needs of its various environments, coastal (Shafiite), or interior (Hanbalite), or agricultural (Imami), or mountainous (Zaidi and Ibadi)...etc. This is what requires an independent study for this sociological comparison of the sectarian geography in the Arab region. Here we suffice with hinting at it in order to bring forth the idea of socio-historical origins of religious sects in general and what is required of contemporary Arabs for freeing themselves of its pure ideological/sectarian influence. Ibn Khaldun referred in his *Al-Muqaddimah*, from [as far back as] his time, that the conservative Malikitete sect suited the conservative North African countries for environmental and cultural considerations,[8] which suggests that such sectarian adoption did not occur for purely theoretical, [Islamic] jurisprudent considerations but is applied for considerations of urbanization, environment and region (given that Ibn Khaldun himself was one of the Malikitete scholars and judges, but his 'jurisprudent' or ideological position did not prevent him from being aware of the nature of the sociological foundation that generates these sectarian jurisprudent developments).

Second: Roots and Objective Factors for Arab Civil Conflicts

1. The Ecological Quadrangle

As the historian Jawad Ali noted, wildernesses[9] – any great desert and desolate gaps – fragmented the urban regions in our Arab region, which prevented it from forming a continuous dense urban society (as happened in China and India, by way of comparison), and this accordingly led to the lack of stabilization and continuity of a state and a fixed central government in a historical continuity as the continuity achieved in the Chinese state for thousands of years, whereas this spatial discontinuity in our Arab region, in addition to temporal discontinuity represented in nomadic invasions – Arab and non-Arab – to the regions of civilization and state, cut its continuity and returned it to an era before the stage of civilization and state.[10] The Arab sociologist Dr. Ali Al-Wadi described these distant urban regions as separated "islands" in the middle of a vast sea of sands. This basic geographical fact represents the first objective factor in the "fragmentation" of the Arab region on several levels: as a result of this factor, several distant ancient civilizations in the Arab east were established, as in the Assyrian, Babylonian, Phoenician, Pharaonic, Dilmunian (in historical Bahrain), and ancient Yemeni (which did not merge with the Arab the North civilization of northern Arabia until after Islam).

These ancient civilizations and states, which were established by stable populous elements did not possess the ability of continuous movement through the desert, were not able to unify among themselves or unify the region that would later become Arabic, even though some aspired to carry out such a role. It was necessary to wait for the historical role of the movement of Arab tribes, both its urban and nomadic parts – before Islam, partially, and after Islam, decisively – to unify the region spiritually, culturally, linguistically – and politically for some time, because of the Islamic mission – morally, and through what these tribes, with their urban leaderships, owned materialistically, and their nomadic/cultural strength, at the same time, and its taming of the camel as a very capable, logistical, and decisive means of commercial, military, human (populous) and cultural (values) movement throughout the region deserts and between its civilizations and its inhabited region. This was not available for any civilization, group or state in the ancient Near East. This is an historical, intensive, and long-term "movement" and continued for centuries after Islam, which resulted in the Arabization of what we call "the Arab World" and the spread of Islam beyond that, although the spread of Islam differed from Arabization by the Arabs themselves carried out in a direct way, as Islam spread beyond the Arabized regions by a relatively different mechanism, by moving first from the Arabs to a non-Arab group that embraced it, who then began to spread it to others, where the effect of this intensive Arab movement did not pass on, for objective reasons, and that is what the Turkish and African groups carried out at the ends of the Islamic world, east and west (Asia and Europe) and south (Africa).[11]

What is worthy of observation objectively, in this respect, is that, originally, Arabization most likely included non-Arab plains (outside the Arabian Peninsula) where the Arabian camel could reach, and that is what explains Ibn Khaldun's note: "the Arabs only conquer the plains,"[12] where they reached as far as open Mauritania, but they stopped near the heights of Kurdistan and Anatolia. These high hills (Anatolia, Persia, Central Asia) did not Arabize, even though Islam moved into them either by Arab elements stationed there not in large numbers – as in Persia which embraced Islam and did not Arabize – or by non-Arab groups, especially the Turks, who were helped in their tribal movement by the Bukhari camel with two humps, capable of climbing heights and hills, to spread into the Anatolian heights and then consequently conquer Constantinople, which was an Arab dream that was not fulfilled and remained waiting for centuries for the Turkish ability to penetrate the high hills where the Arab could not, for logistical reasons, most important of which was the inability of the Arabian camel to climb the hills and push, with large numbers, by land to the capital of Byzantium, and were content with the navel attempts that did not succeed.[13] And this is what returns us to the contemplation of Ibn Khaldun's wise phrase again, and that is that the Arabs only conquered the plains.

However, this Arab-Arabizing expansion over the expanse of what came to be known as the larger Arab World was itself subjected to the natural physical, sociological, and societal fragmentation mechanisms that distinguished this region.

When the Arabs transformed into settled societies in the urban regions and lost the ability of free intensive movement, the frequent crossing of the wildernesses, they began, with the passage of time, to be affected by the effects of ancient civilizations and their distant societies. Each group of them, whether their settlement was in Iraq, Syria, or Egypt, was affected by the characteristics of the region into which they settled. This regional phenomenon was not confined to the areas of ancient civilizations in the Near East outside the Arabian Peninsula, but we find that the Arabian Peninsula itself, due to the vast desert vacuums in its heart from Al-Dahna to Rub Al-Khali, divided long ago into distinguished regions, which still represents different units until today, politically or societally, as in the regions of Yemen, Amman, Najd, Hijaz and Bahrain, as is the situation outside the peninsula between Iraq, the Levant, Egypt, and North Africa, which is divided in turn into its known regions and countries.

Add to this natural geographical factor the disposition of tribal division within the tribal unity or the tribal structure itself, with the appearance of subdivisions, branches, and groups that which branched out throughout the generations between brothers and cousins,[14] etc. with the effects of competition, conflict of interests, and the unsustainability of a society of a stable state uniting and fusing, as happened in the regions of ancient civilizations in Asia (China and India). These civil branches will quickly be divided and shared by the distant Arab regions and areas, and the necessities of the search for water resources and food force them to spread throughout the deserts, oases, and cities, becoming, in the long run, self-established units and societal structures, according to their regional and state adaptation, on one hand, and their ecological adaptation, on the other hand, to be in one of the four environments representing the Arab ecological square with its different sociological and ideological (sectarian) makeup. These environments are: (a) the urban area/city, (b) the open countryside, (c) the mountainous countryside, and (d) the desert. It can be noted that these four environments, as they differ in general in style of production and living, they also differ in a parallel way in their sectarian ideological nature, at the same time (especially in the Arab East):

(a) The city: commercial – Sunnite (and mostly Shafiite along the coasts)
(b) The open countryside: agricultural – Shiite or influenced by Sufi methods if it is Sunnite (to distinguish itself ideologically from the juristic Sunnite in the city!), i.e., that the coastal countryside distinguishes itself either as Shiite or Sufi, and both differentiations are rejected by the Sunnite juristic inclination in the city.
(c) The mountainous countryside: It includes mostly farming tribes, but they are fighters and consequently embrace a rejecting, fighting sect (the Ibadi in the mountains of Oman and North Africa, the Zaidi in the mountains of Yemen, the Druze and the Alawi in the mountains of Lebanon and Syria, etc.).
(d) The desert: It maintains its traditional, roaming, pastoral style and embraces mostly the Hanbalite as it delves into the deserts, by what is suitable with its lofty purifying values compared to the "luxury" of the righteous city, and it is noticed, on the other hand, that the intensity of sectarian tension between the Hanbalite and Shiite – juristically and rhetorically – in particular, is paralleled in the infrastructures of both groups by the chronic conflict between the desert and the countryside, i.e., between the nomadic shepherd (the

Hanbalite) who invades the villages, and the rural farmer (the Ja'farite) who plants and lives in it, where we find that the sectarian difference is only a reflection mostly of sociological, lifestyle, and economic differences that are more ancient in their roots.[15]

In addition to these factors, the vast geographical distribution of the Arab World across the continents has made some Arab regions more interactive with neighboring foreign powers and more influenced by them, where Iraq is still more interactive and reactive to Iran and Turkey than Egypt, Algeria, or Yemen. When this circle widens internationally, we find that the superpowers, throughout history and up until now, can penetrate the heart of the Arab region and penetrate it from a regional Arab or other site (the Baghdad Pact against Egypt, the Gulf alliance in confrontation with Iraq, etc.). It is a phenomenon that, if it takes in our modern age the form of domination, it took the form in the past of complete human invasion (the Tatars and the Mongols).

2. Conflicts in Our History

Of these classifications of geographical, historical, and sociological differentiations and affiliations that we presented, there are basically three:

(a) the regional/nation-state differentiation and affiliation.
(b) the tribal and clannish differentiation and affiliation (within the single tribe and within the single society).
(c) the ecological/local sectarian differentiation and affiliation (the city, the countryside, etc.)

From among these classifications, and in an overlapping intersection between them, Arab Islamic history witnessed (we have to admit!) a long series of "civil conflicts" – and that was before colonial forces or foreign intelligences ignited or fabricated them, as the dominant Arab rhetoric usually goes – (even if it was right in some cases, in the modern age).

Although one meticulous Arab researcher, Doctor Mahmud Abdul Fadil, started from a different analysis, he arrived, from his position, at what is similar to these three differentiations in the Arab societal fabric as a whole, adding to them the affiliation of the profession or craft that overlaps, in our opinion, the ecological/local differentiation.[16]

Civil conflicts from the perspective of the tribal differentiation between the branches and the Quraishi families over authority were the basis of *al-futna al-kubra* (the great turmoil) and the civil wars that followed in the early period of Islam, to a degree that it was feared that the Quraish itself might perish (as a famous poem of the Quraishi poet Abdullah Bin Qais expresses).

In addition, the civil conflict within the house of Umayyad was one of the most important reasons for the fall of the Umayyad state, which was shorter in age – compared to the ages of other states – in spite of what it achieved in important organizational achievements and strategic conquests. The civil conflict between Al Amin and Al Ma'mun led to the domination of the Turks, in the era of Al Mu'tasim, over the destinies of the Abbasid state and the end of its true authority, and that was ninety years after its establishment (between 132 and 220 H), which does not exceed the short era of the Umayyad state.

This tribal civil conflict – the tribal/clannish within Quraish and between Quraish and other competing tribes, at the same time – strengthened, on the other hand, the differentiations and sectarian conflicts, where Umayyad/Hashemite conflict led to the widest conflict in Islamic history between Sunnites and Shiites. In addition, the rebellion of the tribes east of the peninsula against Quraishi authority was the basis of the materialization of the Kharijites sect against both Sunnites and Shiites (who were behind the Quraishi leadership in conflict). Thus we find that each religious sect of the Islamic sects has its tribal and clannish roots and tribal origins

(Sunnite/Umayyad…Shiite/Hashemite…Kharijites/tribes outside the Quraish, etc).

While the factors of differentiation and regional competition (political/interests) between the Arabs of Iraq, the Levant, Yemen, and Egypt overlapped with the tribal and sectarian conflicts, the tribes divided themselves between the Alawi Iraqi camp and the Umayyad Levantine camp in the wars of *al-jamal* (the camels) and *Saffain*, then throughout the Umayyad and Abbasid eras, and some Arabs of Egypt played a big role in the assassination of the Caliph Uthman, and there was a clear inclination of the Yemenis towards the camp of Imam Ali, etc.[17]

3. The Conflicts Reproduce Themselves

Some are fed up with these sociological historical referrals. But as long as this history is still alive and standing, it is unwise to discard them. However, regardless, in order for you to be a good political reader, then you must be a good historical reader, and this saying cannot be truer anywhere in the world than it is in the Arab region. Such a return to the roots of the Arab civil conflicts and their history does not represent, in our opinion, an academic research interest separate from the contemporary Arab reality, because these conflicts, as proven by the experiences of Arab conflicts in the last decades, is still "reproducing" itself in different forms and sometimes in repeated identical forms, whether in the conflict of nation-state on the level of nationalism (the conflict of Mohammed Ali's Egypt with the first Saudi state – the conflict of the Hashemite Iraq with Egypt, Syria, and Saudi Arabia – the conflict of Nassarist Egypt against Ba'athist, Hashemite Iraq and Saudi Arabia – and finally, the Ba'athist conflict of Iraq against the Ba'athist Syria, etc.), or in the conflict with what is lower than the nation-state and lower than the national, which became today a feature of the current stage between tribes, clans, and sects, whether at the recession of the central authority or its disintegration, (Iraq and Somalia), or even when it gets the opportunity of democratic pluralism under the established state (Yemen, Mauritania, Kuwait, and Lebanon), so that the danger to democratic orientations in the Arab World comes from the civil multiplicities, uncontrolled and craning their necks towards conflict, as much as coming from the authoritative regimes and existing governments. Moreover, these groups started giving the justification and argument for these regimes to block the way for Arab democratic growth.

The time has come to focus the light completely – and from a faithful and nationalistically committed Arab opinion – on these multiplicities and the roots of conflict in its "naked" reality, and not with fear or embarrassment of diagnosing it frankly, and treating it realistically, because it becomes "unembarrassed" by expressing its existence, inclinations, and conflicts to a degree that concealing it becomes – under any slogan or consideration – escaping from confronting the Arab reality and an intellectual and practical inability to deal with its facts.

These powers being "civil" and sometimes in opposition to authority (before they get to it) does not mean endearment towards them and patting them on their shoulders, just for being from the people and the masses.

It is necessary to go beyond the dominant rhetoric built upon the defamation mentality of authorities and "praising" the oppositions, regardless to their degree of backwardness and darkness, and to exchange that for a scientific and critical rhetoric harmonious with itself, calling things by their real names, throughout the societal/political map, whether at the top the political pyramid or at its base, that is, if we do not want to be surprised from now on by "popular" regimes taking the people back to the prisons of the previous rulers, with even more severe tyranny, backwardness, and a more tightly closed ideology (and there are many Arab examples among the Arab "oppositions" that are similar to the Afghan Taliban movement).

It is necessary also to have a scientific effort and diligent research to trace the conflict of the sects and clanship back to its true sociological, historical, and humanistic roots, and to remove the mist of absolute sacredness from the vision of those who were born with it – without their own choosing – as they were fed on it in their closed clanship structures. It became an identity and a belonging to them in a time of the collapse of identities and greater cultural belonging, and the conflict and sectarian dialectic became as a clash between the abstract with the abstract, and the truth with the false.

If the advanced natural and humanistic solution is the participation of these structures within the framework of a common civil – national – society, it melts into its unified fabric gradually and progressively, then the Arab thought interested in the materialization of the concepts of civil society is required to have very clear methodological and theoretical criteria that distinguishes between the levels of the desired real civil society and its revelations in the way it accommodates these civil structures in order to open them, bring them closer, and merge them, and between the opposing and conflicting revelations that these civil structures re-secrete in their reversion from the civil society and the entity of the national state to return to pre-modern society by the deliberate and programmed revival of their old clanships. The correct civil society, if exercising its existence and its independence by functional and legal differentiation from official state institutions, it is necessary that it should distinguish itself, by the same degree, from the "civil" clannish multiplicities that can destroy the heart of its fabric.[18] From current Arab experience, the civil-national society in Bahrain, which leans on a common urban sociological base between the different groups representing the main weight in the general societal makeup, proved its ability to absorb the opposing traditional, clannish inclinations and to contain them, whether they were sectarian or tribal, in one national crucible with urban-civil weight.

If civil societies in the experiences of some other nations have supported building a modern civil society, due to their advanced makeup, then that does not mean that any civil structure, regardless of its historical nature, is a positive cornerstone in building the modern civil society. It is necessary to have a methodological and rational criterion specifying where the civil meets the urban in the modern Arab structure, and where it contradicts and invalidates it. No Arab society does not have traditional civil structures wherein its clannish inclinations represent a basic contradiction to the principles of the modern national and civil society and its fundamentals, whether alleging the logic of the group or the logic of the tribe.

The legitimate opposition in Arab thought to the existing "authoritative" national state and its repressive regimes should not put it automatically with backward civil clanships just because it opposes the authority. These clanships will only establish a regime that is more severe in its brutality, that is, only if it is capable of preserving the current state unity and remaining in a state "coalition" capable of continuing with the other opposing clanships, and that is unlikely, in not impossible, in light of similar experiences in Arab Islamic region.

On the other hand, any Arab authority that controls the state and dominates civil society, and does not behave as a national authority to all without exception, regardless of its ancient historical roots and theirs, works actually to transform itself into another clanship among the existing clanship structure – with no arbitrator between them – then it loses consequently its civil and national unifying role, and incites the other clanships, implicitly, to take its place in an open conflict between clanships, ruling or ruled, i.e., it reduces itself from leading the country and the state to a "small group" fighting with other clanships and inciting them to attack it.

That is what actually threatens a considerable number of the Arab regimes unless they rise up to the level leading the common national project and its modern state and surpasses the historical clanship roots of its own establishment.

So, the responsibility is doubled and common between all Arab political powers – official and civil – to surpass their old historical clanship roots (that control the behavior of both the authorities and the oppositions in the Arab makeup), in order to achieve a common escape of the Arab state and the civil society from the swirl of civil conflicts, whether on the internal national level or the general nationalist level.

The resolving, surpassing, and solving of civil Arab conflicts starts with the rational and critical analysis of the deep-rooted and arising clanship structures, whether these structures are ruled or ruling, official or popular, in authority or in opposition.

We must realize that Arab civil conflicts on the level of nation-state start, most of the time, from civil conflict within the single Arab nation-state, where, to "escape" from it, a conflict with neighboring states is fabricated, or the spot of the unrest moves by means of infection. Countries that do not enjoy internal civil peace cannot practice nationalist peace with their "brothers" or regional peace with their neighbors. It is impossible to imagine a "country" in conflict with itself capable of coexisting peacefully with others.

Therefore, any attempt to achieve nationalist closeness (or Arab solidarity) that does not start with the natural logic that is no longer possible to ignore or jump over, for any ideological reasons, and that is the clear and explicit national logic, will not achieve what it aims at.

It seems that nationalist thought (the Arab East, in particular) is the most disabling and incapable in this regard, where it emerged in the confrontation of the divisional Sykes-Picot plan in the Fertile Crescent. It was controlled by the obsession of this plan, and was not able, in the midst of this unequal confrontation, to see the objective factors and phenomena of the nationalisms and the Arab countries except from the point of view of that conspiracy, which is no longer possible to reduce "all" the Arab fragmentation phenomena from it.

From here, the national phenomenon in modern Arab awareness appeared, as though it were a nationalist "sin," the "original nationalist sin," which the Arab could not come close to or accommodate, as if he were caught red-handed in some kind of crime, although the living daily national reality for each Arab – regardless of his country and the conditions of his raising – is his only base and outlet for any other undertaking, whether nationalist, regional, or international, and regardless of his personal feeling towards the lawful or the legitimacy of that national reality from a utopian nationalist or religious point of view.

This conceptual line of thought in the Arab East nationalist thought towards the national dimension and its reality becomes apparent when we compare its position to the position of unificationist Arab West thought which aspires to unite the Greater Arab West, without taking the position of condemnation or incrimination – regardless of the conditions of its raising – of the national reality for the Arab West countries, considering the national structure as a cornerstone towards nationalist construction.[19]

4. National Foundations

Arabs today – realistically and objectively – are the sum of their existing specified countries, with their circumstances, features, power, weakness, positives and negatives...neither more nor less, as they have no significance outside these countries or within them...at least, in international calculations, if it is not even in wishful thinking...and if they do not begin with this nationalist sum, number by number, they will not achieve a position for them in this world that only deals with facts and realities, rather than feelings and wishes.[20]

So the hour has come for confronting nationalist truth, for its liberation and its construction, then for building upon it...for the common Arab (nationalist) tomorrow. There is no other way...neither through Kabul (for 'Islamic *jihad*') nor through Kuwait (for 'nationalist unification')!!

We presume that the current Arab nation-state, and ever since its models appeared in the modern age, whether its development was natural, historical, or was a political reality created by international circumstances and external factors...we presume that this nation-state is the first true experience for Arabs in statehood, unification, and in practicing organized, political society based upon unified citizenship with no discrimination or differentiation, even if it is [only] as far as the declared constitutional principles go, awaiting the completion of its realization upon practice.[21]

It is the first Arab experience of statehood in centuries, meaning that it has, in each Arab state, taken the place of a non-state or the superficial subordination to Imperial Ottoman power, as it covered, in some cases, vast tracts of Arab land that had previously been wasteland, open to moving tribes and their animal stocks. These Arab expanses and the human presence in them are practicing, for the first time in their entire history, the experience of statehood, even in its traditional historical meaning to control security, and the subordination of pluralism to the central authority, after it had witnessed "the war of all against all."[22] The Arab should not be in haste for his political development or political advancement without being in agreement with his own historical reality. He should allow his existing circumstances to become complete and mature without being harsh on himself with despair and doubting himself or others – the important thing is to know which link in the chain of development to hold onto in order to resume the quest with a clear method and realistic vision.

It may seem wrong to say that the Arab nation-state is also the first experience of "unity" for Arabs and that it is the entity considered by nationalist East Arab thought to be the core calamity of fragmentation!

In our modest opinion, however, this Arab nation-state is in fact the first Arab experience of true societal unity, meaning that every nation-state in the Arab World today includes, within its frame and institutional, constitutional, economic, administrative and educational crucible, a group of traditional structures, in its various kinds, working gradually towards comprehending it and melting it into the one national entity. This is a historical mission that requires time, patience, and good management. This is a progressive, qualitative, and very important step towards harmony of the Arab societal fabric in each Arab state, and upon which foundation civilized society is built and the modern nation advances. If the modern nation-state is not able and is not enabled – as authority, citizens, or opposition – to achieve this historical mission, we will then return to our small traditional structures, these *asa'ib* that no state can have control without. We will not only delay the dream of a nation-state but will lose the bet on the nation-state...which, through its completion, maturity, and legitimate reconciliation with it, will provide the healthy, recovered blocks to establish the grand nationalist entity when the time comes. If the age has outgrown the Bismarckian style employing steel and fire to achieve nationalist unity, as we have remarked, for this age presents us with a more tempting and attractive choice, then it is the choice of European nation-state entities which were completed and matured and started to work voluntarily and not by force at building their European unity: France side-by-side with Portugal, Germany side-by-side with Luxembourg, without forcing the branch to join the source or forcing this or that sect or minority to abandon its religion, sect, or language.

The "national" in Arab life, though remaining in strong connection with the reality of the Arab citizen in each state, and in spite of his being the natural, suitable, practical "historical link" to drive forward the wheel of Arab progress and to build a modern society that is able to develop in the long run into an expanded structure, remained either drawn forcefully towards what is above it…to the "nationalist" or the materialistic "ethnic," then the religious, with its being unrecognized, charged, and considered sinful, or threatened by what is below it…with its elements of historical clanship which was supposed to have been, historically, contained and, to an extent, brought together by the launching of the national project, allowing it the chance for living and co-existence on the basis of a civil society and a modern state that is established upon basis of comprehensive citizenship and the equality of rights and duties for all, under the law.

The recent expansion of Arab awareness – intellectually, politically, sociologically, and in terms of movements – of the necessity for the rebirth of the national project, its maintenance, and the return to resuming its quest as the suitable link within the chain of Arab development, in order to halt Arab shattering and fragmentation into ethnicities, factions and tribes, is evidence that the bitter experiences have taught Arabs the worthiness of their national project in each state in order to return to establishing it, then to build upon it as a common organization.[23]

It is time for the Arab to stand upon the natural, practical, and realistic ground of his existence in this world, the surface of the national ground which is capable, by itself, of practical development and construction before all else, in comparison with various other ideological and futuristic alternatives and possibilities. It suffices to observe how any nationalist revival of Arab solidarity at a given moment is not achieved without the concordance of the Arab national units at that moment.

If nation-state conflict has worried Arab nationalists and unificationists a lot, they need to direct their attention to the deeper roots of national civil conflict, since it is impossible to imagine nationalist unity being achieved between states which have not achieved national unity, nor will its national project mature in a natural way without having burned those stages which burn, ultimately, only those who attempt to annihilate them!

Therefore, any solution to the Arab civil conflicts that does not begin with the national solution that is the initiation of the achievement of the form of concordance and common coexistence in the project of the one country between the multiple traditional clan structures – with their differences – of which no Arab society is spared, by one way or another, from clans and tribes to religious and sectarian pluralism, to non-Arab ethnicities – we say that any solution that does not begin with this historical-futurist step simultaneously (the step of the national project and a new national constitution) will not be destined, in our opinion, for the desired success, and will remain suspended with its long-term hopes in the utopian world – whether nationalist or religious – while "the clans" are fighting on the ground of Arab reality, confirming the continuation of communal schizophrenic division of the Arabs between the aspired for unifying tendencies, ideally and emotionally, and the fragmentary conflicts that are carried out in reality, exposing every day the ability of nationalist, reforming, unifying rhetoric in its approach and in dealing with that reality.

Success in the achievement of the national project and the new national constitution in each Arab (and Islamic) country will be the testing ground for all nationalist, Islamic, and liberal/sectarian projects that aim towards unification or unity.

The nationalist, Islamic, and liberal "factions" that are incapable of dialogue and concordance at the limited national level, and are consumed by their own internal conflict...how can they convince anyone – after this – that they are serious in their directions and unification and unity projects on the vast levels of an Arab Islamic nation?...{*"Say, produce your proof if ye are truthful."*}.[24]

There is no proof here, before any proof, except in the extent of the capability of these projects to achieve the national project that is tangible and capable of curbing civil conflict as a true beginning of national construction that can be followed, in a consequent stage, by nationalist and religious construction for those who desire and are capable and able.

If this research confirms the necessity for Arab reaching towards a healthy and effective form to establish a positive balance between the duality of unity/pluralism among them in aspects of Arab life generally, and political life in particular, then what is required practically is to allow enough time and effort to build the national society and its state in each Arab country, allowing for its specificity and distinctiveness, to become a free block in any common construction of the Arab group that is acceptable by the Arabs among themselves on the basis of a free pact, in a time that fears, respects, or accepts only large groups that have strategic, economic, and cultural weight, and at the same time, allows only larger groups whose pluralism and singular units are growing, suffering, free, and equal.

If the Arabs are able to achieve this dialectical "reconciliation" between the "national" and the "nationalist," then this could be a true beginning of their emergence from the whirlpool of civil conflicts that has, until now, consumed much of their energy.

Endnotes

[1] The tragedy of Arab history can be summarized as: "Neither can the smaller units melt politically in the unified conceptual space to form within its framework one stable political entity, nor can it separate or disconnect from it completely so it can stand on its own in entities that have no relationship with it. It is the separation in unity and unity in separation…within a sequence that does not end." See: Mohammed Jaber Al-Ansari, *Political Arab Makeup and the Signification of the Nation-State: An Introduction to a Revised Understand of Arab Reality.* 2nd ed. Beirut: Center of Arab Unity Studies, 1995, p. 178. The challenge that faces the Arabs today is: How are they going to break this empty circle and get out of this swirl?

[2] Mahmud Abdul Fadhil, *The Sociological Formations and Class Makeups in the Arab World: Analytical Study of the Most Important Developments and Directions in the Period between 1945-1985.* Beirut: Center for Arab Unity Studies, 1988, p. 45, footnote 16.

[3] Abu Zaid Abdulrahman bin Mohammed bin Khaldun, *Al Muqaddimah.* Beirut: Al-Hillal Press and Library (Dar wa Maktabat al-Hillal) 1983, p. 11.

[4] It is a role that started to be reconsidered with the increase of Hispanic and Black from African roots multiplicities…until the new balance can be specified between these multiplicities in the future American equation where the white becomes a "minority" in the middle of the new century.

[5] See this author's reference to the phenomenon of increased Western and Israeli focus on the mosaic pluralism issue in the Arab World, in: Al-Ansari, *Political Arab Makeup and the Signification of the Nation-State: An Introduction to a Revised Understand of Arab Reality*, p. 99.

[6] *Al-Arabi*, vol. 455 (October 1996), p. 77.

[7] *The Holy Quran*, "Surat Al-Isra," verse 85.

[8] Ibn Khaldun, *Al-Muqaddimah*.

[9] Jawad Ali, *Al-Masfil fi Tarikh al-Arab qabl al-Islam* (the turning point in Arab history before Islam). Vol. 7. Beirut: Dar al-Hadatha, 1983, pp. 6-8.

[10] Al-Ansari, *Political Arab Makeup and the Signification of the Nation-State: An Introduction to a Revised Understand of Arab Reality*, pp. 37-40. Also see Mohammed Jaber Al-Ansari: *Political Crisis for the Arabs and the Position of Islam: Ingredients of the Chronic Condition*. Beirut: Arabic Institute for Studies and Publishing, 1995, pp. 21-42.

[11] Mohammed Jaber Al-Ansari, "Nationalism and the Nation-State, from the Position of Opposition to Complementation." A lecture presented within the Cultural Conference for Al-Asad Library, Damascus, 23rd September, 1996.

[12] Ibn Khaldun, *Al-Muqaddimah*.

[13] Jawad Ali, *Al-Masfil fi Tarikh al-Arab qabl al-Islam* (the turning point in Arab history before Islam), p. 6-8.

[14] Al-Ansari, *Political Crisis for the Arabs and the Position of Islam: Ingredients of the Chronic Condition*, pp. 75-87.

[15] For more expanded analyses for the phenomenon of the "Arab ecological quadrangle," see: Al-Ansari, *Political Arab Makeup and the Signification of the Nation-State: An Introduction to a Revised Understand of Arab Reality*.

[16] Abdul Fathil. *The Sociological Formations and Class Makeups in the Arab World: Analytical Study of the Most Important Developments and Directions in the Period between 1945-1985*, p. 21. It is an important book in its subject based on primary references in his research, in addition to analysis and critique that it adds to it.

[17] On the ancient tribal factors, see: Fatma Jumah, *Partisan Directions in Islam: From the Era of the Prophet to the Era of Beni Umayyid*. Beirut: Dar al-Fikir al-Arabi, 1993, pp. 37-44.

Returning to the modern tribal concept, see: Mohammed Subuh, *The Concept of the Tribe in Third World Theory*. West Tripoli: International Center for the Green Book Studies.

[18] The book published by the Center for Arab Unity Studies on civil society represents one of the comprehensive Arabic references in its subject. It can be returned to for clarifying many of the concepts of urban and civil societies. See: *Urban Society in the Arab World and its Role in Achieving Democracy: Research Papers and Discussions of the Thought Conference,* organized by the Center for Arab Unity Studies, Beirut, 1992.

[19] See in this regard: Mohammed Abdul Baki Al-Hirmasi, "Society and the State in the Arab West," in: *The Project of Speculation of the Future of the Arab World, The Theme of Society and the State.* Beirut: Center for Arab Unity Studies, 1987.

[20] It is worth remarking that 'national reality' has lately imposed its presence in certain modes of Arab thought that had seemed, until recently, more adamant about the presentation of nationalism and quite contrary to the direction of nation-states. While Mohammed Abd Al-Jabri confirmed a few years back that "the realization of unity is a process that must pass through the realization process of negating the Arab nation-state." (Mohammed Abd Al-Jabri, *Questions of Contemporary Arab Thought*. Beirut: Center for Arab Unity Studies, 1989). Then within a short space of time we find he arrives at the opposite, ascertaining that "the nation-state...can no longer be jumped over, not even on the level of dreams. Thus all thought on Arab unity...not emerging from the reality of the current Arab nation-state is a thought that pertains to a past and terminated stage." (Mohammed Abd Al-Jabri, *A Point of View: Towards a Reconstruction of Contemporary Arab Thought*. Beirut: Center for Arab Unity Studies, 1992, p. 206.) See also in this regard, on the relationship between the national and the nationalist from the viewpoint of revised thought, the writings of Syrian writer Imad Fawzi Shuaibi and Saudi writer Turki Al-Hamad.

[21] Al-Ansari, *Political Arab Makeup and the Signification of the*

Nation-State: An Introduction to a Revised Understand of Arab Reality, p.98-103.

[22]Turki Al-Hamad, "Unifying the Arab Peninsula: The Role of Ideology and Organization in the Destruction of the Socio-economic Structure that Retards Unity." In: *Arab Future*, Year 9, 93rd ed. November 1986, p. 31.

[23]Of this tendency to renew the relationship between "national' and 'nationalist', see for example: Imad Fawzi Shuaibi, "Towards Reinterpreting the Concept of Nation and Citizen", *Al-Hiyat*, 5/11/1992, p. 18.

[24] *The Holy Quran*, "Surah Al-Baqara," 111.

Arab Boundaries: To Get over It…Draw It First! Intellectual Assessment

In: *Alam al-Fikr: Boundary Conflicts and Civil Wars*, vol. 32, no. 4, April 2004. Kuwait: National Council for Culture, Arts, and Literature.

Boundaries beyond Boundaries

Since we will diagnose the phenomenon of "boundaries" in Arab life, it ought to be useful to commence by briefly looking at its abstract dimensions (mental and psychological) and its physical dimensions, as well as the issue of "Arab boundaries, between 'national' nations and pan-Arab unity," where dealing with this aging issue cannot be complete without comprehensively tackling the mentality of a "boundary" and its psychology and social and historic heritage. If the Arabs do not comprehend the dimensions of the comprehensive "boundary complex" that surrounds them, they will not be capable, in my opinion, of scientifically and realistically dealing with the prevailing political boundary issue amongst them.

A. Boundaries with the Age and Reality

The meticulous and comprehensive researcher into the dimensions of this boundary issue cannot ignore the following dimension, as to the relationship of the Arabs with their age, intellectual heritage, and their true history:

Arab Boundaries: To Get over It...Draw It First!

1. In our age, the Arabs suffer a mental and psychological "boundary" issue which separates them from the age and the world. For they have not yet adapted to the basic givens of the modern age from the conceptual aspects: scientific reasoning, rationality, patriotism, civil society, modern state, constitutional, parliamentary, and democratic life. They also live in an inherited fear of the materialism of this age, its atheism and openness, and ignore or are ignorant of its judicial decency, political transparency, and scientific and social frankness. This creates a "boundary" between them and the spirit of the age along with the powerful and progressive potential it possesses. The fallacy lies in the fact that, with their falling into this mental boundary "mix," they failed to draw the limit – which is eminent – between the educated, civilized, progressive West, and the colonial, imperial, greedy, conspiratorial West. This is a positive "boundary" the Arab mind should draw in its thought and practice if it wants to break through this age, after it crosses the boundary between itself and its age and world in general.

2. In continuation to the above, and not less dangerous, the general Arab mentality, due to the abundance of scientists and researchers (most of whom had to immigrate), this general mentality is surrounded by a boundary which separates it from the scientific reasoning that has its roots in Islamic culture itself, and which was the starting point of Western modernity. This boundary should be penetrated and bridges be built over it so that the Arab mentality interacts with modern scientific thought and takes its fundamentals into consideration while formulating its modern ideologies, regardless of whether they are national, Islamic, or ethnic, because basing such ideologies on emotional or abstract fundamentals, or even fairy-tales, is one of the reasons for the current crisis in the life of modern Arabs. Suspicion is not a substitute for truth, as the holy Quran teaches. The

prevalent illusions in the dominant Arab mentality are characterized by this suspicion, which should be overcome by establishing a sound, objective, methodological basis, not prone to error, self-deception, or trying to deceive others. Since the release of the book *Milestones of the Road* in 1965 for Sayyid Qutb, contemporary Islamic discourse has been witnessing a violent reaction against Islamic moderation as preached in the Mu'tazilah sect and by the unitarian Islamic philosophers. It might not be an exaggeration to describe this book as the "manifesto" of the first radical movement, without ignoring the similar contribution of his peer Dr. Mohammed Mohammed Hussain in his publications since the fifties.

3. The dangerous delay in time to comprehend this scientific theory, whose implications have changed human life in civil and military technology, reflected on the Arabs themselves and drew another "boundary" in the contemporary Arab mentality towards revising – scientifically and objectively – the flow of events in the history of Arabs and Islam, and examining it as it happened in reality rather than in the romantic and utopian illusion which prevails in the circulated Arab historical narratives. In addition, the scientific technique in sociologically analyzing the reality of their societies and its implications on the political performance of the state and opposition and the "masses," which forms the cornerstone in the modern science of sociology (which has its roots in the works of Ibn Khaldun!), represents one of the lacking or immature realities in contemporary Arab culture, despite the interest of reputed Arab thinkers, such as Shaikh Mohammed 'Abduh, Taha Hussain, and Dr. Ali Al-Wardi, in the works of Ibn Khaldun. Interest has been directed, since the start of the modern Arab renaissance, to reviving the resurrection of literature and poetry – which is normal at the start of a renaissance – and

historical romanticism and Andalusian literature. After that, partisan political ideologies and its slogans prevailed as the mainstream, in the remarkable absence of socio-historic thought. This thought, in my opinion, should represent the major requirement for the new Arab cultural revolution, which the current Arab situation and its proceedings make highly inevitable [1].

Thus the time has come to remove the "boundaries" between the Arabs and their age and their world, and between the scientific thought of this age and their Islamic civilization, with all that it entails of scientifically reevaluating their history and social reality, including their political systems which lack a great deal of rationalism given the fact that political thought is the weakest contribution of the Islamic civilization to global thought compared to what it has offered in other fields of knowledge.

B. Geographic and Historic Boundaries (beyond Sykes-Picot)

Above was a condensed glimpse at what I consider the "boundary complex" between contemporary Arabs and their age and the world.

As to the reality of the concrete boundaries in the Arab structure, past and present, it is essential to understand it in their historical and geographic context, to overcome their effects in an efficient and objective manner, instead of condemning them using national slogans and clichés without getting rid of the problem in reality[2]:

1. It is historically observed that the unified circle of Arab Islamic civilization never coincided, in historical continuity, with a single congruent political circle, as in the case with China, for example, where the national political circle coincided with Chinese civilization in most of the Chinese historical ages. There is diversity in

the Arab political circles which are contained within the wider civilization circle. This is an historical phenomenon, and not the result of the Sykes-Picot Agreement in the Arab East, which added to the historical fragmentation a new colonial division. It is worth noting and comparing, as many Arab researchers decided, that colonialism divided in some areas of the Arab World, and "united" in other areas, according to its conditions and interests. For modern colonial thought, like the civilization it leads, is characterized by pragmatic thought and not restricted to a single static way of thinking, or as Dr. Ghassan Salamé puts it: "...the colonizer himself has accepted union in many cases where partition was an option...because the rule of "divide and conquer" is far from being absolute...and we see in various places in the Arab World, more like in most of the Arab World, that the established states were a modern extension of (historically) distinctive political structures to a certain extent. This is the case of Oman and Yemen, Egypt and Lebanon, and Morocco, of course." [3]

2. The objective reason for this historical diversity, in my opinion, lies in the uniqueness of Arab geography, for the wide and barren desert spaces naturally separated the centers of civilization and rendered them multiple "political circles" in the general civilization circle, and the caravan routes, with their elements of interaction, during the Islamic era diminished the effect of these "boundaries" and diversities. However, the currently drawn boundaries between the "national" entities and their tariffs, economic, security, and political limitations, have ascertained those boundaries and secured them. We consider the desert areas, along with what they conceived in terms of dispersed clans and quarreling

tribes, as the major "division factor" in contemporary Arab life. The Arabs must deal with this reality in the light of international interests, so as to diminish its effects.

While the nationalist doctrine spoke romantically about Arab unity, a phenomenon deep rooted and manifested in many facets of Arab life that cannot be denied, the encyclopedic Iraqi historian Dr. Jawad Ali warned, in a detailed history of pre-Islamic Arabs, of a parallel truth that should be considered in order to understand the historical roots of the contemporary state boundaries. He wrote, "The wilderness was the obstacle between the Arabs and the formation of large dense societies, as well as the development of communication between the dispersed civil settlements...it [the wilderness] has also dispersed the Arabs in the desert in the form of tribes and clans...and the large dense societies are creative one where life flourishes, and organized governments emerge to work, produce, and deal with the people." [4]

This puts us face to face with an exclusively Arab issue, the fact that they are a nation "united in spirit, divided in structure," and if their united spirit is unable to impose its reality on the ground to form the prerequisite infrastructure of a union, as in an aligned economy, a comprehensive transportation network, and national pan-Arab institutes beyond the boundary of each individual state, then this issue will never part them.

C. "State" Boundaries and Their Nationalist Dilemma

The boundaries represent in the "Arab phenomenon" – physically and abstractly – a very complicated and controversial issue. On one hand, the Arabs talk, and sometimes behave, as if they are a nation surpassing the boundaries created by foreigners, as is commonly described in Arab discourse. Consequently, it is artificial and unnatural boundaries that ought to perish. In some cases, a bulldozer is brought in to destroy it, as Libya did on its boundary with Egypt, in temporary cases of "unification" drives. Except that boundaries become, on the other face of Arab-Arab behavior, a very complicated issue, and a cause of dispute and quarrels. Some Arabs even resort to international courts for a judgment against their Arab neighbors, as Qatar did in its allegation against Bahrain, which cost both countries huge expenses and preoccupied them with tremendous efforts that could have been directed towards the welfare of both peoples. The Qatar-Bahrain boundary crisis, which was not resolved except through a ruling from the international court of law, is not a unique case between two Arab countries. If the wisdom of some Arab leaders is able to prevent a public quarrel over it, long cumbersome negotiations take place behind the scenes to solve those issues. Though drawn by nature in some cases, due to the vast desert areas between these countries, most of those boundary issues are drawn by tribal distribution of clan "fever" resulting from an archaic manner of living, which is the nomadic manner of seasonal migration in search of water and fertility (this is the basic antithesis of a modern stable society and the state).

International and Arab libraries overflow with encyclopedias and volumes of research on the boundary issues among the Arab countries, most of which is derived from British and French documents, for the Arabs live the problem but rarely document it or research this boundary matter in a manner that exceeds the frame of this brief and concise study on the intellectual dimensions of the issue.

From a comparative historical point of view, we observe that agricultural and urban development in water-abundant nations, where the water-abundance contributed to a stable civilization of connected entities, and agricultural communities merged with the feudal system, the feudal manors crystallized into a wider national state, as in the case of some Asian countries and Europe, whereas tribal dispersion, even among the same ancestral clans, leads to a multiplicity of family trees, their struggle and separation. Even if tribal alliances materialize for temporary political interests, the inter-tribal struggle remains apparent or concealed, and with the potential of being exposed in the case of an alliance break, because such alliances are forged with a tribal mentality, and cannot bypass the progression of history, objectively and morally. Despite the huge change Islam incurred on Arab life, tribal factors remained the basis on which armies were divided, cities were planned, and spoils were distributed. Even the political history of Islam in a major aspect is that of struggle among the branches of the Quraish family over power.

It ought to be clearly noted that this historically and geographically inherited tribal "dispersion" due to certain factors that were once present is not a determined destiny for the Arabs and shedding light on this phenomenon – scientifically – does not imply it is among the hereditary genes of their makeup. When the national state starts developing – in the sense of a modern state and its laws and concepts – these diversities will intermingle and be forged into a national fabric through the historic transformation from a traditional society into a modern society, then through the process of comprehensive sustainable development, reaching the fabric of civil society, which is the basic requirement of democratic development in a constitutional state. Among the tangible historical evidence in the Arab World is that Egypt – which Ibn Khaldun described as "sultan and subjugates," i.e., a state and citizens in modern terms, has assimilated the incoming tribes immigrating from east and west, and blended them into a civilized society under a central government. We can see a similar case in the Kingdom of Morocco, where the civilized fabric of Moroccan entities resulted in a central government characterized historically, and to the early twentieth century, as a *"makhzan"* state [literally, a "treasury," meaning a central government or authority which collects taxes], which developed into the constitutional monarchy we have today.[5]

In addition to the space division (the vast barren deserts), there emerged another division in time which weakened the historical continuity of the state and its centers. The historically continuous nomadic invasions, either from the Arabian Peninsula or from central Asia, kept recurring and taking state along with its accumulated civility and political institutions back to ground zero.[6]

Despite that, the Arabs remained, as we have earlier noted, a nation "united in spirit, divided in structure." The experience of the past decades proved that, despite the cracked "national" system, the withering nationalist ideology, the fading common Arab institution and the "cooperation" and "cooperative Arab work," all those regressions and depressions were unable to affect the common emotional spirit between the Arabs or reflect on their daily lives, regardless of the educational, cultural, and informational facets of those quarrels. When the division of space (deserts) and time (nomadic invasions) were coordinating to disfigure a civilized center, the physical urban basis (infrastructure) would naturally collapse, except that the norms and morals were able to escape through the books that were shipped via caravans, and through the individual and collective memory, to areas that were out of danger's reach, so that it was rooted in the emotions and spirit and sprouted to flourish again. That is how invasions and the fall of civil centers caused the physical structure to be ripped apart and perish throughout the ages, whereas the spirit was relocated to thrive in the nation's memory and emotions, and even compensate for the loss of its infrastructure with more vigor.

On an emotional level, the Arab "spirit" is still resurrected, alive and intense, in every national confrontation, relying on its

Islamic roots from which courage and resistance are inspired, except that these emotional "outbursts" do not take long to succumb to opposing factors (like the success of the US invasion of Iraq, and the Israeli military's superiority not only compared to the Palestinians, but to all Arab states combined), so the national structure, which is diverse in its politics, boundaries, institutions, and composition, cannot confront current challenges. This has been the case for many decades, since the conception of the nationalist stream in Arab life, and to a certain extent, even in its prime age during the days of Nassar.

The prevalent thought which aims to remedy the phenomenon of diversified Arab entities and the boundary issue that separate them, be they abstract or physical, concentrates on the pertaining phenomenon of ethnic, religious, sectarian, or sectarian minorities. However, it is useful to notice, while concentrating on another aspect of this issue, that we have a diversified "Arab majority" which is supposedly to be in harmony nationally and "sectarianally," where more than 80% of the inhabitants of the Arab World are classified as "Sunnite Arabs." But this point did not unite this majority, for the "diversified majority" remained the main issue that needs particular attention when trying to sort the boundary problem in its mental, psychological, and "structural" dimensions, and not only in its political or judicial dimensions. This was what we pointed at in our research entitled *The Problem of the Arab Social Makeup: Minorities...or Multiple Majorities?* in a publication about Arab civil conflict released as a cooperative research effort by a team of Arab authors.[7]

Despite the organic unity of the Arab Islamic civilization and the Islamic world, the latter has been politically divided since its very early stages, even during the mandate of Islamic rule when there was no external force controlling it and "conspiring to divide it," as some Arabic literature describes international powers to justify this "division" phenomenon, which is totally Arab!

This was from whence permanent tension emerged in the history of Arabs and Islam, between a comprehensive canonical, cultural, and civil sense of belonging on one hand, and a fractioned political sense of belonging. This tension is still prevalent today between the broad religious or pan-Arab sense of belonging and the limited "national" sense of belonging.

As we previously noted, the unified civilization circle never coincided with the various conflicting political circles, as was the case – for example – with the Chinese civilization circle which coincided with the unified circle of the Chinese state and maintained its unity throughout most of the historical ages and retrieved it early in the modern age with a congruence between the political and civilization circle.

***

If we want to scrutinize the diversity of belongings that are intertwined in the makeup of the Arab identity, we find that there is a tertiary relationship that bypasses the ones we pointed out earlier, a relationship between the general belonging to the doctrine and civilization, social belonging limited to a tribe, section, or area, and the political belonging to the existing systems as a matter of reality.[8] This triangular loyalty was conceived by historical reality and is still valid to date. Moreover, these days, the loyalty to the diverse small communities – such as tribal and sectarian – is growing and even overshadowing the other two aspects, the general civilization and the political. This triangular loyalty is paralleled and accompanied by a resulting congruent tertiary phenomenon in the general Arab Islamic character, for the Arab is a "Muslim" by doctrine, prayer, and spiritual values, "Arabic" by culture, morals, art and literature, and tribal, sectarian, or local in his inclination, social fears, and political alignment. This variety in belonging and in personal expression is not unique to Arabs, for it is a usual human inclination, except that, in Arab society, it remained a detached diversity not organized within a priority scale which forges it into a single entity, and the case remained that minor priorities overshadowed major ones in the most critical situations without any constraint or hierarchical limitation. In other words, it is negatively clashing rather than positively complementing, as in the case of the current European union, where it is important to observe that European nations have negatively clashed in previous stages of European development towards a larger structure, and then were able to place it in a positive hierarchy which was useful to get over differences and eventually unite.

On another front, although we cannot systematically talk about "democracy" before its meaning crystallizes in the modern age (a meaning that bypasses that of ancient Athens), except that the concept of "democracy" in Arab desert life has to be put in the right sociological realistic context – where the natural desert environment and its necessities between the rich, powerful people and the masses, and thus the concept of democracy cannot be generalized to encompass the Arab authority mechanisms. What kind of democracy materialized in the Quraish family, or between the Umayyads themselves, or between the Hashemites (Abbasids or Alawites), or in any other Arab tribe or clan? Even though Islam taught Muslims how to live with and forgive people from other religions, in many cases they have not dealt in the same manner with the political diversity amongst themselves.

It is worth noting that since the conception of political authority in Islam after the demise of the prophet (peace be upon him), the eminent and resolute question was "Who rules?" meaning which tribe or clan. The more important and objective question was delayed: "How will government be in the new state after the prophet? What system and program, based on the political principles of Islam, which is generally flexible and needs preciseness, should be adopted?"

That is how tribal "individuality" transformed the question of ruling in the history of Islam from a "discipline" – how to establish and run a governing system – to a ruler's "individuality" – who should the rulers be, from which tribe or clan, and which "individual" among them is preferred to another "individual" – which accentuated the conflict between the political entities within this single civilization, and the concept of Shura – consultation council – had not be formalized as an effective political institution since the beginning of the history of Islam.

Political and religious Islamic thought drifts behind this sterile "distinction" which preoccupied minds and Quranic interpretations, as well as aroused tensions, instigated biasness, and spilled blood. Moreover, the more imminent issues of political thought and political science calling for constructive politics depreciated, such as the topic of building a state, restricting authority, organizing government and limiting participation, and laying down the rules of reigning in general.[9]

So as not to remain in the context of historical critique, despite its importance for us to comprehend the dimensions, implications, and dangers, we have to reach our tangible reality at the current historical moment of Arab life in the Arab present.

In the Arab present, the national entities represent, regardless of it being naturally or historically inherited or artificially created by colonialism, the only context in which the Arab lives, brings up his children, interacts with other Arabs and the world, and learns the values of nationalism, loyalty, work, and production. The Arab maintained what can be described as an illegitimate relationship with his limited "smaller scale" country due to the comprehensive national tide and the totalitarian religious tide, and this country merely represented a "temporary state" while anticipating the large-scale country or the Grand Caliphate. From this angle, we see the weakness in the civil behavioral values in Arab life, for those are values that a human being can only learn in a definite country which he believes in and is absolutely loyal to. That is why the Arab does not hesitate in vandalizing urban features, public gardens, and lampposts in this "fleeting country" which is seen as having no future. The Arab East nationalist ideology which emerged as an emotional reaction to the Sykes-Picot Agreement in the "Fertile Crescent" contributed to creating a state of pacts under the notion of the "nation-state," which is still a target of anger for most Arab authors because of its tyranny and failure to confront enemies and overcome backwardness. They were probably right in most of what they said. (What is astonishing is that unificationist nationalist ideology continued to denounce "nation-state" entities while its "unificationist nationalist" parties preserved those entities with all its power and wit when they got to power!).[10]

This discrepancy between the concept of a "country" within whose boundary man lives and ought to be brought up patriotically with a sense of modern civil behavior based on citizenship and patriotism, and the consequences of the ruling "nation-state" with all its vices, has led to dangerous and misleading confusion between the country and its political system. The two ought to be differentiated, and the concepts of "country," patriotism, and citizenship should be saved from the negative connotation adopted by the "nation-state," whose vices each and every Arab country should be liberated from through a genuine democratic reformist program that joins the concepts of citizenship and state in a manner beyond the current schizophrenic situation between the "national" and that pan-Arab nation.

This is based on the premises that he who cannot build a "small" country will never be able to build a larger scale nation, while keeping in mind that the "large nations" that were established in Arab history, last of which is the Ottoman empire, were not any better than the "nation-state" in its tyranny, political backwardness, and its dealing with citizens. There is no guarantee that the ruling nature in the larger nations would be any better than that of the "nation-state" unless the proper prerequisite terms for a decent authority are available. The severe criticism directed to the "nation-state" is due to the fact that it is a living witness against itself, whereas the pan-Arab or religious nations remain a farfetched dream. If we went back to history and observed its political heritage, we would notice that the issue is not in the nation's size (small or large), but rather in its nature and core.

If those ultra-national dimensions, like the nationalistic and religious, confront the country to which the Arab is loyal, then the infra-national dimensions of Arab society, like tribal and sectarian, drag the Arab downwards, so that nothing remains for pure patriotic loyalty except a thin margin where a proper country can never be built. To those who fear this idea, we assert that the Arabs will never rise unless they know how to build those national blocks that can mature in the future into the cornerstones of a national pan-Arab structure. As for the zeros and fractions, those do not produce a decent number viable to develop into reliable credit in the making of nations.

Moreover, if it is necessary to distinguish between the concept of a "country" and the political nature of the ruling "national" state's system, primarily for the sake of ensuring the Arab lives a healthy "national" life which plants in his character the basic sense of a citizen's rights and duties, preparing him for a better and wider national life in the future in which he decides to participate with the fellow citizens of his country on the basis of free choice, without annexation or occupation, then it is also necessary to expose the positive aspects of the "national" state in order to reinforce them, bringing this pivotal historical stage to saturation and maturity, thus entering the gradual development of a broader national society, without ignoring its negative aspects, as with any other phenomenon whose reality is governed by historical and social dialectic paradoxes.

Our perception of the historical significance of the "national" state phenomenon, which is, in fact, the first "national" state in which the Arab lives in his history, and which is also the perception elucidating its historical and political facets in our book *Political Arab Makeup and the Signification of the Nation-State*, is based, in brief, on the following premises:[11]

1. Throughout their history, the Arabs were occupied by many empires, the last of which was the Ottoman Sultanate, which represented a majestic empire built upon religious emotions, while its citizens were actually living in miniature sectarian, regional, or tribal societies. They did not intrinsically participate in the state or indulge in its experience and manners as did the Chinese, in the historically intrinsic meaning of a state (not necessarily the modern meaning of the term). It is crucial to note the difference between the state and authority. Authority can sometimes be a contradiction of the state.

2. Arab Islamic history kept swinging between the phase of a state and a non-state, and the Arabs were not permitted to experience a continuous state, which is the school of politics. As many scholars observed, the political dimension on the Arab phenomenon still swings between the merging and detachment of large and small political entities, age after age. The Arab tragedy is summarized as follows: Neither do the miniature entities politically forge into a unified national sphere to form a single solid political structure, nor do they completely detach themselves to establish an unconnected solitary structure. "It is separation in unity, and unity in separation."

3. The practical result of this historical reality is that the modern individual "national" state represents the first true Arab experiment with a state, negative and positive...tyranny and order...right and duty...oppression and liberation...etc. This "experiment" ought to be given its natural role in the exclusive national modern development of the Arab individual and the Arab nation in general. Any attempt to abort this experiment in the name of nationalism and unity before it matures will lead to the hindrance of this natural development, for there is no escape from letting the individual national experiment mature so that it naturally flows into the nationalist development stream. The Arabs, in the modern sense of the national state, are a nation in the course of composition – as some Marxists observed – and it is essential to respect the nature of this composition and mind its singularity, whether we like it or not, or as Mohammed Abd Al-Jabri put it, "Without the theory of the real practical Arab state, the "national" Arab state with all its faces, it is impossible to present a practical theory of Arab unity."[12]

4. Moreover, leaving the Arab waiting for the formation of a larger pan-Arab unity, or the grand Caliphate, like an intangible promise, and an immaterialized one, makes his relationship with his country similar to illegitimacy, carried out in secret, in the dark, and far from any moral legitimacy.

The national and religious sense of belonging is a natural and undeniably real one. However, manipulating it negatively into a notion conflicting with national belonging, instead of complementing it as in the European union where the recognized national European entities merge into a broader European entity – and a project as well – within the larger natural framework of the Western European civilization in its different ingredients, and, we say, developing a relationship of conflicts between the different entities of the Arab identity instead of seriously and intellectually developing it into a complementary relationship, make this identity a battlefield for internal strife, as is the present case, even though it possesses the potential for union if we know how to reorganize the priorities, loyalties, and belonging of its different rich entities. First comes a national sense of belonging, then nationalistic loyalty, then religious and cultural belonging, etc.

5. In the lives of modern Arabs, the absence of civil norms and morals, which can only be implanted through national education, is the cause of the conflict and contradiction that is implanted by national and religious ideologies and slogans – before its proper historic timing – in their feelings towards their countries, which are their only refuge in the present situation. If the country is an illegal structure, an artificial partition, and a colonial division, how then can one be loyal and belong to it, and hence get a proper national education with all that it entails of civil behavioral duties in a national society?

That is why civil behavioral principles remained, in various parts of the Arab World, a deferred principle that will only be established with the conception of the greater unity…and the Arab is still waiting for it! The Arab citizen thus resigned his current national duties – with the excuse of waiting – while the civil behavioral principle mourned itself and revealed its vulnerability. These are principles that should be practiced "here and now"…not at some future time. Thus, it has been observed that the Arab citizen is ready to march in a mass demonstration to sweep away imperialism, considering it a national duty, but he is reluctant to participate in a local campaign to sweep the road next to his house, for Arab civil awareness is deferred until the union state is established. That is how the misinterpreted national "awareness" crystallized in the ideological literature which led in practice to the opposite of what was expected of it and its slogans.

It seems that the national Arab Eastern intellect is the largest impediment and incomplete in this regards where, as we earlier discussed, it emerged as a brusque reaction to the undoubtedly colonial divisions of Sykes-Picot, whereas its remedy needed better and deeper analysis of the flow of events at that time. The Syrian author Imad Fawzi Shuaibi observed, "This romantic nationalism emerged from rejecting every national state, and dissolved nationalism in spiritual and cultural Arabism, and produced economic analysis to prove the failure of nationalism apart from the nationalistic, and it forgot to see that nationalism in the absence of the nationalistic is an urgent necessity. It is sheer foolishness to wait for that which is nationalistic before we start building our countries in a national and collective manner. The notion of a country became an ambiguous one, blurred between knowledgeable identification and the stolen national identity."[13]

This conceptual flaw in the national Arab Eastern notion of a country gets clearer if we compare it to the Arab West unity promoters, the latter of which do not accuse or condemn the national reality of the Arab Western countries, because nationalism is the building block of nationalistic unity, and this is the proper view. [14]

6. The social-historical analysis, past and present, of the practical role of "unification" which the "national" state supports in the merging of the smaller societies – sectors, tribes, and areas – into the fabric of the national body that it governs, even if it were with varying levels of tyranny, control, reaching a civil society in the end, proves that the "national" state, from an historical perspective, represents a "unification" phase for those entities and miniature diversities that are sociologically dwarfed by other entities that were prominent in the days of the empires and whose existence gave the false impression that it "unified" the Arabs into one structure.

For example, the unity of "Greater Yemen" which is still considered a "national" state from a national point of view, is an important historical step in unifying the miniature social Yemeni entities which remained detached due to historical and geographical factors, despite the fact that Yemen is still considered part of the greater Islamic state that is "unified" in prevalent Arab "awareness."

This sort of social historical stability can be applied to the various Arab "national" states within which the miniature social entities interact – offensively or harmoniously – in the process of developing into a homogeneous national society that can provide a solid basis for a larger national structure in the future. These scenarios are detailed and explained in the book *Political Arab Makeup and the Signification of the Nation-State* in a chapter entitled, "With the Perspectives of the Actual Reality of History and Society, the Nation-State: A Fragmentation or Unification?"[15]

Conclusion

If those premises prove correct – and I think they are – it would be useful for the Arab unity stream, in the long run, to have the courage to draw the boundaries of the "national" state in the Arab World, regardless of whether those counties were a byproduct of the history of colonialism, for it is a tangible reality that the Arab lives and in which his destiny and that of his descendants is realized. After drawing these boundaries and acknowledging them and assuring Arab citizens on both sides of the boundary of the end of the struggle over them, we can start planting the seed of trust that is currently missing, through common projects and interests which can lead to overcoming those boundaries for the welfare of all parties concerned.

Five decades ago, the boundary struggle between European countries was as intense as can be, until the boundaries were clearly defined. After drawing and acknowledging those boundaries, common European institutions began to grow, penetrating those boundaries, and working to eventually overcome them.

That is the historical dialectic, in boundaries and other aspects. Arabs are not an exception. Thus we see that the necessary means of overcoming the boundaries between Arabs, which we hope to do for the future, is to draw them first, in order to achieve a unified

Arab state... in the end!

Endnotes

1. Author's articles: "The Arab Culture's Need for a Socio-analytical Inclination," "Towards a Sociological Approach that Views the Crisis at its Roots," and "An Insight into the Roots: The Responsibility of the Past towards the Crisis of the Present," in the book *The Renewal of the Renaissance by Self Discovery and Criticism*. 2nd ed. Beirut: Arabic Institute for Studies and Publishing, 1998, pp. 97, 105, 111. For more detail on the ideas posed in this article, the following are books by the author:

   - *Political Arab Makeup and the Signification of the Nation-State.* 3rd ed. Beirut: Center for Arab Unity Studies, 2000.
   - *Political Crisis for the Arabs and the Position of Islam: Ingredients of the Chronic Condition.* 2nd ed. Beirut: Arab Institution for Research and Publication, Al Shuruq Publishing House in Cairo, joint publication, 1999.
   - *The Arab and Politics: Where Is the Flaw?*, 2nd ed. Beirut – London: Al Saqi Publications, 2001.
   - *Arab Civil Conflicts: The Internal and External Factors.* Beirut: Arabic Institute for Studies and Publishing, 1997. (joint publication with others)

2. Ghassan Salamé, "The Impediments of the 'National' Reality," in the book *Arab Unity: Its Experiences and Forecasts*, Center for Arab Unity Studies, Beirut, 1989, pp 472.

3. Jawad Ali, *The Turning Point in Pre-Islamic Arab History*, Beirut, Al Hadatha Publications, 1983, volume 7, pp. 6-18.

4. Abdul Kareem Ghulab, *Constitutional Development in Morocco*, where we find a condensed and objective elucidation on that development.

5. Mohammed Jaber Al-Ansari, *Political Arab Makeup and the Signification of the Nation-State*. Beirut: Center for Arab Unity Studies, 1994, pp. 38.

6. Adnan Al Sayyid Hussain (coordinator), Mohammed Jaber Al Ansari, Abdullah Balqaziz, and Sasin Assaf: *Arab Civil Conflicts: The Internal and External Factors*. Beirut: Arabic Institute for Studies and Publishing, 1997, pp. 15-46.

7. Burhan Ghalioun, *The Sectarian System: From a State to a Tribe*, Beirut, Arab Cultural Center, 1990, pp. 136-137.

8. *Political Arab Makeup and the Signification of the Nation-State*, pp. 26

9. *The Arab and Politics: Where Is the Flaw?* pp. 138-149

10. *Political Arab Makeup and the Signification of the Nation-State*, pp. 89-103

11. Mohammed Abd Al-Jabri, *The Issues of Contemporary Arab Thought*, Center for Arab Unity Studies, Beirut, 1989, pp. 97-98.

12. Imad Fawzi Al-Shuaibi, *Al-Hayat* newspaper, dated 5/11/1992, p. 18.

13. *The Arab and Politics: Where Is the Flaw?* pp. 139.

14. *Political Arab Makeup and the Signification of the Nation-State* pp. 105-127.

III. CULTURAL PERSPECTIVES FROM BAHRAIN

The Harbor for Memory: The Harbor of Our Lost Reality

Al-Arabi, Issue 487, June 1999. Republished in: *The Harbor of Memory, Al-Arabi,* vol. 54, pp 252-267, Kuwait.

Does Man's memory begin at the moment of the collision of childhood consciousness with the facts of life and other things, or does this memory have a beginning that is far deeper in time and ages?

I am not infringing on the beliefs in reincarnation, which say that humans have previous lives in other times and places, for that is merely talking of an uncertainty, even if such beliefs do not lack excitement for some who are attracted by paranormal phenomena.

But what I meant is: If Man is a mere autonomous self-contained individual, then his memory is nothing but a personal record of his life.

However, if Man transcends his individuality, and his small self, to his deep and far-reaching components in time and place – and that is the destiny of the author, in particular – then he cannot escape transcending the individual memory to the collective memory that formed him – in time and place. Thus, it became his destiny to become an attracting center of its distant dimensions and a fabric reflecting its intermingled threads and colors.

If the "first place" of the subconscious memory of Man – the individual – which precedes the opening of consciousness, is the mother's womb, then the "first place" of the collective memory of Man – the plural – is the country's lap, with its soil, location, and accumulated heritage throughout history.

The "first place" within this meaning has its presence in Man, regardless of the influence of time and other places, for "nostalgia is forever towards the first home." [This quotation is from a line of poetry by ninth century Arab poet Ibn al-Rumi.]

In Bahrain – the country – in the heart of the Arabian Gulf, the crossroads of continents and seas – I received some of the strongest influences of formation: real harmony with the self, openness to the other, and the lust for reaching out and listening to him, the experience of connecting to the self and separating from it at the same time, within a mental and psychological open space that moves farther away only to get closer for an intimacy that is more true and a recognition that is more aware of the self and the other.

That was not a mere personal acquisition, for Bahrain objectively is the only Arab country whose geography is made entirely of islands. It is tightly connected to the Arab World through the waterway of the Gulf that separates the archipelago from the motherland in an amphibious dialectic – it enabled Bahrain's identity to be a mixture and adaptation of deep-rooted desert values and the dynamism of a vigorous sea – and that is, in my opinion, the key to understanding Bahrain culturally and sociologically. This dialectic of connection/separation and distancing/getting closer gave the country geographically and morally what no other Arab country has, a practice of which, I think, the entire Arab World is in dire need, more than any other time. I mean, the practice of getting in touch with the self "from a distance" allows the exploration of the self with serenity of vision that cannot be achieved except with this distancing in order to get closer (and this is what I went through in my personal life, where I have distanced myself from my country in order to get closer to it).

The Harbor for Memory: The Harbor of Our Lost Reality

Through this characteristic Bahraini society and its people gained the ability to contemplate the Arab self to which it belongs with objectivity and neutrality and, even though it is an intrinsic inner part, it can see it contemplatively from the outside. Perhaps Salah Abdul Saboor's comment, "I shun you so that I can know you," explains this idea best, where shunning is a positive manner of turning away from something in order to get closer to it.

Due to the geographically small dimensions of the country, with its sensitive and delicate civilization and culture, Bahrain was able to listen more than be listened to.

The heavyweight Arab countries were keen to make other Arabs hear their calls and ideologies. But Bahrain was preoccupied with listening to its near and faraway regional and international neighbors preaching. It probably learned more by listening than those who were preaching in the large [Arab] world, the majority of whom listen to their own individual voices without listening to other voices.

In the vast, peaceful, open space of the islands, sea, and Man, these variables, and maybe the antagonists, met and learned to coexist and to live in harmony. Bahrain, coastline and islands, represented, under its historic name of "Dilmun," the link between the Mesopotamian civilization and the civilization of the Indian subcontinent, culturally and through trade. As opposed to the dramatic conflicts of Mesopotamia and its surprising changes, the Sumerian legend rendered the adjacent land of Bahrain to the south a magnanimous and serene land of immortality, to which Gilgamesh arrived in search of the black pearl among its white pearls representing eternal immortality.

Considering the coexistence of the variables and the antagonists in Bahrain as opposed to their conflict in Mesopotamia, Sumerian mythology, in the text of a sacred anthem about Bahrain, depicted Dilmun as the land where lambs and lions coexist, as do the sparrow and the snake, where owls do not hoot, and Man does not age.

This anthem baptized Bahrain/Dilmun as "the harbor of the world," and that has been its fate since the dawn of history; a harbor for trade and, consequently, a port of culture and civilization. Bahrain has remained, since the dawn of its Arabism as well – in its islands in particular and its historical region in general – an emblem of the coalition of differences by continuing its openness to the seas of the world and their cultures, on the one hand, and its intimate interaction with the wilderness of the Arabs, both desert and urban. Bahrain was the maritime oasis where, before and after Islam, Christianity coexisted with Zoroastrianism and Hinduism, and brothers of the same household lived harmoniously though possessing different religious doctrines. This is demonstrated in one poet's verse describing his people and his clan:

And I, even if they are Christians, love them.

My heart is in comfort with them and yearns for them.

In modern times, Bahrain was the first place on the coasts of the Arabian Peninsula open to the establishment of churches in peaceful proximity to its mosques and *hussainiyas* [assembly halls for the Shiite sector], the latter two of which also coexist in harmony. That is why the chapter dedicated to Arab Christian and Shiite thoughts, balanced with Arab reason and Persian Gnosticism, in this article's author's book *Divine Thought and the Conflict of the Antagonists*, was not a mere academic interest from the author's side, as much as a personal experience for which Bahrain was the genuine stage.

Throughout the Islamic age, the region of Bahrain witnessed ideological and political tensions of the dialectics between the

Caliphate states and their opposing and rebellious powers, one époque after another. It is here that the Kharijites, the Zinj, and the Qaramites, among others, passed through, thereby molding into its collective consciousness the essence of historic and ideological dialectic without denouncing its Arab and Islamic community principles. Since the Ionians to the present date, the balance has always tilted towards versatile coexistence in the frame of a coalition community.

This image I draw of my country probably tends to be utopian and romantic, especially on the scale of reality and its events. But the noble principles this country has inspired in me and that which I have learned through my vision of thought and the coexistence of ideas in search of a common ground among variables and the differences among similarities, as I have explained in my aforementioned book and other publications.

As for modern Bahrain, I consider it a "*mushraq* (eastern) case" [in reference to Egypt and the Fertile Crescent area] in the Gulf, where one relies on toil and ideas more than on wealth and money. It has only enough oil, as a Western author once described it, to grease the mind. This distinction was the basis for its leadership in the modern Gulf, a leadership I leave for history to detail so that I can go back to my history with the place, time, and thought through these harbors.

As a Bahraini citizen, I am not surprised by this age's globalization, as we have lived with globalization and its heavy reigns, voluntarily and forcibly, negatively and positively, and it was not all evil on the scale of the resident evil we have in our Arab reality. Sometimes, external factors were the better of the two evils. In any case, that was not a globalization to be proud of. It was indifferent to human rights, democracy, and even the slightest labor rights of those oppressed by its gluttonous corporations. My father participated in digging the oil wells that lit the world. Nevertheless, until high school, I never found a single electric lamp whose light I could study by, which reduced the light of my eyes [vision]. Now I understand the Arab poet who said:

From the masses' sweat, oil is distilled,

And from their water wells, oil exploded.

[The author here is making a pun on the Arabic word *ayun*, which means *eyes*, but can also mean *water wells*.]

Despite the luxury and economic booms the Gulf has undergone in the last decades, I cannot divide the Arabs into what some non-Gulf Arabs call the "oil creature" and the "non-oil creature," as they describe themselves. (Such divisions brought nothing to the Arabs except rifts, like regressive and revolutionary, between Assyrian, Phoenician, etc., which are widespread among the ideological classifications in the Fertile Crescent. Many are the divisions of the region, which is divided within itself!)

Given the reality that my father was digging oil wells – since 1934 – sixty-five years ago, and alongside him thousands and thousands of fellow men of the Arabian Gulf, digging as far south as the Sultanate of Oman and as far north as the State of Kuwait, passing through [the region's] depths of Saudi Arabia, and given the fact of our noble toil, we are not in a position to apologize to anyone for the luxuries our new generations reap from the toil of their fathers and grandfathers in the burning sun and hard rocks. And if there is a misuse of wealth in our countries, it is a fact we are courageous enough to admit. But it is an internal affair of our own, which we need to reform and amend without the manipulation of anyone else, just as we have previously reformed our state from stress and toil with humble efforts without anyone's aid, and blessed is the man who builds his own home before extending a helping hand to his brother to build his.

The Harbor for Memory: The Harbor of Our Lost Reality

In any case, when history has its say, none but the Egyptian support of the Gulf Arabs is praised, particularly in times of distress. Egypt was sending educational delegations to our countries in the Gulf and the peninsula, manned by the finest Egyptian teachers – on its own accord sometimes – from the days when it was a kingdom until [the time when] its nationalist liberation struggle contributed to the achievement of many of the national and popular demands of the Gulf Arabs. It is not a coincidence that those who were criticizing Egypt and its liberation struggle back then are the same ones who are criticizing the Gulf Arabs nowadays. It is high time to surpass all these kindest Arab souls altogether, with courageous self-criticism that shows no mercy.

I know this is a thorny Arab issue and I do not intend to argue about it, for it is an internal wound. I hope it is accepted by our kin as a complaint to those with chivalry, and all our Arab brothers are those in their moments of truth with themselves. We have lived with honor in the Gulf while we were digging oil wells with our bare hands and, we maintained our Arabism and confirmed our national belonging to the vast Arab World as peoples and intellectuals.

Furthermore, our brother rewards us with this injustice? What "nationalist struggle" and nationalist honor allows the falsification of the truth to this degree, and generalizes this oil "stereotype" across all the Arabs of the Gulf?

And we wonder if our situation has deteriorated to this extent, as we practice, in the name of nationalism, this injustice on part of our nationalist reality in the Gulf, which has not preserved anything the way that it has preserved its Arabism, despite being stabbed in the back by some brothers in Arabism?!

What is the sin of the Gulf if oil wealth fell upon some groups and some of them were not able to manage it and utilize it wisely and thriftily? Is the behavior of the wealthy Arabs and the Pashas in other Arab countries above suspicion? Is the behavior of the "revolutionary" leaders among them closer to purity and austerity?

Probably it is not a coincidence that the author of the following old verse is a Gulf poet from the east part of the peninsula, Tarfa Ibn Al-Abd:

The injustice of close kin is stronger on the soul...

Than the impact of a sharp sword.

To those Arabs who wish to regain their kinship with their Gulf brothers I say, the Gulf can only be retrieved from within – voluntarily and not forcibly – with a positive majority winning over its negative self, all by itself!

The defeat of June 1967 and the demise of President Abdul Nassar in 1970 were turning points in my life, after which I immediately decided to resign the ministerial position I held in the Bahraini government (1970/1971) just before its independence, to research a doctorate degree in Arab thought; not for the sake of the degree, but to allow myself a period of meditation, research, and scholarly contemplation.

It became clear to me, following our consecutive Arab defeats, that the most dangerous thing we lack is establishing definitions of our causes before promoting them ideologically. Doubt does not negate the truth at all. And I still believe that the present time in Arab history is a "moment of culture," and a moment to reform our knowledgeable awareness of ourselves and *the other*, more than it is a political moment and an external confrontation, no matter how eminent those temporary preoccupations are. Since I started thinking and writing, I was taken by many interests – literature, philosophy, politics, sociology – a craving on my part for the one truth underlying all the sciences – for I have never been a man of a single specialization, or a single interest.

The Harbor for Memory: The Harbor of Our Lost Reality

That is why I found my shelter – finally – in thought, because it is the common ground among those interests, and it is thought that allows an author to cross specializations, but in a contained methodology, even though this did not restrain me from personal writing and debates that show my other face and symbolize my favorite vacation to which I retreat for comfort away from academic and research writings. That is why I ask the critics and readers to make sure whether that which they read is research or a debate, so they do not hold the researcher accountable as a debater, or the debater as a researcher!

I am probably not broadcasting a "professional" secret if I said that the debater in me is alongside the researcher just waiting for a chance to provoke and disturb him, and to push him to get away from the coldness of academic research.

My fleeting interests in specializations are portrayed in books like: *The Renewal of the Renaissance by Self Discovery and Criticism, Western Sensitivity and Eastern Culture, A Quranic View of International Changes,* and finally *The Suicide of Arab Intellectuals and Contemporary Issues in Arab Culture.*

Among these books, I seek your permission to stop a moment at the book *The World and the Arabs in the Year 2000,* which was published ten years ago in May 1988. It was done a true injustice for no other reason than that it was published in Arabic by an author of the Third World, which is now known as the southern world!

I quote the book verbatim: "What is new in the twenty-first century is that, for the first time in three centuries, the Central Powers, the pivot of world balance, will not all belong to the white European race or the Western European civilization. For the first time in the history of the modern world, stands a civilized power that is not linked to the desires of the West, and does not hold a historic feud with Arabs or Muslims. I mean the Asian power in the

Far East. Can the strategic Arab mind comprehend this serious transformation in world power?" The book includes a more elaborate explanation of this view.

This was an attempt to lay the idea of the confrontation of civilizations from an Arab point of view, years before the inception of David Huntington's view, which became known as the theory of the clash of civilizations. In addition to these ideas, the book contained thoughts about the changes in the Eastern camp and the establishment of a unified Germany almost a year and a half before the fall of the Berlin wall.

These ideas were naturally lost in the turmoil caused by Huntington's view in Arab intellectual circles, for it is incumbent for any "new idea" to emerge in the West for it to impress us.

Then we continue to talk about the necessity of independent thinking!

I document this remark merely for the objective historian of our intellectual development, and I do not want, by that, the just recognition, because I know this is one of the rarest things in our Arab life, and we have to live with little justice in most cases, especially from our closest kin!

I finally reach the most important harbor I have stopped at in the last years.

It is the harbor of searching for our Arab reality from both its aspects, the awareness level (upper layer) and the reality level (underlying layer).

Concerning the former, the study of the awareness level, the primary diagnosis for this case is detailed in the book *Arab Thought and the Conflict of Antagonists*: A Diagnosis of the Indecisive Condition in Arab Life," in addition to the book *The Transformation of Thought and Politics* which was published in the early 1980's.

This research project relies, with simplification, on the following assumptions:

First: The primary assumption in the project is that reconciliatory thought in modern Arab life represents the ideology of indecisiveness in this life...and it has been a continuous phenomenon since the dawn of what is known as the Renaissance until this day, because of the diversity of contradictions and antagonists in the reality of this life, where historical decisiveness has not been reached, yet the reconciliatory thought in the awareness level reflected the "state of indecisiveness" in the underlying reality level on the ground of the social, political and cultural reality, which still suffers the clash of those conflicts of the antagonists without any remarkable decisiveness between the state nationalist and below the nationalist, then between the state nationalist and the nationalist, then between the nationalist and the religious, then between the religious and the modern, to the end of this coupled chain of unresolved issues in our modern Arab life.

Second: A methodological remark is eminent here, that this project does not call or preach for reconciliation – as some are deluded – but is a knowledgeable attempt at diagnosis and description, then analysis and critique, of a phenomenon which I think is one of the most dangerous of phenomena in our Arab World and reality, and intellectually. This project is, at its heart, a call to surpass reconciliation, after diagnosing and critiquing it.

Third: This political, ideological reconciliation is not alien to the pervasive intellectual environment of Arab societies and their intellect, from the egalitarianism of the Egyptian Pharaonic writer Tawfiq Al-Hakim to the *madrahiya* (spiritu-materialism) of Antoun Saadeh, founder of the Syrian nationalist movement in the Arab East. In circles that are not open to the religious majority or dominant sectors, this vast reconciliatory prism is still pervasive, where we can classify within this stream political and intellectual movements which look contradictory to us on the political level, but all belong to a common intellectual and social descent that gathers them together, and that is the state of indecisiveness and their inability to control it on the ground of reality.

As for the second research project that grabbed my interest in recent years, it was, on the other hand, a diagnosis of the sociological infrastructure of our Arab societies – after studying the overlying awareness level in the first project. I can claim that I am distinct in this research project from most of my colleagues and mentors of the Arab intellectuals. While their intellectual projects focused on critiquing the "intellect" or critiquing the "thought," this project confronts the critique of reality, the past and present collective Arab reality in the deepest sense of its makeup. This "critique of reality" within this context is my major research goal, because I know that all form of thought and doctrines and behavior is, in the final analysis, the product of this reality, which needs to be broken down and analyzed to release its burden.

The basic assumption of the second project is that the persistent political tension, and the defeats and crises resulting from it, cannot be explained solely by political regimes and enemy conspiracies, even though those are contributing factors, but rather we should investigate the makeup of the Arab "sociological bed" and its tribal and sectarian, etc. makeup, which itself produces those regimes and policies and negative political phenomena. And if this tribal intention continues, which impedes the growth of a civil society and its democratic development and transformation into a state of modern citizenship, institutions, law, and order, then our Arab societies will remain in their current situation of political backwardness and comprehensive cultural backwardness and it will keep producing the exact same sort of regimes, no matter how their

The Harbor for Memory: The Harbor of Our Lost Reality

names change.

This research project is represented in three publications:

- *Political Arab Makeup and the Signification of the Nation-State* (1994)
- *Political Crisis for the Arabs and the Position of Islam* (1995)
- *The Arab and Politics: Where Is the Flaw?* (1998)

This project resulted from the observations that, although the Islamic Arab civilization flourished spiritually, intellectually, and physically, its political history and political thought remained the weakest link and the most dubious.

In brief, this complicated idea can be encapsulated as follows:

1. Nowhere in the world has nomadism and urbanization, or the desert and the city, confronted each other in a structural confrontation the way they did in the Arab region. Whereas desert and wilderness surrounded the outskirts of China, India, and the European continent without directly influencing the interior, the penetrating desert transformed the Arab civilized centers into isolated islands in a sea of sand – according to Ali Al-Wardi – which created a highly tense dialectic that spans from the geographic and economic reality to the core of society, culture, and politics. This is a distinct Arab characteristic carrying with it heavy burdens, usually bypassed by scholars, and was not given proper attention as a subject for keen study – after Ibn Khaldun – except by the late Iraqi sociological intellectual Ali Al-Wardi in his study of the social character in Iraq, in particular, and the Arab World, in general.

2. In the course of Arab civilization, this dialectic resulted in two divisions:
    a. Spatial divisions resulting from the vast desert areas separating the centers of urbanization which hindered the development of an intricately connected urban network, the basic element in the rise and development of a state. This spatial division is the natural separation factor in the Arab World, be it in the social or political makeup.
    b. Time divisions due to the recurrence of nomadic invasions of the capitals of civilization which kept taking it, along with its accumulated cultural and political institutions, back to ground zero, time after time. This is in addition to recurrent waves of desertification that buried civilizations and countries under its sands.

Those two divisions (space and time) contributed as an obstacle to the continuous development of a stable civil society, which is the basis of a state, its development, and unity. This resulted in the currently established multiplicity in the Arab reality: multiple civil centers instead of a centralized one, multiple social structures of tribes and clans and religious sects, and multiple quarreling political entities.

This multiplicity is not a characteristic of other large civil and political entities in Asia with heavy seasonal rains like China or Japan or India, where the river-based civil societies with a unified urban makeup helped contain diversity and contributed to the unity of the larger society and its one state. (In China, for example, we see congruence between its civil circle and its political circle, which is portrayed in the flourishing Chinese state, while this is not the case when it comes to the multiple political circles of various parties and entities within one Islamic Arabic social circle.)

3. This geographic and sociological characteristic of the Arab region influenced its political composition in the following manner: The state's continuity was severed, and the Arabs were fluctuating between the position of statehood and no state throughout their political history. The relocation of the political centers of their states, a phenomenon that did not happen anywhere else in the world, did not allow them to experience living in a stable and continuous state and exercise normal political life within the framework of its institutions, laws, and concepts. If we take into consideration that the state is a school of politics, and that the exercise of politics outside the state's boundaries is futile and ineffectual, we will notice the inadequacy of the political experience of most Arab societies, whose political experience varied from submission to external powers, like the incoming Mamluks, in urban, agricultural, and trade societies, or submission to tribal authorities, which are the antithesis of a state in nomadic societies. In both cases, the Arabic self-practice of politics of the state throughout the ages lacked the positive practice in this important experience, which is critical in the life of nations.

4. In the light of the above, it can be said that the current nation-state in the Arab World, with all its flaws, and while admitting it is a remnant of colonial separation in some cases, from a factual historic perspective and

the comprehensive aspects of Arab societies, it is the first experience for Arabs in statehood and unity. Statehood in the sense of living within a continuously stable state, and state unity in the sense of pursuing the unification of diversified factions and social structures and forging them into a civil society and one national state. It is an inevitable prerequisite historic step for national unity which cannot take place except through the unity of individual national unities [nation-states]. Since the Arab region has not witnessed a real developmental feudal age in its history – in the European and Japanese sense of feudalism – the national state in some aspect represented this missing feudal age and prerequisite stage which prepared for national unity in the history of other societies. For the Arab nation-state can be seen, with objective thought, as a postponed feudal stage in the age of global capitalism and international domination. (*Political Arab Makeup*)

5. The historic choice of this nation-state is characterized by its ability to forge multiplicities and traditional societies and social structures into a unified civil society which relies on urbanization of the countryside and the deserts rather than "nomadizing" the city and presents opportunities for the common national civil powers to practice sound modern politics in front of traditional political inclinations. And if those powers are not rendered civil and merged into a civil society, then the democratic discourse in the Arab World will remain a myth.

On the other hand, Arab unity will remain a utopian slogan if this unity continues to rely on the phenomenon of "moral unity" in culture and Arab emotions without finding, within this unified state, a live reality to unite Arab structures and social multiplicities. This state should represent the practical ability and the historic passage for any possible Arab unity. From this angle we can see, for example, that the achieved Yemeni unity today on Yemeni land is, without a doubt, much more realistic, useful, and lasting than having Northern Yemen join what was once known as the United Arab Republics. From this angle, national striving, even if it seems less festive than the advertisement for nationalist unity, might be more useful in the long run. What might look like an age of Arab decadence in which we currently live, because of the slyness of history and its cunning, can actually be the beginning of a better Arab age, as long as we know how to dismantle this historical cunning, and we possess awareness capable of uncovering its deceiving and cunning tools.

Did this last harbor seem like a heavy burden with its weighty anchors? It might be so, but there is no escape from diving into the Arabic depths to discover one's self, and after the harbor of "Arab reality," I yearn to get in touch with the harbor of "the reality of humankind" and "the reality of the universe."

Nothing lasts except thought that starts from the reality of humankind, and humankind ends with it as a phenomenon of cosmic existence.

That "harbor" I have regarded and contemplated every day since my childhood – I am almost sixty years of age now – but I still have not reached it. I mean the "harbor of ultimate truth," and I wish to write about it in the last of my books, before the end of the journey of life and the passage beyond the horizon.

Television: A New Stone Age? The Culture of Image... And a Caution about Mankind's Mental Backwardness

In: *The Suicide of Arab Intellectuals and Contemporary Issues in Arab Culture*. Beirut: Arabic Institute for Studies and Publishing, 1998, pp. 225-235.

The effects of television have become such a maze of expansion and branching-out that the matter demands an investigation into its various aspects more than the regular generalizations usually made. The aim of this brief article is to study television's epistemological informative effects upon new generations that have depended, during its early formation years, upon receiving information and knowledge – regardless of which kind – by image rather than, as mankind has always done throughout the recorded history of civilization, by word, thought and conceptual abstract symbol.

Given that television has now prevailed over people's lives and their future generations, what is the essential difference between learning visually by image and learning by words within the human mind's formation? Before dealing with this topic, however, we must remark on how, in the course of contemporary life and its concerns, television has become a substitute for the role of parents at home and of the teacher at school in terms of guidance for the child and the adolescent and the shaping of his mentality.

Imagine an electric device that replaces to a great extent the three foremost founding human influences upon a person's life – the mother, the father and the teacher – all simultaneously, as well as the various aspects of both pedagogic and epistemological bases. In other words, it establishes the foundation of educational behavior and mental conceptual information or knowledge.

The issue of founding general educational and behavioral patterns is not included within the purpose of this study. It suffices here to mention that television has an increasingly effective influence upon traditional customs and behavior, as upon the direction of feelings towards evil or good. Perhaps the spread of violence and crime and their influence on the behavior of young generations, as well as the increasing lack of social and family unity due to soap operas and the daily routine of people in the age of television and in societies that were, until recently, considered culturally advanced, are all an indication of an impending dangerous influence.

Parallel to this influence is the hypothesis under discussion in the present research, which assumes that the image that forms and creates a basis for the mental makeup differs from the classical mental formation achieved through recorded history that was created through the word, the concept and the abstract symbol.

Even though the phenomenon that is television provides the viewer with all possible visual dimensions and details, sensual and revealing of the material world, at the same time, it deprives human insight of much it was wont to have as a mental foundation of abstract mathematics, religion and philosophy, aesthetic and linguistic. This assumption, if true, could explain the actual deterioration in contemporary societies in intellectual, philosophic and aesthetic levels of life, even regarding those with advanced cultural standards, after technological progress has gifted them with this amazing invention called 'television!'

Before the invention of the alphabet, man in ancient times used the 'image' to express a concept since he had not yet developed the abstract word, as a symbol, whether physically depicted or mentally conceived.

In these primary languages, the drawing of the sun expressed its actual form or the bird's depiction expressed its actual form and so on. Thus, we cannot say that those signs expressed the significance of these objects, rather merely their material existence, and were void of any metaphoric meaning, which is the case in the age of alphabetic wording, where the human mind went beyond the absolute physical sense of the object and the word it depicted or expressed.

With the invention of the alphabet – that is to say – with the coming of writing and reading, letters became phonetic symbols for meanings that were not necessarily essentially related to the actual physical image of the expressed object. In fact, writing became expressions agreed upon by linguists. Thus, language was freed of necessary material link and became of metaphoric significance, abstract and rich for the intellect and the imagination.

Thus did the human intellect develop gradually towards symbolic, moral and intellectual "abstraction." It became able to transfer the language from its physical, tangible level to a metaphoric one, rich in meanings, connotations, unlettered by limited factual reality.

Human thought, therefore, upon reaching mental maturity and being liberated from the shackles of materialist sense, was able to overcome the infant stage of human thought where thinking depends on the moving image, as has been proven by the renowned psychologist in child education, Piaget. The mind can then soar with philosophical abstractions, intricate and vast, and can establish mathematics and develop it with its formulas, symbolic and with rich possibilities.

Reaching maturity then, mental and spiritual, the mind has the ability to receive divine religions, monotheistic, the belief in one absolute creator – praise be to the Lord – who is beyond the sensual and the material world (where there is no similar being), that is to say, He resembles nothing in the material and physical universe. This, after having developed from the childhood stage of infant worship that could not comprehend religious thought save through statues and icons, because of the physical impulse overpowering the mind and causing its inability for abstract thought.

Perhaps the reservations that Islamic doctrine has regarding physical pictures reflects the commitment to sustain the abstraction of one absolute God, unrelated to the polytheistic physical iconic worship of human practice before the stage of abstract monotheism.

Modern science, experimental and analytical, has returned to what is tangible and material, to analyze, test and articulate its reality, and does not stop at its limits but rather desires to search its deeper material reaches for another 'abstraction'…an abstraction of scientific laws and mathematical formulae, in order to change the material world itself from its heavy tangible physicality to laws, formulae, theories and numerical symbols. That is to say, in order to abstract "materialism" itself by going beyond the literal into mental and mathematical abstracts. Thus, modern science has triumphed over the material world, taming nature into serving mankind.

Iron has been transformed into a flying object…and raw material into energy and intangible electricity. Once nuclear power was reached and was fathomed to its final minutest particle, it was discovered that these material "particles" move on a plain that is neither sensed nor tangible and cannot be governed...at the heart of material nuclear power! In other words, this "zone" is an intangible area even by the finest and most accurate scientific equipment, while the movement within has no one fixed pattern...but is in "abstract freedom" within the deepest core of the material world...just like the motion of the stars within the dome of the sky.

Thus, from the smallest particle to the largest star in the universe (microcosm) to the greater cosmos (macrocosm) does the physical sense finally halt, unable to explain or use its own material analyses, and surrenders once more to abstractions, its images and possibilities from what the developed human mind possesses of energy and ability to deal with sublime abstractions, including the spiritual, the mathematical, the philosophical and the abstract arts.

Naturally, the "physical image" remains a means of communicating abstract meanings and has not lost its significance completely. Rather, it has become a means of expression of what lies behind it, as in visual poetry, plastic arts, the cinema and the theatre...but it is not an end in itself.

Literary and art criticism requires the visual artist – whether poet, painter or director– to give the image its significance, its expressed suggestiveness, and what lies behind it of abstract thought. The principles of great creative art in literature and in art depend upon the extent to which figurative language and images were charged with deeper meanings, else it (the image) would remain a literal photographic rendering of reality having lost its true artistic value. Thus is the literal photographic picture considered among the lesser artistic levels of depiction, and less than paintings and impressionistic portraits.

It still holds that a painter's rendering of your features by hand gives meanings and connotations that go beyond the physical material barrier, and it is far more valuable than having your photograph taken for a passport or identity card by an automatic lens.

The truth of the difference between the portrait and the photograph is the starting difference between sublime abstract meaning and tangible reality in its raw form.

***

Television arrived – it was certainly a radical revolutionary invention in the history of civilization – and the transference of true live scenes became a possibility that was not present with journalistic writing or by description over the wireless, while educational television brought scenes concerning the human anatomy, surgical operations, geographic depictions, societal documentation in rural as well as in urban areas, and other similar instances regarding communication by image, without which direct visual experience would not be possible. Without doubt, there are areas and fields of science and life which we cannot fathom and comprehend without the physical visual image.

Up to this point, television or communication by image represents important scientific progress in human communication and knowledge. It could have retained this progressive role had its influence been limited to those aspects needed in human life to be understood in terms of the visual and tangible, rather than transforming into the tool and comprehensive means of communicating that has taken over various areas of human knowledge and the mental formation of humans starting from childhood, so that communication with images overtakes the various paths of life.

Man returned – especially as regards the young generation – to thinking with the tangible image while the talent of intellectual abstract thinking began to suffer, as well as the talent of linguistic metaphoric description, and he enjoyed the leisure of watching tangibly any subject as much as he refrained from the difficulty of intellectual reading, abstract thought, spiritual meanings or significance...and other similar factors basic to morality and abstract thought in our lives as in the universe and without which a human being cannot be a cognitive, spiritual being.

I talk of this in such detail, yet I am not certain as to whether the kind reader will receive my intangible "communication," since the image has become the means of understanding in today's world and whosoever does not have pictures cannot effectively address the public to his content.

This issue of the televised image being a conqueror of fields of knowledge and human communication and which should not have the power of conquering moral thought or mental and abstract significance is an issue that needs to be analyzed and clarified...and still the infatuation with televised communication spreads throughout the world, even within the realm of knowledge and universities, so that new mental and intellectual development depends upon visual communication, whether the image is necessary or not, and here's the crux of our problem.

The simple truth is that the image itself, whatever it is, cannot deliver an imaginative or intellectual, a mathematical or spiritual significance, or any abstract thought (independent of the sensual and pictured vision). In order to comprehend the meaning of the language that is metaphoric and abstract, it is necessary to be liberated from the limitation of the camera lens. It is remarkable, for example, that when the literary text of stories and novels with the psychological or social or philosophical dimension is transferred to a television film or series, it mostly fails to deliver the deeper meanings and thoughts of the original text, just as it cannot bring to light any other than the already tangible personalities and scenes, without the suggestiveness and deeper meanings present in the book since these abstractions cannot be rendered through a visual image but only through metaphoric language. What happened – under television's influence – is the overpowering of the sensual image over the figurative metaphoric language and over all that this language bears of human treasure. The overpowering of the sensual image that is…habitual…lethargic…routine over the metaphoric language which is… imaginative…deep…liberating and bears all the linguistic possibilities that is the human treasure hoard.

If television directly fails to deliver meanings and psychological and intellectual depths within the visual, then what could we say about philosophical works and abstract thinking, moral and spiritual significance, and mathematical symbols?

Educators and thinkers have complained that younger generations ignore classical masterpieces of thought and art in the heritage of human civilization, and have wondered how these works that have inspired generations and driven them to great deeds no longer mean anything for the coming generations that are infatuated only by the tangible image, and have been demanding of it only what is strange and exciting, and the departure from the usual…only for the sake of departure.

Furthermore, it is an almost unanimous opinion of specialist scholars that these generations have lost the finest levels of linguistic talent in reading, writing and expression and even direct social dialogue because of prolonged intake of the mechanical television, and the lack of their usage of language except within the narrowest of circumstances so that it becomes closer to silence and passivity than it is to speech or articulation.

Those educators and thinkers offered many interpretations for this demeaning phenomenon in the minds of youthful generations.

And we say: search for the destruction that has been caused by the lethargic televised image over that abstract aspect that is sublime in the human mind.

If the influence of the physical image upon the human mind has been reflected in advanced societies which have a large share of populace cultured in the written word, in reading and in the significance of the intellectual and the abstract, then the governance of the physical image that depends on oral communication in backward and developing countries, where illiteracy prevails and where they already depend on oral (unwritten) communication, will make of illiteracy a natural condition that needs no change since it is naturally adequate to receive television through audiovisual senses requiring no development through the practical educational activities of reading and writing.

Thus, it is possible to implant and firmly establish extreme advancement, in the form of satellite television, within extreme backwardness, in the form of illiteracy, as its way of life and thought. This is a phenomenon we must become accustomed to, with all its ironies, within the fabric of the contemporary world, from north to south, especially whenever the gap increases between technological progress in the north and age-old sedimentation in the south, and what results from the conflict between the two worlds because of this hybrid. It is of course not unknown to us where our societies in the Arab Gulf and the Arab World stand in terms of this encounter.

To conclude, these hypothetical suppositions of thought that we present need the coordination of statistical fieldwork for support, modification or for opposition. They also require extensive discourse from different viewpoints. Until this takes place, I tend to believe that the continuation and the establishing of the reception of general knowledge, information and media through television will result in the deterioration of mankind's mental capacity at the heart of contemporary scientific progress. This, by virtue of the noted addiction of the new generation, especially regarding the dependence of knowledge on images in most areas of general knowledge and, specifically, intellectual knowledge.

Therefore, it would seem that the decline of civilization occurs once it has reached its peak, from whence it loses its voluntary intellectual focus and direction.

God help us.

Labor
A Short Story

The maternity ward at the hospital is clearly marked by different sorts of noises; the continuous coming and going of nurses, the pushing of beds, the bringing of medical tools and medicines by aids, the parents and families awaiting behind doors, yelling for every little sound, explaining each and every movement, and looking anxiously at every nurse's exit. The most touching sound remains that of the irregular moaning of pregnant women fluctuating between yelling and whispering for the unbearable long hours of child birth, into which the woman puts all her mental and physical power. Then we hear the peak of the symphony filled with hope, expectation, and compassion: the crying of babies shocked by the severe, careless world and its unknown, unlimited, and entrusted expansion!

He was standing with the expectant fathers in the corridor of the ward as observers, reacting to this astonishing symphony as though they were participating in its creation, despite the silence around them, marked by tension, and the noise of the agitated, repressed thoughts isolated from this entire environment that people used to embrace with hope and optimism since ever.

An hour and a half has passed since she went inside, enduring – as he is waiting outside – afflicted by hope and fears together. He had his own reason to be more anxious than the others.

He put out his cigarette stub, burned out with his nerves

within a few minutes, in the ashtray quickly with indifference, as if he wanted to get rid of the heavy weight on his chest. He looked out of the ward corridor's back window overlooking the hospital's internal garden standing with its heavy lazy trees under the June sun, turning hotter by noon.

The grass overspreading the ground was decorated with palm trees, a few almond trees, and bushes of red and white roses. Circling the garden's corridor was basil, spreading randomly all over it.

"How quickly days and months seep, as if it is yesterday, or even today. The day of our wedding. A romantic legendary violent love joined us together; a love written about in old stories. She was the most beautiful girl in the neighborhood and even in the whole city. All the boys were struggling just to have her. I did the impossible to win her heart. I proved my capacities in every educational professional field, even in fighting…and of course in matters of love!

The wedding night was like the tales of *A Thousand and One Nights*. Exaltation filled the neighborhood. All the opponents and rivals admitted their defeat. Hatred killed the envious, but all our friends were delighted. She proved that she is a real woman, perfect in everything. And our longing for our first baby born, the symbolization of our pure love, was endless. She got pregnant a few months later.

We shared with each other happy moments just waiting for the infant to come, spending hours of great happy moments together, dreaming of our future. Happiness surrounded us. She was full of life, working day and night at home to make for him a small paradise. She believed that the baby, fruit of this true love, would not follow the rules of growth like all the others. He was a creature, so she thought, who had his own rules. He grew through endless happiness. He was nourished by love and moved through hope filled with trust.

I started to fear this surplus of trust. I told her that with love and faith, we need to take the real world into consideration in order to materialize them in this world. So we must consult the doctor and follow his instructions. But she would face this with a big smile and a joyful childish gesture, leaving no place for any doubt in her heart, neglecting any fears or unpleasant possibilities.

Months went by so fast. She was in her seventh month of pregnancy and we were spending our days and nights imagining how our baby will look, what gestures and voices he would make. One day I went with her to do the shopping for our baby and we bought him the loveliest clothes and materials ever. Every corner in the house was waiting and everywhere we could feel the big dream, the dream of the arrival of our dear little visitor.

Just a few days earlier – she had not yet completed her seventh month – she was standing on a little chair cleaning the dust on the window when she suddenly slipped and fell violently to the ground. Then began a long road of suffering.

He suddenly closed his eyes and imagined the trees of the garden as if they were terrifying devils trying to kidnap him from inside the window. He looked inside the corridor and stared at a man standing on his right to whom he had not said more than a brief greeting.

"Tell me, is there any hope for a baby born in the seventh month to live?"

"Yes, they say so."

The man stopped talking for a while to catch his breath, then continued.

"Yes, such things happen."

He did not feel like continuing the conversation with the man. He gazed again at the garden, trying to breathe a gust of wind in through the window.

He looked at the branches of trees where green was still predominant over yellow and he could see a bird cheeping so loudly that he could hardly hear the moaning from inside the hospital.

Suddenly all the ears were attracted to the inside. A new severe voice protesting against this world – a newborn.

Hopes were revived in the hearts of all the people waiting. The crowd turned into eyes, devouring the door. After a while, the nurse came out and called for the man sitting on his right. He was just about to follow her to ask about his wife, but she shut the door behind her and disappeared.

The tension returns to the others waiting for the coming of another baby into this tiresome world, to bring with him serenity and hope.

As for him, he needed a miracle for his baby-to-be and its mother healthy, and for both to survive.

Does this kind of thing usually happen...or it does need a miracle?

The doctor came out in a hurry. He followed her spontaneously, demanding of her in a severe anticipating voice, "Tell me. What about my wife?"

The hurrying doctor gave him a brief fleeting look and noticed his psychological state. "Until now, everything is under control," she said. No need to worry. The birth is progressing normally. We hope for the best." She smiled gently at him and left without giving him a chance for another question.

He was shocked by hearing her saying "until now." What did they expect after that? But he forcibly rid himself of that worry and made a voluntarily effort to hold onto that which made him feel tranquil and reassured. He looked again through the window towering over the garden, trying to distract himself.

The gardener was holding a transistor radio listening to enthusiastic loud tunes and to violent strong sounds. He remembered that today was the third day of war. He didn't believe he could possibly have forgotten it, although his interest in following it up. The merging of sounds coming from the transistor with those from the delivery ward made him loose his concentration.

He heard the opening of the door. He looked behind him and was sure that the nurse's hand was pointing at him, asking him to come over. He rushed like the wind towards the nurse. He was surprised by a man from behind pushing him, and by the voice of the nurse telling him nervously, "I didn't ask for you. I called for him."

He withdrew sadly and disappointedly, like a defeated soldier who was sure a little while ago that he had triumphed.

Minutes passed by, followed by hours, carrying from time to time hope and desperation. Hours became heavy, painful with no meaning, with only desperation, with no hope, nothing at all. He felt himself approaching nonexistence. He was nonexistence itself!

Two days passed while he was still waiting. He came everyday to the hospital and went back, hoping to come back the next day to receive good news. The doctors cannot determine anything, becoming less and less optimistic.

Labor: A Short Story

In the afternoon of the fifth day, he was standing as usual in the corridor of the ward, where the faces surrounding him had been replaced by others waiting for their luck. He has lost his belief in good luck.

Tired of the ward's melancholic atmosphere, he looked out the window as usual and contemplated the trees.

Something odd had occurred. For the first time, he felt that green had turned to yellow. Even the basil had lost its color. While he was still in the first week of June!.

There were not any birds on the trees. Even the shadows of scattered trees on the grass seem to be defeated and faded.

Finally, the door opened and the doctor appeared. He looked at her, his eyes filled with caution and compassion. She told him to come. But he wanted to be sure. He asked her breathlessly, "Me?"

"Yes, you. Come in please."

He came near her. She took him aside and, trying to reduce the impact of her words on him, said, "The mother is fine and is out of danger. as for the baby…he came out malformed and died."

He didn't feel like saying anything. Things could have been worse. The mother could have been in danger too. Or even dead with her baby. But there was no use. Everything was over now.

The doctor looked at him, encouraging him to talk

"Is my wife really fine?"

"Despite being tired from the childbirth and her psychological state, she isn't in danger at all."

He looked at the floor, looking as if he were about to fall from exhaustion.

The doctor told him, "You can come and look at your wife from behind the glass. She is sleeping now for the first time in days, and we don't want to disturb her."

He remained still without saying a word. Heavy long seconds passed by. The doctor held his forearm and shook him violently. She looked him in his eyes and said, "What's the matter with you? Why are you so down like this? Aren't you a man? Can't you have a second child? Will your offspring die out forever? Are you going to be infertile? All you have to do is to follow the doctor's instruction to avoid any rashness and foolhardiness because the fetus doesn't grow healthy without supervision. Do you understand?"

Afflicted by the feeling of sadness and loss before this woman, he felt shyness arise from deep inside and embrace him with shame. He restrained himself. His self esteem revived he looked at the doctor with pride trying to be a firm man controlling his destiny.

He said, "No, I'm not infertile."

Considering it enough, he didn't add anything.

The doctor regarded him with encouragement and compassion. She was unable to decide if at this moment he looked like a man of endurance or a man on the point of depression. The contradictory feelings struggled and intermixed confusedly. He restrained himself and went with the doctor to where his wife was lying. He looked at her tired pale face with sorrow, tenderness and hope, then thanked the doctor, asking her to take care of his wife. And he left.

When he exited the hospital, he saw the streets crowded with people tortured between confusion, anger and sorrow. He understood from what was said that something horrible and disastrous had occurred. It was total defeat. He simply accepted the reality and didn't feel surprised.

Labor: A Short Story

It was a legendary romantic love from the tales of *One Thousand and One Nights*. An intense violent feeling overwhelmed him and faded away. These days, children of this world don't grow easily. Stories of genies and magicians can't exist anymore. Everything must run under its rules.

While the main street was crowded, he walked slowly on an empty side road that led to his home. He went quietly, slowly, and felt the need to contemplate, to return the situation to normal.

Yes. We must start all over again.

He pictured his wife sleeping quietly in the hospital. He imagined her awake entering a green garden where bushes of flowers and jasmines sway. Healthy little children surrounded her. The lightly falling rain was more or less like dewdrops. The moist aromatic leaflet of flowers sprinkled and crowned children's heads. The sun arising brightly and transparently shone on their foreheads while they stretched out their hands towards it firmly.

Desert Journey for a Sea Bird
A Poem

Al Bayan, Issue 22, 1968, p. 19.

A sea bird was buffeted by the wind

Towards the thirsty desert,

With no companion in the air

No sail in sight,

And no sound of friendly voices of pearl divers' singers.

Nothing.

There is nothing

Except the hum of grasshoppers....

And on the rocks,

Between the empty caves

The wolves howled,

Their eyes invading the sky.

And the sea bird…

How wonderful was this distinguished creation!

Feathers of pure gold.

And its wings…

Like the wonder of lovers.

And its friendly voice…

A tune from paradise.

The sea bird,

With a broken wing,

Grew weary of its infertile wanderings

With no safe harbors along the way,

No lighthouses for the drowned,

And no shores to return to.

And in the morning,

The wind carried with it over long distances

Strange colored feathers,

Scattered in every direction

Like the waves in the middle of the sea.

IV. INTELLECTUAL INTERVIEW

Mohammed Jaber Al-Ansari's Intellectual Project: An Inquiry

An interview conducted by Turki Ali Rabeao, *Al-Moustabal Al-Arabi*, vol. 314, April 2004/2005, pp. 6-34.

Rabeao: Al-Ansari is a model for the Arab researcher seeking to acquire knowledge concerning the Arab reality and its disappointments, as well as its future and its possible renaissance. Since his earliest writings, he has been occupied with transformations of thought and politic, not only on a western level but on a global one as well. He went beyond this to search for the flaw in Arab political formation, the flaw in the conduct of Arab intellectuals and their choices, and on political strains. Most significant is his call for the inquiry of defeat, which is within the framework of his search for the deep roots of the Arabic flaw.

Within this context, he published many books: *Were They Giants?* year 1988; *The World and the Arabs in the Year 2000*, year 1988; *The Transformation of Thought and Politics in the Arab East between 1930 and 1970*, year 1980; *The Renewal of the Renaissance by Self Discovery and Criticism*, year 1992; *Geographical Paradox of Arabic Culture between the Arab East and the Arab West*, year 1992; *Western Sensitivity and Eastern Culture*, year 1998, whilst in politics, he wrote: *Political Arab Makeup and the Signification of the Nation-State*, year 1994; *The Arab and Politics: Where Is the Flaw* in 1998, *Arab Thought and the Conflict of Antagonists*, in 1999; *Political Crisis for the Arabs and the Position of Islam*, year

1999; *Inquiry of the Defeat*, in 2001; then he wrote: *Nassarism through a Critical Perspective*, year 2002.

These are in addition to dozens of intellectual articles published in the most important Arab intellectual magazines, newspapers, and journals. I conducted this interview with him in order to shed light on this rich thought in his methodological approaches to the issues of Arab thought and the potential of the rise of the Arab nation. The final judgment is left to the reader.

Rabeao: In your masterpiece book, *Arab Thought and the Conflict of Antagonists*, (1996), we can find a diagnosis analyzing the state of indecisiveness in Arabic life, and a reconciliation encompassing the prohibited dialectic. You have noted how both idealism and romance left their marks on nationalist Arab thought in the eastern part of the Arab World, particularly in the case of Michel Aflaq, where he borrows most of his origins of self-expression from the German idealism, romance, and nationalism found in the writings of German intellectuals such as Herder and Fredrich Hegel (1770-1831) regarding his opinions about nationalism and the state. Moreover, you must have gone further than that to make a comparison reaching the level of congruity between the thought of Michel Aflaq and the concepts of Herder, and you said, "Michel Aflaq adds to the Arab nation the same distinction and uniqueness that Hegel added to the Russian state." The question is, do you see Arab nationalist rhetoric, the rhetoric of the end of the century that has witnessed numerous nationalist conferences and intellectual reviews of our nationalist rhetoric, as surpassing the German one and bringing an openness towards new emerging developments and a reality far away from what Anderson calls "nationalist imaginings," and is there a possibility to renew this nationalist rhetoric?

Al-Ansari: There is a notable accumulation in the last decades of research about the phenomenon of nationalism in Arab life and their history. However, this research did not yet mature theoretically. I think that the most distinguished writers who scientifically documented this phenomenon, generally and specifically, are two pioneer Arab intellectuals, Sateh Al-Husari and Munif Al-Razaz, who surpassed the romanticism of Aflaq and the idealism of Zaki Al-Arsuzi. With Al-Husari, we see the objective documentation of the nationalist phenomena among nations, especially on the linguistic level. As for Munif Al-Razaz, author of *The Features of the New Arabic Life since 1954*, he has significant sensitivity for the specificity of Arabic geographical, historical, and social parameters that we do not find in the writings of other nationalist intellectual "ideologists," Ba'athist or others. Munif Al-Razaz pointed out the dialectic on urban and nomadic influences on the formation of the Arab. This dialectic, in my opinion, should be taken into consideration in any attempt to "philosophize" nationalistically or socially about Arab thought. We also should not overlook the role of Dr. Abd al-Aziz Al-Douri as a sober historian who considers the theory of nationalism in his writings.

I do not want go on in this regard, as I have explained it many times in several of my publications. However, regarding the "nationalist imaginings," I am not sure that our contemporary nationalist rhetoric has overcome its meanderings. It is necessary to intellectually "clear the accounts" from these imaginings and meanderings to establish an Arab rhetoric that is able to deal with reality and facts.

Rabeao: The nineties of the last century witnessed more than one call to "Arabism, farewell" on the argument that Arabism had become a corpse, and the wise is he who buries his dead, as Hazim Saghiah said in *Arabism, Farewell* and in *The Nationalists of the*

Arab East where he conducted a critical trial for the leaders of nationalist Arab thought, especially Michel Aflaq (who is obsessed by his Christianity, according to Saghiah). The question is, since you are considered one of the contemporary nationalist Arab intellectuals, do you see that the present situation, where Zionist occupation threatens to swallow all of Palestine and the American occupation of Baghdad, as well as the hopelessness overtaking contemporary Arab rhetoric, is pushing towards *Arabism, Farewell* or, as some see it, is pushing from the migration of Arabism to Arabism, or – in a more precise way – from the Arabism of romance, idealism, and ethnicity, as some see it, to an Arabism that is more open to the other, internally with the problems of minorities, and externally where the nationalist and Islamic rhetoric are identified in ideological perspectives with hatred towards both the occupying and imperialist West?

Al-Ansari: I would like to point out that, under the reign of narrow regional fundamentalist confrontations, nationalism only become extinct as a phenomenon in our minds. It is enough to look at the political map of our world today…Japan…India…China…Russia…. What are these? And the European Union came about only through the different nationalities and their interaction.

To surpass any specific examples as mentioned in your question, the phenomenon of the "the Arab hating himself" became repetitive and noticeable with the increasing regression of nationalism. In fact, denying facts is a terrifying trend in the Arab mind, especially among the "classical national intellectuals," (and their fundamentalist heirs and others who are not better anyway!). It is like the old saying, "It's a goat even if it flies!" This trend is responsible for the birth of a generation of almost illiterate party members who drafted "Arabism" and today, they are drafting

"Islam" within the small crucible of their illusions.

The problem with the "romanticism" of nationalism is not in its romanticism only, but in this schizophrenia from which it suffers with the Arab reality. This is what put us between the best principles and the worst conditions, in both nationalist and religious points of view. What is the explanation for this huge gap between the two? Where is the missing link?

There is no escape from "Arabism" except with Arabism that is true to itself and its reality, with openness to the problems of minorities that we have to face, like all our nationalist problems that were frozen by romanticism and nationalist idealism in the refrigerator…I mean the refrigerator of the denial of reality and escapism.

The new "Arabism" must accept the challenge for survival, and survival is for the fittest. If it survives, that is fine, and that is our destined gamble… and if it does not survive, then the truth deserves to be followed…. In the statements that have been lost and diminished of Michel Aflaq, his significant and correct statements, he says, "What is right stays above Arabism… Arabism must use right as its reference for arbitration…but unfortunately, those who call for Arabism, in reality, arbitrated in its name to injustice, despotism, and oppression, and denial of the facts and the "rights" on which truth is based…this is how they lost "human rights."

On the other hand, it is necessary to whisper in the ear of partners of our destiny – the minorities – to let them know and realize that they, in the darkest night, will only find an open, welcoming, kind heart – I mean, true Arabism, that is truthful to itself, as the meaning of the question implied.

Rabeao: In your above-mentioned masterpiece book, part of which found its way into Arab thought in the early 1980's through the series *Alim al-Marifah* (*world of knowledge*) under the title of *The Transformation of Thought and Politics in the Arab East between 1930 and 1970*, 1980, you ascertained reconciliation as being one of the most important components of Arab thought, which gained an historical track without reaching the state of decisiveness in Arab history and thought. In your opinion, intellectual religious reconciliation that was awoken during the early 1930's of the last century prevented the division of the Arab intellect between pure secularism and decisive fundamentalism. The reconciliation of the 1950's, led by the Free Officers and ending with Nassarism, came as a reaction to the challenge of this division, as well as to meet Eastern Arab needs to prevent tearing and polarization, as well as an expression of the disinclination of its societies towards – or maybe its incapability until now to confront – the sacrifice of the fundamental decisive choice, "the un-reconciliatory," between the basis of its inherited civilization and the fundamental modernization requirements that cannot be fragmented or for selective adaptation. The question is, if this reconciliation became a dividing mark in our cultural and political lives, to what extent can we overcome this reconciliation towards a fundamental solution enabling us to catch up with modern civilization? Would it be possible for this fundamental solution to find its way, especially after the failures of radical fundamental ideologies of the past decades of the last century? And would you say the reconciliation, that hides within it the spirit of conspiracies, is an explanation for the retrieval of Nassarism and its death by the death of its leader, meaning the death of the leader Jamal Abdul Nassar? And to what extent are the modern forms of reconciliation able to cope with contemporary Arab rhetoric while hindering the hoped-for renaissance? And then, to what extent is the relationship between reconciliation and the "moderate nation" which is explained by some as one type of reconciliation, although neither the Quran nor the books that explain it take that direction?

Al-Ansari: First of all, I would like to underline that I have studied reconciliation as a phenomenon, but I do not call for it. My remark that reconciliation is the dominant trend in the Arab region is only a description of a reality and not a call for an ideology, as understood by Dr. Nathir Al-Athma.

In the experiences of other nations, we do see possible and effective reconciliations, if they reached the level of synthesis that is able to survive. But there are reconciliations that are so frail, reaching fabrication, that they are subject to cracking in front of the boldness of logic and the seriousness of an event that puts it to the test. This is what happened to several Arab reconciliation attempts, especially after the June defeat and the explosion of the forbidden dialectic between the antagonists in Arab societies, including the revolutionary ones like the Nassarism experience.

You might notice that my book *Arab Thought and the Conflict of Antagonists* presented subtitles on its cover. It says, "How reconciliation contained the prohibited confrontation between fundamentalism and secularism, and the postponed decisiveness between Islam and the West," and "The diagnostics of the condition of indecisiveness in Arabic life and the containment of reconciliation for the prohibited dialectic."

But what is happening today in our Arab and Islamic World?

The prohibited conflict imposed itself at last between fundamentalism and secularism, and the postponed decisiveness is closer, the reconciliatory containment of the forbidden dialectic is no longer capable of "containment."

There is a fact in the dialectics of history that there has to be a conflict between antagonists that cannot be reconciled until we reach reconciliation or the targeted synthesis. The attempt to impose reconciliation on facts of the historical dialectic is a syncretism to gain time, but it does not stop the dialectic of history, and I am afraid that the Arab authorities, whether political, religious, or social, are trying until this day to gain time and to postpone the inevitable historical dialectic which includes conflict between the old and the new which cannot be avoided. If we fear this conflict, events of violence will come to us without equivocation. This is an inevitable result of avoiding "true" historical dialectic, by measurements of progress to the empty bloody cycles which more than one Arab society is going through today.

It is necessary to point out that "moderation" is an expression that does not move souls, but the call for "reform" is stronger. The thought of "moderation" that was presented by different ancient and modern philosophies, and which was considered by Greek philosophy as a virtue and moderation between the two vices, is similar to reconciliation. As a matter of fact, it is its essence and core, containing positive elements and others that are syncretic. We have to verify what we are talking about. "Moderation" is not a monopoly held by Islamic thought, as it is widespread. In addition, Islam is "moderate" in certain aspects and not in other aspects. It is important to establish ideologies and calls on solid facts in logic and reality. Otherwise, it would be susceptible to cracks once again.

Rabeao: Looking at your historical and intellectual track, extending for many decades and including numerous books, and, to be precise, from your masterpiece book *Arab Thought and the Conflict of Antagonists* to *Inquiry of the Defeat* in 2001 to your recent book, published at the beginning of the new millennium *Nassarism through a Critical Perspective* in 2002, Nassarism as a phenomenon and a practice, as well as the most significant historical embodiment of Arab romantic revolutionary nationalism, remained a subject in which you are exceptionally interested, if we can say that, from seeking for the reconciliatory project of the Nassarist movement, its tragic, heroic, cultural, romantic content to its progressive content and its ability to reconcile between the forbidden dialectic to ascertain that "conservative" reconciliation dealt the fatal blow to "Nassarism." Nassarism's project remained a carrier for reconciliation of renaissance between Islam and modernism. It did not exceed it nor overcome it. What is strange is that Nassarism, for you, represents a project that can be developed (*Inquiry of the Defeat*, p. 52) as the most capable project to overcome civil wars and their projects in the Arab region. The question is, do you see any new Arab renaissance initiative using Nassarism as a model? What is the way to develop Nassarism to develop a successful renaissance project capable of crisis management and transforming it into a comprehensive Arab renaissance?

Al-Ansari: I mentioned the lessons for the future in the introduction of *Nassarism through a Critical Perspective*, a book I published for the occasion of the fiftieth anniversary of the movement of June 23, 1952. "If Nassarism is the phenomenon of the individual ruler and the control of his authoritative systems, then this is a history that must be overcome by all Arab regimes. But if Nassarism is a stimulus for Arabs to build their progressive, modern identities with honor and freedom in this era, then this cannot be ignored in any project for the renaissance of Arabism and Islam where Egypt must be its leader."

I would like to stress the necessity of distinguishing between the new Arab self-awareness, the phenomenon of military coups, and the Nassarism phenomenon. It is true that Nassarism was born from the womb of a military coup d'etat, but it was an attempt to overcome and topple it, yet it failed in the end. Whoever takes power through a particular means (the army, the religious institution, tribal or sectarian fervor) will remain under the control of the "means" that gave him that power. These "means" will not relinquish their control even if the one they brought to power defeats them, and even if the one in control is Abdul Nassar!

These "means" with their machineries and centers of power remained practicing all they could, pressuring but without any direct open confrontation with the leader and his masses. Abdul Nassar was very sensitive towards criticism and contrary opinions in practicing authority (as long as the discussions remained under his control). He naturally was not a democratic liberal leader. He came after a weak factional democratic experience, though having a parliamentary constitutional aspect, and a higher ceiling regarding freedom of speech. However, the masses began to doubt it and believed in its corruption. It failed in reforming itself. Therefore, all the elements of change gathered against it. This is a very important lesson which I hope all Arab regimes benefit from and will seriously work on to reform themselves and to minimize the amount of corruption that rots them, and any regime that hesitates to do so will end. If reform is absent, revolution will take place. The targeted reforms must have an Arab identity card. Otherwise, they will end up holding foreign passports. That is the logic of history and modernity, and it will not be changed by the attempts of Arab official media!

Returning to the coup d'etat phenomenon, the Egyptian army, after the loss of Palestine in 1948, and its retreat to its capital, like the other Arab armies, was the most capable of mobilizing to avenge its honor.

As shown in numerous historical and documented indications, the 1952 Egyptian coup was not far from American influence against British domination of that time. Abdul Nassar himself, as an intelligent politician, "engineered" the utilization of this existing international situation.

But Abdul Nassar, with his historical vision, honesty, and sincerity towards the aspirations of the majority of his people and the Arab masses, improvised the script. Yes, he improvised the American script. Just as he had used the American-British conflict in the beginning, he tried to take advantage regionally and internationally of the American-Soviet conflict. He managed to achieve some success in this, but the Soviets were also playing their games behind the scenes with the American power that controlled the global economy and military supremacy. Moscow used the Egyptian card in the face of Washington to gain its own goals from the Americans. This is how Nassar paid the price for improvising the script and maintaining his independence in a world that was accelerating towards the loss of independence by small and medium-sized countries.

It is a long history…the most important issue being that the Johnson Administration took the decision in 1965 to hit Nassar. The Soviets were drawn into this "game" not to hit him but to bring him down to size, because, in their perspective, he was hindering the proletarian popular revolution's triumph in the Arab World, since he was petit bourgeois himself.

That was a wrong and pathetic analysis, to which most of the Arab Marxist parties were driven, as well as some other pro-Marxist wings of Arab nationalism. I do not call it the unification movement because it was not sincere in spite of its claims of nationalism going above and beyond Nassar.

After the strike of June, 1967, which was a devastating, crushing defeat, it became clear that Nassar's leadership was the true instrument of building the Arab progressive movement. The traditional opponents realized that completely, but their revolutionary allies realized that after it was too late. Their turn for elimination came, except for those who believed in the eternity of their "nation-state" entity and stopped improvising and went back to the script in one way or another.[1]

The important thing is that "the summer lost the milk"...the summer of June, 1967. [from a proverb meaning, what was good was lost.]

Everything in our world is urging the Arab to affiliate with such a "project," because we are in an era of grand entities where there is no place for midgets. As a matter of fact, there is no security for them! If the Nassarist unification project failed in that time, there are countless models in front of the Arab to choose, the most distinguished being the European Union project, if they are able to undertake that. The most important thing is that they "invent" a proper project for them and for the historical moment that they are passing through.

What did Egypt discover after the "Camp David" experience? And what did other Arab countries discover when they tried to take its role in vain?

Therefore, it is not the "Nassarism" of the project that is important, but its "unification." This is the goal for which Nassar struggled and improvised the script, but was dismissed from the arena! What is required is to benefit from this lesson, in thought and in application.

We should have no "illusion" in the current moment. The Arab region is moving towards further division and fragmentation.

But this is the required "objective" condition in theory, to hold onto the rope of Arab unification with a new vision and methodology. The end of the night will be...daylight!

I would like to add, without hesitation or ideological bias to anyone, that safeguarding Saudi integrity is a trust to be fulfilled by all Arab unificationists. We have had enough of our mutual political conspiracies.

Rabeao: From your book *Political Arab Makeup and the Signification of the Nation-State*, 1994, to *Political Crisis for the Arabs and the Position of Islam*, 1995, to *The Arab and Politics: Where is the Flaw? The Deep Root of the Failure*, 1997, we see that your interest is directed towards opening the "file" of the comprehensive political problems of the Arabs and the search for the deep root of the failure, and then a call for a scientific explanation that goes beyond weeping and depression, as you expressed it, and to go beyond the surface and what is current in Arab political rhetoric, going towards digging through the social geological layers that made the terrain and this historical political inheritance that still represents an impediment that prevents the discovery of the deep roots of the abeyance. The question is, to what degree have you succeeded in this digging through the layers of Arab political rhetoric and political awareness? To what extent have you succeeded in initiating a scientific explanation for our repeated political failures? What is the way to build a new Arab political reality? And is that possible? Is it possible for these excavations to prepare to build this new Arab political reality, which is different and gives us hope that it is possible?

Al-Ansari: Many nationalists and Islamists did not receive well these historical sociological "excavations" that I used as an approach in my books.

Many people told me they cause depression! This was described by Dr. Mohammed Amara, an Islamist scholar who was an ex-leftist, who said, "This is an analysis of reality by the methodology of chronic disabilities."

What I meant and still mean is to show objectively why our progressive unification projects failed and for reasons that do not go under the classification of self- or moral incrimination or hang our failure on the rack of "conspiracy." These would not have succeeded if it were not for the socially inherited barriers that need to be remedied, shattered, and removed. I wish that people like Dr. Amara would realize that one of our tragedies is our zealous language which sells optimism and promises in vain. This is also one of our "chronic disabilities" that we have to remedy and overcome!

One of the Arab intellectuals who was able to realize precisely what I targeted is Dr. Abdul Hamid Al-Ansari, (and the relationship between us is the relationship of readiness for intellectual exchange) who was Dean of the Faculty of Sharia and Law in Qatar University, and today is one of the Arab writers that we may agree or disagree with, but we can only respect his concern to be truthful to the self in judgment and evaluation.

He was able to show in transparency that which I am trying to show, the barriers that prevented our progress, diagnosing the truth and removing these barriers, not to make anyone despair, except maybe those who are searching for good news on cable TV that ends as soon as they are broadcast, and our situation stays the same, if not worse!

It has to be clarified that I abide by the method of analysis, but not to the results literally. These can be discussed and proven wrong, but by the same method of analysis, not by the method of wishing. I do not sell promises and illusions, but I search for the truth, which I might be wrong or right in reaching, like any other researcher, as it is not a holy sacred text, nor a "critique" that is above criticism.

My methodology is to go back to Ibn Khaldun to surpass him…he is still the closest in description for the historical and sociological facts and tribalism hindering progress and unification.

Twenty years ago, I called for Khaldunism and not Marxism (this with all my respect to the wise interpretations derived from Marxist sociology that still contains many bright spots that are beneficial and analytical for understanding the progress of history and modernity, in spite of the collapse of authoritarian communist regimes).

The problem of misunderstanding and communication between Khaldunism and Marxism is the problem of the distinguished Iraqi sociologist, Ali Al-Wardi, in his debate with Iraqi communists and their attack on him for fifty years! The man used to say, in all simplicity, that tribalism, for us, is not the feudalism the Marxists face in other societies. Wardi adds, "I hope I am wrong, and the communists are right!" This is the scientist's modesty, but the truth is something else. It was not by accident that Al-Wardi went back to Ibn Khaldun.

Rabeao: Whoever follows the contemporary Arab intellectual movement, starting from the first half of the 1980's of the last century, notices the call to bring together Arab intellectuals and decision-makers, to make peace between the intellectual and the prince, as expressed by Saad Al-Din Ibrahim in his writings about this problem. This was followed by many calls to bring about a new Arab partnership between the prince and the masses, as was expressed by Ghassan Salamé in his book *Towards a New Arab Social Contract,* published by the Center for Arab Unity Studies, and who was nominated as the successor of Saad Al-Din Ibrahim in the Arab Thought Forum in Amman. This was followed by many other calls, the last being yours, to have "a unified national front" in order to establish a civil and national society and to adopt a program of gradual reform. The field of reform, as you mentioned in your book *An Inquiry of the Defeat*, is the civilized field wherein all the rulers and their masses can "play" a friendly game where its goal is progress in harmony and peace. The question is, is disciplined Arab reform possible through a new Arab social partnership? Could the veil of Arab reform with the slogan of "reform" from the inside, be hoisted, under the pressure of exceptional external conditions, to turn into a true banner of reform under which all (the prince and the masses) can find shade? Or is it a worn veil that protects neither from the sun nor the cold? Do you notice, within this partnership, any concessions from the prince and his old and new guards to yield or to come down and play on the field of reform, or is it that the Arab rulers, like the kings of olden days, if they enter the "field," they corrupt it and humiliate the most honorable of its people? How do you evaluate what is happening and what has been accomplished on this issue, especially since you occupy a leading position in this matter?

Al-Ansari: We should distinguish between true reform and the "veil" of reform. The two possibilities are there, naturally. If it is a veil, then there is no value in it, and whoever hoists it will, by his own doing, come to regret it, because the movement of history and the will of nations do not joke and cannot be occupied with veils, except for a short time.

After pointing this out, we have to agree, rationally speaking, that reform has been the greatest "revolutionary" incentive throughout history. A revolution does not occur unless the door of reform is closed or becomes a veil. But revolution itself cannot be a magical remedy, and it has to go back to the logic of reform, as the French Revolution learned. After decades of revolutionary upheavals in France, from the "terrorism" of Robespierre and the execution of intellectuals by guillotine – because the revolution did not need them! – to the dictatorship of Napoleon and his European wars, France discovered that it had to reform its conditions through gradual democratic parliamentary methods. And that is what happened. The catastrophe of the French monarchical regime was its inability to reform itself at the right time (like the Arab monarchies that collapsed in the 1950's). As for Britain, it progressed democratically through radical democratic reforms over eight centuries – during which there was the failed dictatorship of Cromwell for a few years – while the country was ruled by a constitutional monarchy that continues to this day! Does Britain today live in backwards, despotic conditions? Do you need a revolution like the Arab "republic" revolutions, or do you see that its experience, as we can see, is still coping with time and progress? Why does our political rhetoric not "contemplate" this superlative constitutional monarchy in its progress and democracy?

The problem with the Arab revolutionary republicans and the conservative monarchists – on the same level – is that they are living an historical illiteracy in their political thinking, feeding their people literacy with these illusions. The reference to the kings in the Holy Quran should be understood on its true merits and within its historical frame. That holy verse, used and abused by the media of the Arab "republican" regimes while it was upholding their despotic rules, similar to those of the backward kings, was not meant to champion a monarchy against a republican regime, because at the time of its descent, all the regimes were monarchies whether they were despotic or not. What was meant is the rulers of those big nations in control to which the Arabs were not subject. It is not true that any republican revolutionary governor is better than any king at all. I do claim that King Faisal the First, the king of Iraq, was much better in terms of culture, vision, conduct, and humanity than some of the "revolutionary and republican" rulers of Iraq and the Arabs. This is not a testimony in favor of Imam Ahmad Hamid Al-Din, the former Imam of Yemen. The handicap of the traditional Arab regimes is that some of them, with their own incapability of reforming themselves, allow the gamblers to reform it by the harmful and common "revolutionary way" in our Arab World. This applies to the monarchies in both Egypt and Iraq. We are afraid it might apply to other monarchies. The message of thought should be delivered to whom it may concern – whether a monarch or a republican – in our present Arab moment with all that it holds. This message is either a true reform or a destructive revolution. Two options, and there is no third. The strange thing is that we hear all the Arab regimes, with all their differences, repeat today with one tongue: "Reform starts from the inside and does not come from the outside." Fine. Then why, sirs, did it not come from the inside in all this time, except for very few Arab countries that can be counted on one hand?

Rabeao: With the July 1982 defeat, when the Zionist state invaded Beirut, Edward Said regrets the absence of the term "defeat" in Arab political rhetoric. (Note from the translator: *The term "defeat" is used to refer to the 1967 war, while the defeat of 1982 is referred to as the "invasion."*) An expanded symposium was held under the supervision of the Center for the Studies of Arab Unity, to evaluate the Arab progressive movement, and more precisely, to evaluate the performance of the Arab Left, and the result of this evaluation was that the Arab Left (Ba'athist, Nassarist, Arab nationalist and communist) failed in achieving two things, independent development and democracy. In other words, not for a bite nor for democracy. In your book *The Arabs and Politics: Where is the Flaw?* published in 1998, you said that regimes that came after national independence betrayed the trust when it was entrusted on the country and its assets, and it lacked the capability when it failed to establish an option of renaissance aimed at catching up with western civilization or modern times, in general. The question is, what is your evaluation of the performance of the Arab Left? Do you see that this Left possesses the capability for a culture of reevaluation that can limit the backwardness and become a gate to discuss the deep root of the abeyance? What is your evaluation for what has been accomplished within this frame of work?

Al-Ansari: There are inherited social obstacles that the Arab Left and Right keep producing. I can assume that the Arab Left, in some circumstances – and it is a Left that sometimes does not hold the characteristics of the Left except in name – destroyed and lost what the traditional "Right" achieved in some Arab societies, such as modest educational, economic, and political programs before the cycle of military coups, especially in some centers of Arab weight, like Egypt and Iraq.

The historical predicament is that the incapability of the "Right" to proceed with reform, as required by the movement of history, and because of its chronic corruption, the Arab masses lost their patience, especially after the 1948 defeat. And they thought the "Left" was the answer. The result was to reproduce historical backwardness that needs to be tackled and remedied in our societies, Left and Right. It became common to us that any revolution of the masses was a progressive revolution, and this is not true. We have to be sure whether the main power within the revolution is progressive, or it is backward, which will reproduce backwardness in the name of the revolution this time!

The experiences of the Japanese renaissance, and then the Chinese, having parallel to them the Indian, how do we categorize them, Right or Left? We remained for a long time repeating that imperialism supports the Japanese Right, and that China is the leader of the Left (in opposition to the Soviet Left, of course) and that India is liberal and bourgeois and is not a model to be followed!

In the three big successful Asian cases, there has been an "historical renaissance" and a transformation from the traditional community to a modern society, according to the specificity of each of those nations, by Right, by Left, by moderate liberalism…terminologies that the Arab ideologists are still fighting about. But the renaissance nations "achieved," overcoming the Byzantine ideological argument. May God have mercy upon the soul of Shakir Mustafa, the distinguished nationalist historian who wondered a quarter of a century ago why did they achieve, "those Asians," while we did not? What is required is a movement seeking knowledge and an intellectual renaissance of reevaluation that is capable of thinking Right and Left. As a matter of fact, that is capable of freeing itself from the ignorance of the Arab Right and Left, as neither carries much credibility.

Rabeao: In your book *The Arabs and Politics: Where is the Flaw?* you stopped at what you called the judicious remark of Malik Bennabi, who spoke about the predisposition of imperialism (and its equivalent), which now a lot of people talk about. You generalized that to say that there are several predispositions (the predisposition for foreign interference, the predisposition for dictatorship, the predisposition for shattering and dismantling, the predisposition for myths and illusion, etc.) The question is, is imperialism the only truth in our contemporary history? Does this mean that there is no renaissance without imperialism? Are these predispositions becoming part of our fundamental characteristics alone? Then, don't you think that talking too much about these numerous predispositions are perceived judgments that make the possibility of our renaissance impossible? Can we not say that this rhetoric is a living expression of an ideology for despair that you had repeatedly refuted and tried to overcome? Then what does this rhetoric represent after the occupation of Baghdad and the return of imperialism and colonialism from the eastern gate of the Arab World?

Al-Ansari: As I pointed out, the purpose is to demonstrate the objective "obstacles" which, until now, prevented us from achieving the goals of the Arab renaissance, as well as all of the various national, nationalist, and Islamist movements in the Arab countries. These are legitimate objectives. But why were they not achieved? And why does the backwardness continue in Arab life?

There has to be a scientific explanation for not being able to achieve these goals. There has to be frankness in this regard, even if it is painful. Otherwise, we are just hiding our heads in the sand.

What is the meaningful intellectual alternative to confront the crisis of failures? Should we keep playing the record of "conspiracy" and the Zionist and imperialist powers? Naturally, these are avaricious hostile powers, but had we not already discovered that? Until when are we going to continue, after many efforts and disasters, to explain imperialism by saying it is imperialism, and Zionism by saying it is Zionism? Do we expect these powers to behave in any other way than conspiracy, betrayal and evil? Why does our Arab rhetoric remain only a repetition of the faults of these powers? The question is, what can be done about it? And before anything else, what can be done to build the Arab self and Arab power? I mean, constructive work, not emotional screaming! Are the Arab authors required to continue "promising" rosy dreams? Until when? Does the attempt to say what we believe is closer to the truth represent despair? Naturally, the shining superficial rhetoric of optimism cannot bear that because it reveals its weakness. But again, what is the alternative? Should we continue self-deception, justifying it simply by saying, "We waited for them to come from the east, but they came from the west"? We are still repeating this logic, so is it permissible to continue in this verbal triteness like this?

Is not "the occupation of Baghdad and the return of colonialism and imperialism through the eastern gate of the Arab World" a reminder and new warning that we do not face our issues "intellectually and practically" in the required way and at an adequate level?

Were the prevention of the occupation of Baghdad and safeguarding the eastern gate issues that the U.S. was expected to take care of? Or should Israel do it? Why was this not expected seriously and wisely? Why did the officials not warn about it?

If we proved again verbally that these are hostile powers, then what is the "accomplishment" that we achieved? Are we incapable of action? Have we seen international powers, either in the past or the present, in which some are ascetic and abstinent while others are avaricious? Does not each power have its own coveted things? So what is the explanation for this naivety? Why do we hang our incapability on the hanger of others who are neither angels nor saints?

Nothing can scratch your skin better than your own nails. Do you not agree with me that this extended to become a tongue instead of a nail for the majority of the Arabs?! For the truth and history, the "eastern gate" collapsed on August 2, 1990, by the attempt to annex Kuwait by force. For history, too, the women of Kuwait used to donate their gold and jewelry for the Iraqi war efforts [against Iran]. Many of the children of the Gulf bear the name of "Saddam." This "Arabic condition" that emerged at the "eastern gate" for the first time between Iraq, the Gulf, and the Arabian Peninsula was not to the liking of the controlling powers in the region. And what is strange is how Saddam ended this accomplishment for Iraq and the Arabs. Is Arab awareness able to contemplate...just contemplate on that? Or is it going to remain part of the "unspoken issues" under the dominant emotionalism?

Rabeao: Within the framework of your sociological excavations inside the Arab political mind, you stopped repeatedly at the term "tribal solidarity" as it represents one of the most important components of the Arab political mind, which prevents its launching and its establishment on logical political awareness. You said that, "in the beginning was the tribe, and it still is." The question is, does the tribe still represent a sociological and developmental barrier preventing the construction of a modern civil society? And what is more important is, how can we explain the continuation of the tribe and tribalism together in our modern thought and in our civil organizations (parties and societies), and why did our radical parties fail to overcome the tribe and tribalism? The question that remains is, in the absence of serious studies of nomadic sociology and political sociology – except for the work of Mohammed Abd Al-Jabri regarding *assibiya* and the state, which you praised – to what extent can we straighten out our impressions that we convey about the tribe, either in our developmental rhetoric or in our rhetoric of renaissance? On the basis that tribalism is a political and organizational unit, how can we explain its rejection and its resistance to occupation? And how can we explain that while we have the current situation in Iraq in front of us?

Al-Ansari: The tribal organization represented the only living opportunity for individuals who lived as shepherds and moved in an arid, dangerous desert, seeking grass for their herds, which were their only possible "means" of living, since they transformed their products into dairy, meat and wool, as was pointed out by the philosopher of history, Arnold Toynbee, among others.

This tribal organization based on blood ties and a unified dynasty – whether it is true or assumed – was an alternative to the rules of the state, city, and law. These laws can only be established by sedentary people living in one place, where the experience of urbanization accumulates and develops until it is complete. The word "village" in its Arabic root – as well as its Quranic one – is not the small rural unit as we understand it today. A village is a sedentary, urban settlement. (Note from translator: *In Arabic, the word "village" is derived from the verb that means "to settle."*) Hence, Mecca is described as "the mother of all settlements." The nomad who spent his life on the move would mock the urban dwellers for being settled and lacking the courage of the nomads. Nomad women would refuse to marry sedentary men.

The Islamic movement represented a revolution against nomadism. Islam worked with all the instructions and laws to urbanize the nomads as a required condition to accept their full conversion to Islam. The nomads are more infidel and hypocritical than the infidels of the urban areas, as documented by the best explanations of the Quran. "The nomads say, 'We believe.' Say, 'Ye have no faith; but ye (only) say, 'We have submitted our wills to Allah,' for not yet has faith entered your hearts.'" (Sura 14: *Al-Hujurat*) After the migration to Al-Medina, returning to a nomadic life after settlement in the city was considered a major sin. The companions of the Prophet prayed to God to save them from such a lifestyle.

It is clear here that faith – according to the Quranic concept – has its urban sociological requirement. What is odd is that this insinuation was dropped from jurisprudence and intellectual thought in the history of Islam until our day. But this is the Quran, and our preachers use just a word from it to pass judgment on what is forbidden and what is allowed. So what about these verses in regards to the dialectics between nomadism and urbanization in the Quran?

Do you believe in some of it and do not believe in some? And what is the punishment for whomever does that?

We go back to the tribe, which was the boundaries of the [social] entity, which was equivalent to the boundaries of the state and its soil. Moving from one land to another was an ordinary common matter. Territorial boundaries were not forbidden to cross. But there were new boundaries that became a symbol of nobility, the boundaries of honor, blood and dynasty within the entity of the tribe, which no stranger was allowed to violate as in stable countries where national boundaries cannot be violated.

Honor before the land? This is the law of the nomadic tribe. It was, and still is. From it come the "crimes of honor."

Islam fought tribal zealotry. The Prophet, peace upon him, warned against its detriments, saying, "Leave it. It is rotten." Islam in its practical reality absorbed the tribal organization and benefited from it in the planning of cities and in the organization of armies. In spite of the great difference between the tribal means of production and the urban one, the tribal bond remained a reality and became the only moral bond that could cross the living boundaries between nomadic life and urban life. A part of it might have stayed here while another part stayed there, as happened in the biggest tribe, the "Quraish," and the two parts would exchange "calls for emergency" whenever the tribe needed that. What is noticed is that the "identity" of the tribe became the reference for ruling in Islam, because the biggest question in *Al-Saqifah* after the death of the Prophet, peace upon him, was "Who has more right for governing and authority, the Ansar (the Prophet's supporters in Al-Medina) or the Quraish?"

The answer was ready, whether its attribution to the Prophet, peace upon him, was correct or not. Then the problem became: Which branch of the Quraish had more right to become the successor? No historian can escape the truth that the historical conflict between the Sunnite and Shiite started when one Quraishi branch was favored over another with regard to the right of succession! Even the rise of "Al-Khawaraj" has its tribal roots. It started from that, and we can use this as a measurement of what came afterwards. So do we exaggerate when we say, "Search for the tribe!"

Great states in Islam were established on the basis of tribal alliances. When the alliance began to crumble, the tribe remained as the base. If the tribe itself crumbles, the conflict begins between its main branches and clans. This phenomenon summarizes long chapters in the political history of Arabs and Islam.

For this reason, it is possible to say that the Arabs did not live within the crucible of one continuous stable historical state, as did the Chinese within the crucible of the historical Chinese state. This swing was continuous in the history of the Arabs between the condition of statehood and no state. That is why the tribe remained the only continuing moral entity, at least in the soul of its people, between nomad and urban areas in front of the challenges that resulted from the absence of state authority.

These are observations and historical facts. We either make sure scientifically that it is correct, or say it is wrong, by seeking judgment through the approach of rationality and research. But to say that pointing out this creates despair and affects Arab morale and other self and ideological considerations, will not change the truth, and will only lead to self-deception and hiding our heads in the sand of wishing that gets to be blown away every time a crisis and calamity occurs. This wishful thinking is responsible for the empty circles that we live in today with no results.

After all this on the subject of the tribe, we have to face one of the realities of modern times, and that is the establishment of the state and its development – as a political materialization of a state –

requires that the priority be toward loyalty and the belonging of citizenship. The tribe as a social and moral reality, and even as a virtue, can remain, but under the submission of the logic of the state and its statehood "that has to be modern and constitutional." If the absolute priority remains to the tribe in loyalty and belonging over the country and the state, then it is just going backwards and diminishing the project of the country and the state.

This is one of the realities of modern times. If we do not face it with frankness and clarity, we remain moving in place.

The Iraqi situation, after the occupation or before it, is not an exception. It is not a secret that the ruling partisan elite, before the occupation, were all members of one tribal branch and, like these tribal branches, will remain influential in the current political scene. This matter needs long-term construction of the entity of the country and its statehood to overcome tribalism, either on our eastern gate, or other gates!

There are no fast magical solutions for any problems in the movement of history, and I repeat, that shouting on cable TV will not convince history to change its course.

Rabeao: There is a lot of democratic noise that the Arab arena is witnessing. It cannot actually be described as anything but that, accompanied by magical talk on democracy as the key and the door for everything. This noise attempts to establish democracy undermining the Arab state. Let us say, undermining the Arab authority because it is the one that contains the state. This is what you indicated in your book *Political Arab Makeup and the Signification of the Nation-State* in 1994, one of your books on political excavations. This led you to wonder, as part of your works criticizing the political mind, is it possible to establish a stable democracy before establishing a fully developed state? The question is, what is your evaluation of the Iraqi condition, which was meant to be a model to be followed as in the writings of Fouad Ajami in *Iraq and the Future of the Arabs* which seeks to establish a democracy outside the borders of the state? What is more important from an establishing point of view is, if the weak Arab authority is what contains the state, what are the chances of the Arabs building a democratic model within the borders of the state, especially when you call on the Arabs to start the reform of their states first?

Al-Ansari: The issue of internal reform will remain, in each Arab country, the issue of all issues. Any correct beginning has to start from there.

Internal reform should not be linked to the general noise in the Arab or the international arena, even if you are talking about democracy with all its facets. Internal reform in each Arab country should start by examining the existing specific practical problems in that country, whether it is the backwardness of education, corruption of administration, or weakness of the economy, etc. or all of these together.

It is not possible for democracy to sprout and develop and sustain itself if the basic problems remain in any society. The test of democracy itself is the extent of its ability to solve these problems and contradictions. Otherwise, the society will bypass it for another system. That is what gave the excuse for the phenomenon of military coups in the 1950's to become the savior in the eyes of people in front of the incapability and corruption of the previous Arab regimes, which had been classified as democratic, constitutional, parliamentary, and liberal.

One of the shortcomings of the dominant Arab attitude is its tendency for generalization, simplification, and reduction.

The Arab intellectuals enjoy debate regarding "post-modernity." But, did we understand how modernity began before shifting to "post-modernity?"

I started with the methodology of "status quo" which looks into the existing conditions of the status quo and the current reality of society first, without generalizations!

But our intellectuals have a lot to say against the status quo, which is a methodological concept after the development of the way of thinking. But I am afraid that some of those got an "F" in the lessons of the status quo from its emergence at the beginning of the scientific revolution until now.

Why do you only ask about the Iraqi case? The Iraqi condition is only an example of many similar Arab conditions in its sociological base and political formation.

What is odd is that we only notice danger when we see a foreign flag, since it embodies occupation.

There are conditions under the national flags that prepare for foreign occupation in one way or another, so why do we not notice these and talk about them?

If Fuad Ajami, from another point of view, calls for the establishment of democracy outside the state, he is dreaming. I am not even going to answer him. But I am going to refer him in this regard to the objective analysis of Abdallah Al-Arwi, from whose writings I benefited in this matter.

In regards to the weakness of authority and of the Arab state and the possibility of its inability to establish democracy, this is an open history and an existing challenge. It is for the social Arab powers to prove themselves in reforming the authority and state.

And this is the test for any project of reform, at the end of the day.

We should not wait to achieve all this in the lifetime of our generation. But we have to try to plant good seeds, and to put the correct foundation, but the completion of the results and the harvest is subject to many objective parameters. As man can reform whatever is under his control or whatever his hand can reach, then he will be more able to control what he wants to achieve. To insist on liberating Palestine from a distance, to the last Egyptian soldier, and to defend Baghdad to the last Iraqi soldier, where did this enthusiastic watching take us to while our situation under our feet is more than bad?

Rabeao: The mid-nineties of the last century witnessed more than one call to doubt the usefulness of the intellectual. What was the use of someone being an intellectual? Everybody talks about the illusions of intellectuals (Ali Harb) and the focus is one criticizing the progressive intellectuals who have been shot with more than one bullet of mercy. Also, increasing criticism has been aimed at the debate mentality that dominated Arab intellectual culture and prevented any creative interaction, leading to the division of the existing Arab intellectual culture into intellectual militias, as someone described it. The talk increased about the death of the preacher. Within the same talk about the end of the preacher and the death of the intellectual, some said magical praises about the thinker who was considered the heir of the intellectual. The question is, where do you place your book *The Suicide of the Arab Intellectuals* (1988), which was explained as an invitation to bypass the role of the intellectual and to endorse the role of the thinker. The question which we need you to clarify is, what are your views on the role of the intellectual and his ability to tell the truth? What is the capability of the Arab intellectual to renew the Arab intellect, and the role of the thinker in this renewal process, though you described him as being a weak and fragile creature? Do you really see that thinkers are the heirs of the intellectuals, after their failure in achieving that which was expected from them, or because they betrayed the objectives that they dedicated themselves to, as some critical studies say?

Al-Ansari: "Faith-based ideological" Arab parties started within the atmosphere of school and university, meaning the educational environment, while the masses were outside the school walls. In the past, preachers were the protectors of the truth and guidance in the face of the rulers in the name of the silent subjects. From here, the feeling was magnified for the role of the intellectual and the thinker, in the past and in the present.

We have to realize that the movement of history depends on the effect of effective social powers in all countries and not just the "ideas." If the power of the French middle classes – and these of the holders of the torch of development in Europe – had not comprehended the ideas of their enlightened and encyclopedic thinkers, what would their role have been? If the Russian Bolshevist Leninist organization had not adopted the ideas of Marx, would Marxism have any mention in the memory of the world?

This is the way of thinking of Ibn Khaldun! He said in his *Introduction*, "The revolutionists – from the public or the preachers – who are working to change corruption make themselves vulnerable to mortal doom. The conditions of kings and states are strong and stable, and cannot be shaken and its buildings collapsed, except by strong demands made by the loyalty of tribes and clans that stand behind them." Or, naturally, what he means is effective social powers.

On the other hand, we have to realize that not everyone who

sits in a coffee shop or a forum and argues on general issues becomes an intellectual. The real intellectual, meaning thinker or scholar, is a producer of knowledge, first and last. By it, he stands or falls. And we should not confuse him with the fighter, the activist, or the politician. He can be that if he decides to. However, he is not then producing knowledge, but taking a brave position like the others. We should not burden the intellectual with more than he can bear. Societies change with their effective powers, not by students, teachers and intellectuals.

Rabeao: In the aftermath of all the defeats, and there are a lot to which this nation has been subjected, there is a search for the sociological root of that defeat, and they are explained by the traditionalism of Arab society. This is what explains the call, for many years, for the burning of the dying pelican, meaning traditional Arab society, in a way similar to the Marxist call to burn Indian society and redraw it anew in a way that looks like the Western image. As far as the backwardness of Arab society, and there are people who talk about the discipline of backwardness, you spoke, at the beginning of the millennium, about the backwardness of awareness, and you classified it into three interrelated categories, "social backwardness that leads to backwardness of political endeavors, the mental backwardness that leads to backwardness of intellect, culture, and scientific innovation, and last, to moral backwardness that leads to backwardness of conduct. This explains your later call to form a "Front to Confront Arab Backwardness." The question is, do you see the possibility of overcoming Arab backwardness in the near future to catch up with modernization or is Arab backwardness like an immortal backwardness germ, as claim some pessimistic scholars filled with the ideology of despair?

Al-Ansari: In social sciences, there are no immortal backwardness genes. Whoever says or believes that makes himself a victim of superstition. This self-doubt comes to us from our lack of self-confidence due to defeats and retreats – and they are numerous, as you said – when we are faced with serious analysis of our reality and its inheritance.

Naturally, we are not promised national celebrations soon, as we have been promised by some regimes in their propaganda, and as some of us, from different categories and positions in our society, look forward to. We must have the tenacity of the generations that were renaissanced on the promises of "statement number one" on the radio (*Hamzah: the statement Arab radio employed to state that a revolution had taken place*), or the shining or inciting propaganda whose podium still exists today.

Backwardness as measured by the epoch movement and progress of humanity, east and west, still exists in our Arab societies. Our people proved that they don't lack courage of sacrifice and that they reject foreign occupation in all its forms. But we are required to have the ability for alternative internal self-construction and the ability to resist internal tyranny as well, instead of transforming its bloody personnel into heroes in the public imagination that is drowning in illusion. This is the real battle, to resist backwardness in all forms. We have, from our experiences in resisting the enemies, honorable pages, but I look forward to an honorable page showing our ability to build modern civilized constructions, and not to come up with excuses on the glory of the past, because imperialism leaves from the door of resistance just to enter from the window of backwardness.

Comparative observations become very important. For several decades of the twentieth century, everything modern that entered China panicked its stomach, while its rival Japan grew more powerful with the same things. But China took its ultimate decision after that, bypassing the worries of backwardness and the Ideology of despair, to the battle for construction. This can happen to us! China witnessed even "terrorism" in conditions similar to ours, as I wrote lately. The matter that indicates that the phenomenon of terrorism should be studies out the domain of the confrontation between Islam and the West.

Rabeao: It can be said that you are one of the first Arab intellectuals who called for the study of the Japanese phenomenon back in the early eighties, when you published important research introducing the Japanese civilization that found its way into your book *The World and the Arabs in the Year 2000*. You visited Japan and established close relationships with Japanese in order to get better acquainted with this phenomenon. These writings were explained by us that it is an attempt to bypass the gap between us and the West, to have the openness that was referred to by Anwar Abd Al-Malik as "the wind of the East," sending warmth to us after getting bloody from the trembling of the West and its endless wars. But, after two decades or more, you went back to evaluate this experience in two articles published in "Al-Hayat" newspaper on February 23, 2004, to talk about the weak Japanese in the Arab East and in the Arab World in general. Even more than that was the warning against the Asian danger when you said, "We waited for them from the West, but here they come from the East." The question is, what is your evaluation of the Japanese experience as of now? What is your evaluation of the Arab studies of the Japanese phenomenon where several conferences were held and many books published in this field, and what is the reality of the dangers that Japan and the southeastern Asian countries represent against the Arab World, especially the Arabian Gulf?

Al-Ansari: I still think that it is important to have comparative studies of the experiences of Japan, India and China, in the Asian East, which I consider the "other East." It is not the East of wonders and strange things that some Oriental studies hinted at and we believed. It is unfortunate that serious intellectuals, on the level of Taha Hussain and Salama Musa, fell hostage to this direction of thought. They tried to cut any connection between the Arab East and the Asian East, not connecting it with Western tradition, and considering the Far East as the "East" of myths and the unknown, far from logical reality. But this other East proves the opposite today. Where is the myth in Japanese technology, the achievement of China, and the Indian Silicon Valley? Isn't the opposite the truth? I mean, the preciseness of the mind and the hand and fingertips to the minutest details of knowledge and its application.

That is what's behind the rise of these countries and their competition to the West in their scientific and practical approach. We have to overcome the myths and dervishism of the East. I'm afraid we will remain that East.

What happened in Japan, as I pointed out in my "second" analysis, is what happened in all capitalist economies with cycles of ups and downs. Some of our ideologists are waiting for the collapse of Japan as just an American "capitalist" pocket to confront the Soviet Union. The historical reality says that Japan had all the necessary requirements for development and progressiveness since it opened itself to modernization. Even while it was under American Occupation, for the first time in its history, and looked as though it were surrendering to the occupation, in reality it was "resisting" in its own way. It used the strategic American umbrella to build a technological economy that invaded America and the West, and the whole world on their own turf.

Naturally, the Japanese are not angels. Japanese power is a power that has its own calculations like everyone else, outside of the duality of good and evil which still dominates our naïve way of thinking.

Arab studies in regards to Japan and the Asian phenomena are numerous, but they did not yet mature theoretically. I find it strange that the nationalist intellect and the Islamic intellectual awakening remain outside the domain of these vital experiences as if they don't exist. This ignorance is on the level of intellectual scandal!

And why? Because we have this overwhelming scary and deadly feeling that we are totally "different" from others and that we are from another planet. And that is a catastrophe.

As long as we don't reach a conviction that we are a nation like other nations, having positive and negative sides, and this nation is not beyond criticism and objective analysis – as long as we don't reach this modest conviction – we will remain in a world of illusion. "May God have mercy on a nation that knows its own capabilities," and I mean specifically contemporary Arabs, good and bad, without hiding under the cloak and turbans of our ancestors. We have to expose our heads to the sun, the sun of the truth, the sun of the epoch we live in. Did we accomplish any intellectual and civilized achievements when we called the Iranians "the Magus Persians" and when we called the westerners "bandits?"

Danger, whether it comes from East or West, will always remain a danger if the one confronting it does not have self-immunity. It goes without saying that Japan, China, and India have important experiences worth looking at, and these, like other nations of the East, as we said, and have their own calculation. They are not charities to help and rescue the helpless.

In the early twentieth century, the Egyptian national movement thought of France as the country of revolution and freedom against England, the country of aggression and imperialism. Shortly, they were awakened to the rosy agreement between France and Britain to divide the influence in North Africa so that England could have Egypt and France would have the Arab West.

Today we comfort ourselves that some European countries are good with virtues that will stand in the face of American evil.

It is the duality of good and evil that we have to free our minds from so that our minds can understand the truth regarding the "Asian dangers" that we are confronted with. Everything is relative in sciences, even in humanities. Once again, I'm afraid our minds do not enter the stage of the "status quo!"

Rabeao: In the early eighties, you expressed an unprecedented concern about the dialogue between the Arab East and the Arab West and you wrote a series of articles on this topic in *Al-Doha* magazine. One of the noticeable titles was *The Sun of the Arabs Shines on the Arab West,* which precedes in a similar way to the book of Zaghred Hounka, *The Sun of the Arabs Rises from the Arab West*. It seems you were happy and excited about the intellectual renaissance in the Arab West, which would foresee the birth of a new renaissance. You wrote in your book about the intellectual interaction between the Arab East and the Arab West in 1992. You went further in the beginning of the millennium and, within your inquiry of the defeat, you wrote a chapter in your book *The Inquiry of Defeat*, on "an Arab West taking the reins from an irresolute Arab East." You praised the efforts of Abdullah Al-Arwi and his distinguished work, which had been noticed by the Arab East at an earlier stage, but this chapter contained a sharp attack on Al-Jabri and showed bias toward George Tarabishi.

The question is, do you still see a place for the resurrection of the (Arab) nation through the resurrection of one of its wings, meaning the Arab West? Is it true that the intellectual renaissance in the Arab West cuts into the stagnation of the Arab East and its ideological tendency? Does the procedural division between the loquacious and conversant Arab East and the objective and analytical Arab West, as Al-Jabri said, have more historical and intellectual reality? And if Al-Jabri is one of the knights of this West Arab renaissance, then how can your judgment of it be sound while you attack Al-Jabri's work, except for his book, *Al-Asabiyyah (clanship) and the State*, which you praised as one of his most important books? And don't you see that this type of debate, overwhelmed by a rivalry that has to end in a knockout in order to win, is futile?

Al-Ansari: My comparison between the Arab East and Arab West is limited to comparing current cultural conditions that can change here and there. I'm not here to pass judgments that are general, decisive, and eternal, like the ones made by Al-Jabri on the "loquacious and conversant Arab East and the objective and analytical Arab West." This is similar to my talks about Arab social barriers at a particular stage in history, understood by others as passing a final judgment of backwardness!

I still think that Al-Arwi in his objectivity in explaining the basic concepts of the mind, history and the state is the closest to the requirement of the current Arab stage. Georges Tarabishi, in his reply to Al-Jabri, dug the graves for Al-Jabri's point of view in his reference book *The Critique of the Critique of the Arab Mind*. (Hamzah: Al-Jabri's book is entitled *The Critique of the Arab Mind*.) Therefore, Tarabishi is the true champion of the critique of the Arab mind.

Regarding my reservations concerning the "critique" of Al-

Jabri, I was very precise and detailed in my book *Inquiry of the Defeat*. If there is one correction, it has to be made point by point, not by a knockout, as you say. I'm afraid that the refusal of Mr. Al-Jabri to respond to this critique detailed and precisely, and categorizing their personalities and not their intellect, cancels the other and establishes the culture of the "knockout," which I agree with you, threatens any culture to the core.

Rabeao: With the prevalence of the dominant doctrine that establishes the divisions and historical cultural confrontation between the West and Islam, which led some in the West to talk about the confrontation of civilizations while leading those in Islam to impossible equations (either us or them) you worked on igniting a positive utopia, foreseeing the possibility of a renaissance, and depending on a Quranic point of view of international changes based upon your own explanation of the Sura *Al-Rum* (*The Romans*). What captures one's attention is the increase of this positive utopia that foretells a renaissance. I specify, for example, Hassan Hanafi, in his book *Introduction to the Science of Occidentalism*, which draws a cycle of seven stages for a renaissance where the tracks of the "I" and the tracks of the "other" run in exchangeable lines. If the cycle of the "I" is at the top, then the cycle of the "other" is at the bottom. This complete cycle takes seven centuries, and is a historical destiny. The question is, do these utopias represent a form of running away to the front and a differentiating mark in this regards? Or is it within the context of the political doctrine of renaissance, establishing itself in what is mythological and holy, and this is a characteristic of the political mind on the long historical track, as concluded by Regis Dubray in his points of view and his critique of the political mind?

Al-Ansari: First of all, and in reference to the Quranic point of views for the international changes, my remark is limited to the core of the Islamic movement from an historical point of view in addition to its religious point of view, and it was an urbanized, civilized movement at the core. The Quranic verse, "The Roman Empire has been defeated in a land close by: but they, (even) after (this) defeat of theirs will soon be victorious." (Sura 30: *Al-Rum*) alludes to bringing in the Arabs into international interactions to prepare themselves to carry the civilized message of Islam to the world surrounding them.

What I mentioned in my book *A Quranic View of International Changes* did not exceed the frame of this meaning. It has nothing to do with the expected utopia of the Arabic renaissance. I have to clarify that the title of the book might have led some people to think I'm trying to ride the religious wave. What I meant is for this wave to reduce its flow behind the supernatural and wonders, and to look at the movement of history from a Quranic point of view based upon the understanding of God's laws of nature in the universe and scientific and realistic adaptation with its logic.

That's why, when I published the second edition of my book, I was careful to assure, in its introduction: "This book is not an attempt to ride the religious wave and to put on a turban, like some might have thought upon publication of the first edition. For those who want to ride that wave, there are several procedures and tricks that go beyond the intellectual issues for this book…

"As Islamic studies were monopolized by self-proclaimed religious scholars and preachers of political Islam, who would not allow individual Muslims to contemplate their own religion, this is an attempt, by my humble person, to challenge this "ban" without a turban or a beard!"

Is it a "sin" for Muslims – with no beards or turbans – to

contemplate Islamic studies?

This is what makes this book an experimental attempt to search for a common language – thought and expressed – between the two opposite directions confronting contemporary Arab life: the religious and the modern – as they are called – according to whatever issues are put in front of Muslims.

Our Arabic language had been divided into two, a special language for modernists and one only for traditionalists. There has been no common reference anymore – not in expression nor in thinking – between the two "camps" which we have forgotten both belong to Islam!

Is it possible that we – as Muslims – can go back to a common agreed-upon language to determine what exactly it is that we "disagreed upon?"

A Quranic View of International Changes is an attempt to communicate with the two parties – in a language of the Quran and modern times – but without camouflaging any of it...with a turban...or a hat!

On the other hand, I'm not keeping it a secret that I'm not pessimistic regarding the renewal of the Arab renaissance, in spite of others' conclusions of despair concerning sociological vision and the possibilities in the current inherited Arabic formation that led us to where we are now and we haven't yet been able to bypass completely.

I believe that there are several Arabic examples of scientific, literary, and accumulated development that are multiplying in the Arabic arena which haven't yet been continuously bridged, but they are like dispersed "islands" in the Arabic ocean. We have to build the bridges to connect them. What hides these examples and successes is the Arab political incapability in Palestine and Iraq, and the incapability, too, of practicing successful politics in most of the Arab countries. As I have already stated in many books, the political crises broke the back of Islamic civilization from the beginning, in spite of its being a beautiful and civilized civilization in intellectual and physical development. This civilization has continued to suffer from political "anemia," and we are still suffering from it.

But in regards to historical mythology and what is associated with it of seven centuries – or any seven cycles up and down – I do not believe in it, and I do not trust the conclusions based upon it, whether it was discussed by Dr. Hassan Hanafi or others, with my respect to his intellectual efforts. If Regis Dubray found, along the long historical track, the establishment of the political mind based upon mythology, is it possible to say that the current European political mind is filled with these sanctities?

Rabeao: With the expansion of the phenomena of current resurrection movements, and I mean the phenomenon of political Islam, there has been an increase in political explanations that interpret things with a conspiracy mentality, and economic explanations that limit it to a bundle of misery and poverty, making that the reason for the conditions of social misery and poverty. What is noticeable is the domination of the ideological vision in explaining these movements that stands on negating these movements by passing more ideological judgments. What's noticeable in your book *The Inquiry of Defeat*, is that in your explanations and points of view on that, you appear to be worried, not only in your views, but in your rejection of the sociological explanation for the birth of these movements, while ascertaining that they are "an existing fact in this moment of history" which cannot be ignored. Here we go back to the same questions that you previously confronted, "Does this phenomenon, though dangerous, own the elements of success and establishment? How much do you think are true these analyses published by centers of research in the West on the failure of political Islam? To what extent does the political conduct of the West and the politics of double standards that the United States carries before and after the eleventh of September help in expanding the base of political Islam?

Al-Ansari: I don't think it's possible to reject the sociological basis and explanation for any social or religious movement (including the major religions, as we notice in the issue of nomads and civilization since the beginning of the Islamic message). I repeatedly warned against accepting the monopoly of Marxist sociology as the only sociological analysis. I called on Islamists and others to get out of the cave of intellectual and religious fear regarding this point of view. The divine revelation represented in the Quran, and also many documented sayings of the Prophet, cautions us about the effective sociological and historical norms in the development of societies, and of the sociological parameters behind them.

I want to remind people of the saying of the Prophet Mohammed (PBUH) mentioned in the documented Al-Bukhari and in a similar *hadith* by Al-Bukhar and Muslim, which says, "The messenger of God observed: There have come the people of Yemen; they are tender-hearted, the belief is that of the Yemenis, the understanding "of the faith" is that of the Yemenis and sagacity is that of the Yemenis." (Al-Bukhari, Hadith 8834)

What are the common aspects between these three elements (the people of Yemen, the owners of camels, and the shepherds? Did the Prophet (PBUH) mean *Yemen* only as the geographical Yemen in the south of the Arabian Peninsula or is it some other social phenomenon closer to the Arab north?

What is the explanation of our honorable Islamic scholars and the scholars of the saying of the Prophet for this particular saying? In the light of this, is it possible for an Islamic writer to ban sociology, even the Islamic part of it? (Ahmad Khudhar, *The Scholars of Sociology and their Position on Islam*. London: Islamic Reform, 1993)

In my opinion, any movement, if it complies with the truth and considers the objective parameters in the reality of the world, might succeed.

There is no doubt that the West has a double standard. It is not a charity or moral society. All international powers have their own calculations and interests that favors this standard at one time and the other standard at another time. If we get rid of the double standard in the Western position, would we expect a logical and moral position in the Japanese, Chinese, and Indian positions in the dealings with us?

Any phenomenon, like political Islam or others, cannot expand in any society through external factors unless the internal situation helps in that and complements its effects. This is why we have to consider in the long-term building and planning, as did the progressive Chinese movement from Sun Yat Sun (1912) to Mao Tse-Tung (1949) in spite of the division, occupation, and historical fall of China, which was only remedied by long-term planning, a progressive way of thinking, and civil programs that considered Chinese conditions before all else.

Rabeao: Contrary to what others say about the farewell to Arabism concluded from the repulsion in Arabic common dialect, where understanding, harmony, and interaction between the people of one nation is absent, you noticed the emergence of a new intermediate dialect that is in the process of interacting between the people of one nation. This is what is materialized by the epic of visual imagery, where television shows and songs, in addition to other forms of media, became an intermediary to expand the promotion of this new dialect. The question is, what is the future of this new dialect enhancing the exchange among people within the same nation? To what extent would this new language complement the mother language to reunify the nation and its interaction from the concept that the language is the residence of man and his country?

Al-Ansari: I see that, in approaching the phenomenon of Arabism, we have to distinguish between two issues. First, the objective parameters in terms of time and place of this phenomenon. Second, what has been presented by the ideological and emotional literature in its regards at one particular stage. For the first instance, we are before parameters that would bring us closer to the constants that gave Arabism its existence and continuity. This is what we reconstructed Arabism upon, even when Arabs was under the control of foreigners from the Buwayhis, the Seljuks, and the Ottomans, and after that Europeans, and today Americans and Israelis. What made Arabism reemerged at the end of the Ottoman regime? What brought it back in spite of the severity of French occupation, which tried to eliminate the Arabic language and culture in Algeria? What made it survive until today, alive in our emotions and minds in spite of the severity of the current attacks in Palestine and Iraq and other places?

There are some objective requirements for Arabism that make the basis for it continuation. These requirements include the Arabic language, in spite of its weakness and the spread of foreign expressions and accents, and the domination of its being well spoken on the surface but its style is lacking in content. Despite all this, the language did not remain solely in books and used only for writing but stayed alive on the tongues of the general population, and that is the secret of its power. It is true that it is spoken with numerous dialects, but they are all derived from classic Arabic in one way or another. Much linguistic research has appeared around the field of "bringing the dialect back" to the classic language. Let us look at, among many other examples, how the illiterate are fond of Al-Mutanabbi, and at the obvious fact that Arabic is the language of the Quran. We notice, too, that Arabic churches, at the beginning of this current epic, decided to say their prayers in Arabic even though their Holy Book was read in a different language.

Today, in spite of the calamities of division and dispersion, the factors of global development impose an ideological national plan that interacts with the Arabic dialects in one common Arabic dialect, derived from the classic language, without the complications of its grammar and its rules and is closer to it than any other historical dialogue within a very limited geographical environment. (Even in the smallest Arabic countries like Lebanon and Bahrain, there are many spoken dialects!)

This is a critical positive development in the living Arabic language and in the linguistic life of the Arabs, and this is, before anything else, just a description for this phenomenon. I hope that linguists in the field study this deeply to decide if this is really what is happening in our linguistic reality. I personally believe, from watching discussions on cable television, conferences, commercial businesses, songs and tourism in all the different Arab countries, that a new linguistic creature is being born and formed. It is bypassing the local dialects and getting closer to the classic language, which will open a door, present and future, for all Arabs from the ocean to the Gulf, to communicate in one close common dialect understood by them all. This is how the "Quraishi dialect" began historically its formation in the effects of classic Arabic.

I repeat, all I hope is that this hypothesis and theory will be judged by capable expert linguists, because the impressionist critique that comes from writers of compositions living the worries of the confrontation between the classic and the dialect, living within the frame of mind of the imperialist conspiracy theory and looking for popularism, are the last to judge the language's development and sciences.

Rabeao: In Richard Perle and David Frum's book entitled *An End to Evil: How to Win the War on Terror* (2004), Perle, known as the intellectual adviser for foreigner politics of the new conservative movement, says that "time is running out." This means that the American empire has to occupy the world in order to extinguish terrorism. The worrying question is, facing the absolute hegemony of Jurassic Park dinosaurs (a well-known film by Steven Spielberg) or the male sheep of Thomas Freedmen that threatens to butt the whole world if it doesn't stand aside or stand with it, what is your vision of the future of the world under this absolute hegemony, as well as your vision of the future of global civilization, especially that there are true fears expressed by many of the end of man and humanity, as concluded by Francis Fokoyama's in his book *The End of History and the Last Man* (1992)? Can the future find its path with all this terrorism (the terrorism of the superpower and its deformed copy Zionism) that stands on the same ground as the terrorism referred to as the terrorism of the international organizations?

Al-Ansari: There are no guarantees of a rosy future for anyone, but the course of human development, especially what has been achieved in modern times in different aspects of life, is able to reform itself, especially within its imperialistic alternatives, even if its course were disrupted by the "terrorism of the superpower and its deformed copy Zionism," as you expressed, which is really the truth. The decision of the International Court of Justice about the illegitimacy of the Zionist racist isolationist wall is proof that the international conscience is still alive. We know that the International Court of Justice is not a religious court and it's not formed from the Third World judges in particular, but it is an international forum for rights belonging to the international society, and its judges are mostly from Europe and new Asian East. In other words, the superpowers of the world today. All of these adopt the methodology of modernization intellectually, scientifically, economically, socially and politically. I think that the West will reform itself internally. Even America will reform itself internally, and when it comes to Israel, if it does not reform itself internally, it is destined to collapse. This also means the Arabs should reform themselves internally.

The establishment of injustice or justice does not mean giving the rights back, but it is the beginning. But even that establishment is subjected in reality to terrorism. The truth about the Arabs and Muslims, and the rights of the Palestinians people are facing American Zionist propaganda terrorism. The truth about how bad are the Arabic conditions and their backwardness is forbidden in our Arabic doctrine…even in the popular and progressive ones!

The matter stays (for both parties) as it was described by the poet Al-Maari, "If I said the impossible, I talked loudly. And if I said the truth, I prolonged my whisper."

So the world is threatened by aggressive power and aggressive marginalization, and they talk a lot about "human rights." I think the most fundamental right is the right "to know" before anything else. We have to call to stop terrorism against the truth, with them and with us.

Rabeao: On the occasion of choosing your book *The*

Transformation of Thought and Politics in Egypt and its Arabic Surroundings (2003), while receiving the award from the minister Farouk Al Husni, how did you feel as you received this award? To what extent do this book and your other books contribute to strengthening your call for the culture of self-evaluation upon which you built the hopes for stopping the Arabic backwardness and collapse?

Al-Ansari: The most significant things about this honor I received from the Minister Farouk Husni for my book is my feeling that this book will reach a wider audience among Egyptian readers and the cultured class in Egypt. This is the hope of every Arabic writer.

As you know, I said in my book *Inquiry of the Defeat* and my other books that culture is the last line of defense for Arabic existence. We witness that today. I think that Egypt in particular, no matter how some evaluate its political role, can play a fundamental role in the cultural interaction between the Arabs, East, Gulf, and West.

Perhaps Egypt does not have the opportunity to compete with the Japanese, European, and Chinese industrial products in the Arab markets, but no one can compete with Egypt in its Arabic cultural product in all forms. Beirut can print and publish, and it has had a vital role since the beginning of the renaissance, but this role cannot be complete except with the Egyptian role.

The "Egyptianized Syrian" school, as referred to by Professor Mohammed Yusuf Najm, was not able to express itself intellectually or culturally except through Egyptian institutions. Of course, history may not repeat itself, but we see different forms and styles for this phenomenon in our day.

The Nassarist political unification tide did not come except after the Arabic cultural tide coming from Egypt. Among its instrumental leaders, intellectuals that are Arabists, is Taha Hussain.

Endnote

[1] Mohammed Jaber Al-Ansari, *Inquiry of the Defeat: The New in the Arab Mind between the Shock of 1967 and the Turn of the Millennium: The Culture of Assessment in the Face of Regression.* Beirut: Arabic Institute for Studies and Publishing, 2001, pp. 39-46.

About the Author

Dr. Mohammed Jaber Al-Ansari is a leading Arab intellectual widely read throughout the Arab World. He received his Ph.D. in Islamic and Cultural Studies from the American University of Beirut in 1979 and joined the Arabian Gulf University in Bahrain as a professor of Islamic Studies in 1985. He became the Advisor for Cultural Affairs to His Majesty the King of Bahrain. Dr. Al-Ansari's intellectual treatises have been honored by numerous Arab governments and intellectual organizations, and he has received numerous prestigious awards for his social, political, and cultural contributions to modern Arabic intellectualism. He is the author of more than twenty books, several of which have been designated as assigned readings for social and political science courses in universities throughout the Arab World and appear as references in many academic tomes. For over five decades, he has written articles for the most prestigious journals in the Arab World.

About the Translator

Dr. Riyad Y. Hamzah is a leading figure in higher education and a well-known Arab scholar greatly concerned with the issues of the scientific renaissance in the Arab World. He received his Ph.D. in Biochemistry from the University of Houston in 1984 and joined the Arabian Gulf University in Bahrain as a professor of Biochemistry in 1985 where he was a leader in developing the academic programs and founded the programs in Biotechnology and Technology Management. He has served as the Vice President of the Arabian Gulf University, the General Director of the Higher Education Council of Bahrain, and as the President of the University of Bahrain. He has served on the Boards of many international scientific organizations and journals. He has received numerous accolades for his contributions to education in the Arab World, has numerous publications in international scientific and educational journals, and is active in the translation of literary and scientific works between English and Arabic.